RELIGION and LITERATURE

A Reader

Robert Detweiler &

David Jasper, editors

with S. Brent Plate & Heidi L. Nordberg

Westminster John Knox Press
Louisville, Kentucky

See Acknowledgments, pp. 184–91, for additional permission information.

Book design by Jennifer K. Cox
Cover design by Mark Abrams

First edition
Published by Westminster John Knox Press
Louisville, Kentucky

This book is printed on acid-free paper that meets the American National Standards Institute Z39.48 standard. ∞

Library of Congress Cataloging-in-Publication Data

Detweiler, Robert.
  Religion and literature : a reader / Robert Detweiler and David Jasper ; with Heidi L. Nordberg and S. Brent Plate.— 1st ed.
    p. cm.
  Includes bibliographical references.
  ISBN 0-664-25846-8 (alk. paper)
    1. Religion and literature. I. Jasper, David. II. Nordberg, Heidi L. III. Plate, S. Brent, 1966– IV. Title.

PN49 .D44 2000
808.8'0382—dc21

                                                    99-047561

Contents

Contents

Contents

Preface

This book has grown out of the classroom and is intended for classroom use. Its purpose is, therefore, practical. It is a project that is infinitely expandable and therefore, inevitably, limited. Each reader will have his or her own ideas of literature that could have been included, and there are many different notions of the discipline of "literature and religion." Indeed, part of its attraction is that it is a field which is always changing its shape and form.

As teachers who have been toiling in this field for many years, we are profoundly aware of its elusive nature and the differences between traditions on opposite sides of the Atlantic. At the same time we are acutely aware of the lack of resources for teachers and students who try to find their way into this many-sided and many-splendored arena of study, and how easy it is to get lost or stray too far into one corner of the meadow, forgetting the demands of literature in an overemphasis on religion (or even theology), or vice versa. It is all too easy to lose one's balance, and there are many who would say that "literature and religion" is too narrow a term—perhaps religion and culture or religion and the arts is really what we are concerned with. Perhaps our emphasis, some would argue, needs to be more theoretical, more visual, more immediately focused on issues of gender, ethnicity, ethics, or politics.

There is much truth in all of these comments. However, our purposes are limited, and for that we make no apology. In an age that has been obliged to admit its own postmodern condition, there is, more than ever perhaps, a need to acknowledge the texts and traditions that have endured and culturally formed what we are as thinking, feeling, believing, or skeptical beings. For this reason we have included many of those texts which it is all too easy to avoid or neglect—from classical literature, from the Bible, from the classics of English and European traditions of writing. For it is only with a sense of these (and many have been omitted—Dante, Rabelais, Cervantes) that we can go on and make sense of the rich traditions of our own time in a world that is becoming more complex and at the same time smaller. Religion and literature, like all disciplines, needs a shape and a way in, and that is what we have tried to provide. Each reader must then move on and carry these suggestions and proposals into the next stage, we hope a little wiser and more wary.

The preparation of this book has been a long and sometimes difficult road, strewn with much pain and not a little laughter. Many people have made it possible, in spite of all the difficulties on the way, and in particular Heidi Nordberg and Brent Plate, who have been unstinting and selfless in their labors; without them it would have been utterly impossible. At Westminster John Knox Press, Davis Perkins and Stephanie Egnotovich have borne with us throughout the long process. Finally, Sharon Greene and Alison Jasper have given us far more than we deserve of their love, time, and encouragement.

ROBERT DETWEILER AND DAVID JASPER

Atlanta and Glasgow

Introduction

Literature and religion lie at the very roots of culture. Since the dawn of history, long before the development of abstract, critical, and methodological thought, before philosophy and systematic theological reflection, human speculation on the self and the universe was expressed through myths, stories, and poetry. The thought of the ancient world was wrapped in the imagination and emerged in the oldest written texts that have survived, much of it in the familiar stories of the Hebrew Bible and in the even older texts that lie behind them. Later these literary traditions survived in exchanges with the emergent Western philosophy of the Greek world. And they continue to enliven reflection within Christianity and Judaism to the present day. Religious experience and reflection have always engendered poetry and literature, prompting the imagination and moving beyond speculative thought.

This book is intended as a textbook for students and general readers, with those engaged in courses in literature or religion in colleges and seminaries particularly in mind. It offers an anthology of primary source readings (poetry, drama, prose fiction, sermons, criticism) with commentaries that provide sufficient guidance for further reading and study. In no sense can this be a comprehensive collection. Rather, it should be only the beginning for those who are prepared to think and look further.

We have generally limited ourselves to the Western literary-religious tradition, emphasizing the influence of Christianity and Judaism in their interplay with the Greco-Roman tradition of thought and culture. From time to time we make reference to the other major world religions by way of comparison, and to indicate the extraordinary ability of stories, beliefs, and myths to cross cultural boundaries, even in the most ancient of periods.

Furthermore, we have limited ourselves generally to the English language literary-religious tradition as it grew out of Middle Eastern and European sources, with some emphasis on North American orientation and concerns, though, again, it would be arbitrary to exclude other texts from other traditions and languages in translation.

In no sense is our work intended to be confessional. Inevitably it will reflect our own backgrounds in American Protestantism and Anglicanism, but as far as possible we have sought to avoid religious biases. Indeed, an aim of this book is to demonstrate the value of the interdisciplinary study of literature and religion for those who do not have a religious orientation as well as for those who do. Theological discussion, therefore, while inevitably present in our concerns, does not play a major part in this reader and is certainly not employed to argue for a particular confessional ideology. Further, although we emphasize the Bible as probably the single most important literary influence on Western culture and still its major sacred text, we do not do so from any doctrinal or dogmatic position.

The study of literature and religion is a veritable minefield for the unwary student. It makes double demands of reading and tends to break down the assumptions usually built into the academic study of either religion or literature. Each field has its own vocabulary, its own strategies of reading, and its own claims for commitment. The same texts and the art of reading itself are often viewed in very different ways. We are acutely aware of these potential difficulties, and have structured this course of reading with them much in mind. The book is divided into eight chapters that in various ways approach the study of the interdiscipline from theoretical, philosophical, historical, and applied-interpretive perspectives. Of these four, the applied interpretive is central; the emphasis of the book is on the educated interpretation of important representative texts, guided by theoretical explanation and historical contextualizing. Each chapter is prefaced by a short essay that draws together the various excerpts that follow, and each author is briefly introduced. Finally, a brief list of suggested further reading is added, although this is in no way comprehensive and is intended merely as a guide for more developed study. The first and last chapters are the most theoretical, the first giving an explanation of the nature and development of the interdisciplinary study of literature and religion, and the last exploring wider theoretical questions from other fields of study and looking toward new developments in the future. Chapter 1 is also strongly historical, in order to present the modern genesis of the academic study of literature and religion in their interactions, as are chapters 2 and 3, which address respectively the matter of the common origins of both religious expression and literature itself, and the major stages in the literary-religious interpretive tradition in the West. Chapters 4 to 7 consist mainly of applied interpretation. They identify the kind of texts and themes that have been prominent in the interdiscipline and show, through close readings of examples of these, how various literary-religious hermeneutical strategies were employed to both explicate them and shape the field.

We hope that this book will raise fundamental issues in a very difficult area of study. Approaches to the study of literature and religion vary enormously, depending on where one begins. Even between ourselves as authors there is a vast difference, one of us being American, the other British. What we have tried to do here is to propose a course of study that will begin to ask the questions that really matter, and to inspire others to take them further in their own way. Our aims may be summarized under seven headings as follows:

1. To introduce the study of literature and religion as a contemporary academic interdisciplinary field of inquiry to those who are unacquainted with it, and to systematize and deepen such study for those who have already begun to be aware of the questions it raises.

2. To explain and illustrate the nature and theoretical strategies of a literary-religious interpretive approach to texts, and to encourage an appreciation of it as a way of reading that is both valuable and productive.

3. To demonstrate the importance of literary readings of the Bible, to outline recent scholarship of such readings, and to emphasize the still pervasive influence of the Bible on modern Western culture.

4. To demonstrate the value of religiously aware readings of representative great texts within Western culture and to introduce to the reader other less well known texts that suggest and embody changing attitudes toward religion.

5. To illustrate the importance of incorporating texts from the Native American and African American traditions into the study of literature and religion.

6. To show how kinds of texts and actions normally associated with religious worship (such as liturgies, prayers, sermons, rituals) have literary dimensions that influence the way in which we think and behave beyond the context of worship and religious practice.

7. To show how relatively recent concerns in academic thinking and Western culture more broadly (such as the significance of the unconscious, technology, questions of gender, the body, ecology) are conveyed in writing that is often undertaken in a combined literary-religious mode that prompts literary-religious responses.

Much has been written and said about the secularization of the European mind since the Enlightenment, and the demise of religious perspectives under the pressure of the great ideologies of progress in the nineteenth century. The result, it may be suggested, is the postmodern crisis of thought, belief, and identity with which contemporary art and literature struggle in their obsession with theory and the failure of theoretical processes after the apocalyptic experiences of our century (the Great War of 1914–18, the holocaust in Germany and its horrific "final solution," the threat of nuclear oblivion). Perhaps, however, this sense of the "secular" is too simple—what we are suggesting here is a persistence of the religious spirit and its insights which still must be taken seriously, its incorporation into our culture still acknowledged by all those who either fear it, continue to subscribe to its power, or celebrate its apparent demise. The energy and difficulty of the interdisciplinary debate that lies at the heart of our concerns may yet be central, even crucial, for us and for those who will follow us.

We might suggest three concepts that lie at the heart of our endeavor in writing and editing this book. They are beauty, narrative, and community.

First, *beauty*. It is said that Pico della Mirandola, the Renaissance philosopher, planned to write a book on poetic theology, believing that the artist as poet is the best theologian and that aesthetics and religion are properly inseparable. Our approach to literature and religion here might best be described as a hermeneutic, or interpretation, which takes up both the forms of aesthetics and the content of knowledge, and holds them in tension, not discarding either too quickly. To know, to see, and to feel the beauty of divinity are to be taken together and can never, finally, be separated. In this tension is played out the telling of the story—that is, *narrative* lies at the center of our task.

Thus the Bible, the collection of texts which lies at the heart of our anthology, continually returns to narratives and the telling of stories that draw the reader into their dramas, so that art (including poetry, fiction, and drama) becomes an experience that is radically life changing. One of our purposes is to introduce our readers to the particular activity of religious reading, a celebratory event that is finally never solitary or merely academic but enables the construction and realization of *community*. As one of us put it in an earlier book, "A religious reading could seek to regain the group-celebratory nature of story enactment by transferring it to the reading experience."

What we learn from the practice of religion and the experience of literature is the root and origin of community and culture. In liturgy (that is, formal worship), the drama, or the reciting of sagas, ballads, and stories, and finally in the confrontation between the reader and the text, we learn that process of interaction from which narratives begin to develop. From these narratives communities begin to form, in turn appropriating the narratives—as we see, for example in the earliest stories of the Bible or in the Gospels—and it is within these living communities that we realize ourselves and our identities. When the narratives congeal into the power structures of false ideologies, we can see also how the dangers that have haunted our modern and postmodern societies are closely associated with the matter of literature and religion.

We hope, therefore, that this book will help to form individuals and communities that will be, precisely, better readers—more aware of the beauty and the danger inherent in what they are doing. No doubt we will leave behind many questions, but perhaps learning to ask the correct questions is a major step that is all too often missed as we strive too quickly to find answers.

Further Reading

From the huge literature available, the following list represents some of the more important or useful studies of recent years in the field of literature and religion.

Three journals are dedicated specifically to the field of religion and literature:

Christianity and Literature (Journal of the Conference on Christianity and Literature)
Religion and Literature (University of Notre Dame)
Literature and Theology (Oxford University Press)

Alter, Robert, and Frank Kermode, eds. *The Literary Guide to the Bible*. Cambridge, Mass.: Harvard University Press, 1987.

Apostolos-Cappadona, Diane, ed. *Art, Creativity and the Sacred*. New York: Crossroad, 1984; second edition, 1996.

Detweiler, Robert. *Breaking the Fall: Religious Readings of Contemporary Fiction*. Basingstoke: Macmillan, 1989; Louisville, Ky.: Westminster John Knox Press, 1996.

Detweiler, Robert, ed. *Art/Literature/Religion: Life on the Borders*. Chico, Calif.: Scholars Press, 1983.

Frye, Northrop. *The Great Code: The Bible and Literature*. New York: Routledge, 1981.

Gunn, Giles, ed. *Literature and Religion*. New York: Harper & Row, 1971.

Jasper, David. *The Study of Literature and Religion*. Basingstoke: Macmillan, 1989; second edition, 1992.

Jasper, David and Stephen Prickett, eds. *The Bible and Literature: A Reader*. Oxford: Blackwell, 1999.

Josipovici, Gabriel. *The Book of God: A Response to the Bible*. New Haven, Conn.: Yale University Press, 1988.

Kermode, Frank. *The Genesis of Secrecy: On the Interpretation of Narrative*. Cambridge, Mass.: Harvard University Press, 1979.

Scott, Nathan A., Jr. *The Poetics of Belief: Studies in Coleridge, Arnold, Pater, Santayana, Stevens, and Heidegger.* Chapel Hill: University of North Carolina Press, 1985.

Spencer, Richard A., ed. *Orientation by Disorientation: Studies in Literary Criticism and Biblical Literary Criticism.* Presented in honor of William A. Beardslee. Pittsburgh: Pickwick Press, 1980.

Of the numerous anthologies of religious poetry, the following are some of the more useful and accessible.

Atwan, Robert, and Laurence Wieder, eds. *Chapters into Verse.* Oxford and New York: Oxford University Press, 1993. (This two-volume work relates passages from the Bible to later poetry. Volume 1 is entitled *Genesis to Malachi*, and Volume 2, *Gospels to Revelation.*)

Bly, Robert, ed. *The Soul Is Here for Its Own Joy: Sacred Poems from Many Cultures.* Hopewell, N.J.: Ecco Press, 1995.

Curzon, David, ed. *The Gospels in Our Image: An Anthology of Twentieth-Century Poetry Based on Biblical Texts.* New York: Harcourt Brace Jovanovich, 1995.

Davie, Donald, ed. *The New Oxford Book of Christian Verse.* New York: Oxford University Press, 1981.

Gardner, Helen, ed. *A Book of Religious Verse.* New York: Oxford University Press, 1972.

Impastato, David, ed. *Upholding Mystery: An Anthology of Contemporary Christian Poetry.* New York: Oxford University Press, 1997.

1

History of the Field
and Theoretical Issues

Literature and religion are ancient and natural partners in the literature of the West. The Bible, still perhaps the seminal book of our culture, has, on the one hand, been the most influential text in the development of the art of literary criticism through such figures as Augustine of Hippo and, on the other hand, been interpreted apart from othePr literature in the past two centuries in a curious backwater of literary studies known as "biblical criticism." There are many reasons for this, the most important being its status as the supreme "sacred text," set apart from all others as "the Word of God." As a result, the Bible is rarely studied in literary courses, while those studying the Bible are often woefully underfed when it comes to reading poetry and literature more broadly.

However, in spite of this, since the beginning of the nineteenth century there has been a stream of influential writers, critics, and scholars who have continued to reflect on the interaction between literature and religion, often with particular reference to questions of biblical interpretation. Samuel Taylor Coleridge's posthumously published *Confessions of an Inquiring Spirit* (1840) promotes the reading of the Bible in the context of Shakespeare, Goethe, and the great literature of the world, warning against what Coleridge calls "bibliolatry"—the false worship of the Bible as a text not to be interpreted by critical tools employed on other texts. More generally, William Wordsworth in his 1815 "Essay, Supplementary to the Preface to *The Lyrical Ballads*" compares poetry and religion, which share close affinities while at the same time rest uneasily together in "kindred error," so that, he warns, nothing is more difficult and subject to "distortion" than "religious poetry."

Thus, we shall find that religion and literature coexist in a necessary and highly tensioned relationship. Arguably the most influential work of biblical interpretation of the nineteenth century, David Friedrich Strauss's *The Life of Jesus Critically Examined* (1835–36), argues for a "mythical-poetical ground" from which the Bible is to be read and understood. Despite the title of his work, Strauss was frankly uninterested in the life of the historical Jesus, presenting the authors of the Bible—along with the classics of Greek literature like Homer—as writers in whose works some kind of poetry or fiction will be intentionally mixed up with history. His own work, it has often been noted, reads, not unlike the Gospels themselves, as a kind of

1

investigative novel, and it is not by chance that Strauss's English translator was none other than Mary Anne Evans, more generally known to the literary world as George Eliot, one of the greatest of English novelists.

Through the nineteenth century, as the "higher criticism" of the Bible, largely from Germany, developed sophisticated techniques of interpretation in such ventures as the "quest for the historical Jesus," scholars and literary artists outside the academy of biblical critics were laying the foundations of what was to become in the twentieth century the more formal study of literature and religion. In England, the poet and critic Matthew Arnold wrote three major studies arguing that the language of the Bible is "literary, not scientific," and that the authors of the Bible used language in a "tentative, poetic way." The studies are *St. Paul and Protestantism* (1870), *Literature and Dogma* (1873), and *God and the Bible* (1875), the last displaying his considerable knowledge of German scholarship. In the essay excerpted in this chapter, "The Study of Poetry" (1880), Arnold, in a way that betrays the influence of German thought on him, argues that "the strongest part of our religion lay in its unconscious poetry" and looks forward to the rise of the humanistic study of literature in the academy, which sets it at the heart of our culture and civilization.

A writer and thinker of far greater profundity than Arnold, and one whose effect on the twentieth century has been incalculable, is the Danish existentialist Søren Kierkegaard. He, perhaps more than any other individual, has influenced the study of literature and religion (though an inveterate critic of the established church in Denmark), not least by his indirect, often ironic, style of writing. To read Kierkegaard is not so much to read about philosophy or theology as to engage in a literary experiment in religious thought, and later in chapter 3 we shall study his reading of Genesis 22 (the sacrifice of Isaac) in *Fear and Trembling* (1843), which was to attract the attention of no less a writer than Franz Kafka.

It might be argued that the formal study of literature and religion begins in the twentieth century with T. S. Eliot's 1935 essay "Religion and Literature," in which Eliot, arguing from an overtly Christian perspective, attempts to overcome what he calls the tacit assumption "that there is no relation between literature and theology." Despite its title, the Englishness of Eliot's essay lays down what has become a continuing difference between British and North American studies, the latter focusing on religion and literature, while the former has remained committed to theology—a distinction to be observed in two major journals, *Religion and Literature* (published by the University of Notre Dame Press) and *Literature and Theology* (published by Oxford University Press). Eliot maintains that, for Christian readers at least, literature must be read "with explicit ethical and theological standards," and he is part of an English tradition that numbers, among others, C. S. Lewis, Dorothy L. Sayers, and W. H. Auden, all of them both critics and creative writers.

The great German Protestant tradition of the nineteenth century was translated to North American scholarship largely by the work of Paul Tillich, a German who fled to the United States with the rise of Hitler in Germany in the

1930s. Hugely influential as a theologian through such important works as his *Systematic Theology* (1951–63), Tillich also wrote major works on theology, culture, and the arts, standing, as he put it "on the boundary" between the church and secular culture. His work embraces not only a concern for literature but also attention to expressionist art, modern dance, and the theory of art.

During the second half of the twentieth century, more formal study of literature and religion has gained a significant place in the academic curriculum, particularly in North America, through the work of scholars like Nathan A. Scott, Jr., Northrop Frye, Stanley Romaine Hopper, and more recently, Frank Kermode, Harold Bloom, and Robert Alter. Unlike most of their predecessors such as T. S. Eliot, these are professional academics with few pretensions to be poets or creative writers. In Chicago, Scott introduced the field into the mainstream of European philosophical and theoretical thought through his discussion of figures such as Martin Heidegger and Paul Ricoeur, while Northrop Frye engaged with studies of the Bible and literature from an initially structuralist perspective in literary criticism. Both Scott and Frye are Christian ministers and share a sense of a world in religious decline, or, as Scott would express it, "defiguralized." Others, however, like Kermode and Bloom, together with feminist critics such as Mieke Bal and others associated with varieties of postmodern thinking, stand outside traditions of faith and confession and truly follow Coleridge in his injunction that the Bible be read like any other text, without critical let or hindrance.

WILLIAM WORDSWORTH,
THE LYRICAL BALLADS

The Lyrical Ballads of William Wordsworth and Samuel Taylor Coleridge first appeared in 1798. They constitute a landmark in English Romantic poetry after the classicism and stylization of the eighteenth century. Coleridge described Wordsworth's contribution as "to give the charm of novelty to things of every day, and to excite a feeling analogous to the supernatural, by awakening the mind's attention from the lethargy of custom." In his 1800 preface to the poems, Wordsworth himself states his intention "to follow the fluxes and refluxes of the mind when agitated by the great and simple affections of our nature." The extract that follows is taken from Wordsworth's Supplementary Essay of 1815, in which he discusses the links between poetry and religion. Influenced by the German philosophers Kant and Fichte, and by the traditions of Platonic thought, Wordsworth draws a close link between theological and poetical inspiration, perceiving "intuition" as the link between them.

From "Essay,
Supplementary to the Preface to *The Lyrical Ballads*"

As Poetry is most just to its own divine origin when it administers the comforts and breathes the spirit of religion, they who have learned to perceive this truth, and who betake themselves to reading verse for sacred purposes, must be preserved from numerous illusions to which the two Classes of Readers, whom we have been considering, are liable. But, as the mind grows serious from the weight of life, the range of its passions is contracted accordingly; and its sympathies become so exclusive, that many species of high excellence wholly escape, or but languidly excite its notice. Besides, men who react from religious or moral inclinations, even when the subject is of that kind which they approve, are beset with misconceptions and mistakes peculiar to themselves. Attaching so much importance to the truths which interest them, they are prone to overrate the Authors by whom those truths are expressed and enforced. They come prepared to impart so much passion to the poet's language, that they remain unconscious how little, in fact, they receive from it. And, on the other hand, religious faith is to him who holds it so momentous a thing, and error appears to be attended with such tremendous consequences, that, if opinions touching upon religion occur which the Reader condemns, he not only cannot sympathise with them, however animated the expression, but there is, for the most part, an end to all satisfaction and enjoyment. Love, if it ever existed, is converted into dislike; and the heart of the reader is set against the Author and his book.—To these excesses they, who from their professions ought to be the most guarded against them, are perhaps the most liable; I mean those sects whose religion, being from the calculating understanding, is cold and formal. For when Christianity, the religion of humility, is founded upon the proudest faculty of our nature what can be expected but contradictions? Accordingly, believers of this cast are at one time contemptuous; at another, being troubled as they are and must be, with inward misgivings they are jealous and suspicious;—and at all seasons, they are under temptation to supply by the heat with which they defend their tenets, the animation which is wanting to the constitution of the religion itself.

Faith was given to man that his affections, detached from the treasures of time, might be inclined to settle upon those of eternity;—the elevation of his nature, which this habit produces on earth, being to him a presumptive evidence of a future state of existence; and giving him a title to partake of its holiness. The religious man values what he sees chiefly as an "imperfect shadowing forth" of what he is incapable of seeing. The concerns of religion refer to indefinite objects, and are too weighty for the mind to support them without relieving itself by resting a great part of the burden upon words and symbols. The commerce between Man and his Maker cannot be carried on but by a process where much is represented in little, and the Infinite Being accommodates himself to a finite capacity. In all this may be perceived the affinity between religion and poetry; between religion—making up the deficiencies of reason by faith; and poetry—passionate for the instruction of reason between religion—whose element is infinitude, and whose ultimate trust is the supreme of things, submitting herself to circumscription, and reconciled to substitutions; and poetry—ethereal and transcendent, yet incapable to sustain her existence without sensuous incarnation. In this community of nature may be perceived also the lurking incitements of kindred error;—so that we shall find that no poetry has been more subject to distortion, than that species, the argument and scope of which is religious; and no lovers of the art have gone farther astray than the pious and the devout.

DAVID FRIEDRICH STRAUSS, *THE LIFE OF JESUS CRITICALLY EXAMINED*

David Friedrich Strauss (1808–1874) published his *Leben Jesu* in 1835–36, and it was translated into English ten years later by the young Mary Anne Evans, later known as the novelist George Eliot. It is one of the most important nineteenth-century books on the Bible, denying the historical foundations of all supernatural elements in the Gospels and describing them as "myths" developed in the earliest years of the Christian church. Strauss, strongly influenced by Hegel, emphasizes the "purely mythical-poetical" ground of the Gospel narrative, opening up the Bible to a literary understanding in a radical way.

Strauss's *Life of Jesus* critically introduces the fascinating problem of the nexus of history, fiction, and myth. "Myth," from the Greek term *mythos*, means both history and story, and in this ambiguity lies one of the central problems within the study of literature and religion. George Eliot carried Strauss's thinking into the mainstream of English literature through novels like *Middlemarch* (1871–72) and *Daniel Deronda* (1874–76).

From The Life of Jesus Critically Examined

Truly it may be said that the middle term of this argument, namely, that Jesus was the Messiah, would have failed in proof to his contemporaries all the more on account of the common expectation of miraculous events, if that expectation had not been fulfilled by him. But the following critique on the Life of Jesus does not divest it of all those features to which the character of miraculous has been appropriated: and besides we must take into account the overwhelming impression which was made upon those around him by the personal character and discourse of Jesus, as long as he was living amongst them, which did not permit them deliberately to scrutinize and compare him with their previous standard. The belief in him as the Messiah extended to wider circles only by slow degrees; and even during his lifetime the people may have reported many wonderful stories of him (comp. Matt. xiv. 2). After his death, however, the belief in his resurrection, however that belief may have arisen, afforded a more than sufficient proof of his Messiahship; so that all the other miracles in his history need not be considered as the foundation of the faith in this, but may rather be adduced as the consequence of it.

It is however by no means necessary to attribute this same freedom from all conscious intention of fiction, to the authors of all those narratives in the Old and New Testament which must be considered as unhistorical. In every series of legends, especially if any patriotic or religious party interest is associated with them, as soon as they become the subject of free poetry or any other literary composition, some kind of fiction will be intentionally mixed up with them. The authors of the Homeric songs could not have believed that every particular which they related of their gods and heroes had really happened; and just as little could the writer of the Chronicles have been ignorant that in his deviation from the books of Samuel and of the Kings, he was introducing many events of later occurrence into an earlier period; or the author of the book of Daniel that he was modelling his history upon that of Joseph, and accommodating prophecies to events already past; and exactly as little may this be said of all the unhistorical narratives of the Gospels, as for example, of the first chapter of the third, and many parts of the fourth Gospel. But a fiction, although not undesigned, may still be without evil design. It is true, the case is not the same with the supposed authors of many fictions in the Bible, as with poets properly so called, since the latter write without any expectation that their poems will be received as history: but still it is to be considered that in ancient times, and especially amongst the Hebrews, and yet more when this people was stirred up by religious excitement, the line of distinction between history and fiction, prose and poetry, was not drawn so clearly as with us. It is a fact also deserving attention that amongst the Jews and early Christians, the most reputable authors published their works with the substitution of venerated names, without an idea that they were guilty of any falsehood or deception by so doing. . . .

So that we stand here upon purely mythical-poetical ground; the only historical reality which we can hold fast as positive matter of fact being this:—the impression made by John the Baptist, by virtue of his ministry and his relation to Jesus, was so powerful as to lead to the subsequent glorification of his birth in connection with the birth of the Messiah in the Christian legend.

MATTHEW ARNOLD,
"THE STUDY OF POETRY"

Matthew Arnold (1822–1888) was one of the greatest poets and cultural critics of Victorian England. Arnold wrote widely on education, politics, religion, and poetry, drawing the latter two fields into a close relationship in works like *Literature and Dogma* (1873) and *God and the Bible* (1875). He valued poetry over prose because of its "practical" use in the fashioning of the beautiful soul, and throughout his life he wrote poetry and argued for its value in his criticism. He also criticized Christian theology for its lack of inquiry into the literary elements of religious language, close in some ways to the thought of Strauss. Thus Arnold becomes a key figure in the nineteenth century in the study of religion and literature. The passage below was published several months after his death and shows his continued interest in the value of poetry in the service of humanity.

From "The Study of Poetry"

"The future of poetry is immense, because in poetry, where it is worthy of its high destinies, our race, as time goes on, will find an ever surer and surer stay. There is not a creed which is not shaken, not an accredited dogma which is not shown to be questionable, not a received tradition which does not threaten to dissolve. Our religion has materialised itself in the fact, in the supposed fact; it has attached its emotion to the fact, and now the fact is failing it. But for poetry the idea is everything; the rest is a world of illusion, of divine illusion. Poetry attaches its emotion to the idea; the idea is the fact. The strongest part of our religion today is its unconscious poetry." Let me be permitted to quote these words of my own, as uttering the thought which should, in my opinion, go with us and govern us in all our study of poetry. . . .

We should conceive of poetry worthily, and more highly than it has been the custom to conceive of it. We should conceive of it as capable of higher uses, and called to higher destinies, than those which in general men have assigned to it hitherto. More and more mankind will discover that we have to turn to poetry to interpret life for us, to console us, to sustain us. Without poetry, our science will appear incomplete; and most of what now passes with us for religion and philosophy will be replaced by poetry. Science, I say, will appear incomplete without it. For finely and truly does Wordsworth call poetry "the impassioned expression which is in the countenance of all science"; and what is a countenance without its expression? Again, Wordsworth finely and truly calls poetry "the breath and finer spirit of all knowledge": our religion, parading evidences such as those on which the popular mind relies now; our philosophy, pluming itself on its reasonings about causation and finite and infinite being; what are they but the shadows and dreams and false shows of knowledge? The day will come when we shall wonder at ourselves for having trusted to them, for having taken them seriously; and the more we perceive their hollowness, the more we shall prize "the breath and finer spirit of knowledge" offered to us by poetry. . . .

At any rate the end to which the method and the estimate are designed to lead, and from leading to which, if they do lead to it, they get their whole value,—the benefit of being able clearly to feel and deeply to enjoy the best, the truly classic, in poetry,—is an end, let me say it once more at parting, of supreme importance. We are often told that an era is opening in which we are to see multitudes of a common sort of readers, and masses of a common sort of literature; that such readers do not want and could not relish anything better than such literature, and that to provide it is becoming a vast and profitable industry. Even if good literature entirely lost currency with the world, it would still be abundantly worth while to continue to enjoy it by oneself. But it never will lose currency with the world, in spite of momentary appearances; it never will lose supremacy. Currency and supremacy are insured to it, not indeed by the world's deliberate and conscious choice, but by something far deeper,—by the instinct of self-preservation in humanity.

SØREN KIERKEGAARD,
THE POINT OF VIEW FOR MY WORK AS AN AUTHOR

Søren Kierkegaard (1813–1855) was one of the nineteenth century's most influential thinkers in the fields of literature, theology, and philosophy. Part of his genius was to write philosophy through the medium of various literary forms and styles. Early in his short but extremely productive career he published a number of books under pseudonyms. In these books he played with the possibilities that a variety of positions and attitudes might bring to life. Kierkegaard assumed different personae to examine the possible ways that one's individual existence could take form. Along these lines he developed three categories of human existence: the aesthetic, the ethical, and the religious. While many scholars have thought of these categories as a linear development—from the aesthetic through the ethical to the religious—Kierkegaard was clear that all the categories were possible at any moment, and in the essay excerpted below he claimed: "The religious is present from the beginning. Conversely, the aesthetic is present again at the last moment" (p. 325).

Kierkegaard's religious thinking is self-consciously literary—perhaps best exemplified in the early pages of *Fear and Trembling* (1843), which deal dramatically with Genesis 22, the sacrifice of Isaac. The excerpt below is taken from a book that was published posthumously and describes Kierkegaard's literary methods of writing. In particular, he was interested in developing what he called the "indirect method of communication," a method that finally had a certain evangelistic mission to it. The goal of all his writing was to bring the reader to a true Christianity. This could not be done by stating what "true Christianity" really was and forcing the reader to move toward it, but rather by nudging the reader from behind, through "indirect" writing, toward a freely chosen Christian life. Kierkegaard would have agreed with the poet Emily Dickinson when she said, "Tell all the Truth but tell it slant."

From The Point of View for My Work as an Author

No, an illusion can never be destroyed directly, and only by indirect means can it be radically removed. If it is an illusion that all are Christians—and if there is anything to be done about it, it must be done indirectly, not by one who vociferously proclaims himself an extraordinary Christian, but by one who, better instructed, is ready to declare that he is not a Christian at all. That is, one must approach from behind the person who is under an illusion. Instead of wishing to have the advantage of being oneself that rare thing, a Christian, one must let the prospective captive enjoy the advantage of being the Christian, and for one's own part have resignation enough to be the one who is far behind him—otherwise one will certainly not get the man out of his illusion, a thing which is difficult enough in any case.

If then, according to our assumption, the greater number of people in Christendom only imagine themselves to be Christians, in what categories do they live? They live in aesthetic, or at the most, in aesthetic-ethical categories. . . .

The religious writer must, therefore, first get into touch with men. That is, he must begin with aesthetic achievement. This is earnest-money. The more brilliant the achievement, the better for him. Moreover he must be sure of himself, or (and this is the one and only security) he must relate himself to God in fear and trembling, lest the event most opposite to his intentions should come to pass, and instead of setting the others in motion, the others acquire power over him, so that he ends by being bogged in the aesthetic. Therefore he must have everything in readiness, though without impatience, with a view to bringing forward the religious promptly, as soon as he perceives that he has his readers with him, so that with the momentum gained by devotion to the aesthetic they rush headlong into contact with the religious.

Assuming that there is a prodigious illusion in the case of these many men who call themselves Christians and are regarded as Christians, the way of encountering it which is here suggested involves no condemnation or denunciation. It is a truly Christian invention, which cannot be employed without fear and trembling, or without real self-denial. The one who is disposed to help bears all the responsibility and makes all the effort. But for that reason such a line of action possesses intrinsic value. Generally speaking, a method has value only in relation to the result attained. Some one condemns and denounces, vociferates and makes a great noise—all this has no intrinsic value, though one counts upon accomplishing much by it. It is otherwise with the line of action here contemplated. Suppose that a man had dedicated himself to the use of it, suppose that he used it his whole life long—and suppose that he accomplished nothing: he has nevertheless by no means lived in vain, for his life was true self-denial.

This is the secret of the art of helping others. Anyone who has not mastered this is himself deluded when he proposes to help others. In order to help another effectively I must understand more than he—yet first of all surely I must understand what he understands. If I do not know that, my greater understanding will be of no help to him. If, however, I am disposed to plume myself on my greater understanding, it is because I am vain or proud, so that at bottom, instead of benefiting him, I want to be admired. But all true effort to help begins with self-humiliation: the helper must first humble himself under him he would help, and therewith must understand that to help does not mean to be a sovereign but to be a servant, that to help does not mean to be ambitious but to be patient, that to help means to endure for the time being the imputation that one is in the wrong and does not understand what the other understands.

Thus it is, as I believe, that I have rendered a service to the cause of Christianity while I myself have been educated by the process. He who was regarded with astonishment as about the shrewdest of fellows (and this was attained with *Either/Or*), he to whom the place of "the interesting man" was willingly conceded (and this was attained with *Either/Or*—precisely he, as it turned out, was engaged in the service of Christianity, had consecrated himself to this from the very instant he began that pseudonymous activity: he, personally and as an author, was striving to bring out this simple thing about becoming a Christian. The movement is not from the simple to the interesting, but from the interesting to the simple, the thing of becoming a Christian, which is the place where the *Concluding Postscript* comes in, the "turning point," as I have called it, of the whole authorship, which states the "Problem" and at the same time, by indirect attack and Socratic dialectic inflicts upon the System a mortal wound—from behind, fighting the System and Speculation in order to show that "the way" is not from the simple to the System and Speculation, but from the System and Speculation back again to the simple thing of becoming a Christian, fighting for this cause and vigorously slashing through to find the way back.

T. S. ELIOT,
"RELIGION AND LITERATURE"

T. S. Eliot (1888–1965) was born in the United States and brought up in a liberal-minded Unitarian household. He was educated at Harvard University where, among other things, he studied Eastern religions. In his early twenties he moved to England, eventually becoming a British citizen and converting to Anglicanism. In England he established himself as a prominent poet and critic. His great early and preconversion poem *The Waste Land* (1922), portraying a godless landscape among other things, helped mark the beginnings of modernism in English literature, while his last poems, *The Four Quartets* (1943), reflect his later deep adhesion to Christianity, even as they maintain a strong sense of the existential struggle and journey of his early pieces. Indeed, in many ways, Eliot is close to the existentialist arguments of Paul Tillich's *The Protestant Era* (1957).

In this spirit, Eliot believed that poetry should pose the existential questions, and religion or theology should answer them. His essay of 1935, "Religion and Literature," has been enormously influential, although its argument is not always clear; he makes a clear distinction between religion and literature with an emphasis on the priority of the religious and the theological.

From "Religion and Literature"

What I have to say is largely in support of the following propositions: Literary criticism should be completed by criticism from a definite ethical and theological standpoint. In so far as in any age there is common agreement on ethical and theological matters, so far can literary criticism be substantive. In ages like our own, in which there is no such common agreement, it is the more necessary for Christian readers to scrutinize their reading, especially of works of imagination, with explicit ethical and theological standards. The "greatness" of literature cannot be determined solely by literary standards; though we must remember that whether it is literature or not can be determined only by literary standards.

We have tacitly assumed, for some centuries past, that there is *no* relation between literature and theology. This is not to deny that literature—I mean, again, primarily works of imagination—has been, is, and probably always will be judged by some moral standards. But moral judgements of literary works are made only according to the moral code accepted by each generation, whether it lives according to that code or not. In an age which accepts some precise Christian theology, the common code may be fairly orthodox: though even in such periods the common code may exalt such concepts as "honour," "glory" or "revenge" to a position quite intolerable to Christianity. The dramatic ethics of the Elizabethan Age offers an interesting study. But when the common code is detached from its theological background, and is consequently more and more merely a matter of habit, it is exposed both to prejudice and to change. At such times morals are open to being altered by literature; so that we find in practice that what is "objectionable" in literature is merely what the present generation is not used to. It is a commonplace that what shocks one generation is accepted quite calmly by the next. This adaptability to change of moral standards is sometimes greeted with satisfaction as an evidence of human perfectibility: whereas it is only evidence of what unsubstantial foundations people's moral judgments have. . . .

But it is certain that a book is not harmless merely because no one is consciously offended by it. And if we, as readers, keep our religious and moral convictions in one compartment, and take our reading merely for entertainment, or on a higher plane, for aesthetic pleasure, I would point out that the author, whatever his conscious intentions in writing, in practice recognizes no such distinctions. The author of a work of imagination is trying to affect us wholly, as human beings, whether he knows it or not; and we are affected by it, as human beings, whether we intend to be or not. I suppose that everything we eat has some other effect upon us than merely the pleasure of taste and mastication; it affects us during the process of assimilation and digestion; and I believe that exactly the same is true of anything we read.

It is our business, as readers of literature, to know what we like. It is our business, as Christians, as well as readers of literature, to know what we ought to like. It is our business as honest men not to assume that whatever we like is what we ought to like; and it is our business as honest Christians not to assume that we do like what we ought to like. And the last thing I would wish for would be the existence of two literatures, one for Christian consumption and the other for the pagan world. What I believe to be incumbent upon all Christians is the duty of maintaining consciously certain standards and criteria of criticism over and above those applied by the rest of the world; and that by these criteria and standards everything that we read must be tested. We must remember that the greater part of our current reading matter is written for us by people who have no real belief in a supernatural order, though some of it may be written by people with individual notions of a supernatural order which are not ours. And the greater part of our reading matter is coming to be written by people who not only have no such belief, but are even ignorant of the fact that there are still people in the world so "backward" or so "eccentric" as to continue to believe. So long as we are conscious of the gulf fixed between ourselves and the greater part of contemporary literature, we are more or less protected from being harmed by it, and are in a position to extract from it what good it has to offer us. . . .

My complaint against modern literature is of the same kind. It is not that modern literature is in the ordinary sense "immoral" or even "amoral"; and in any case to prefer that charge would not be enough. It is simply that it repudiates, or is wholly ignorant of, our most fundamental and important beliefs; and that in consequence its tendency is to encourage its readers to get what they can out of life while it lasts, to miss no "experience" that presents itself, and to sacrifice themselves, if they make any sacrifice at all, only for the sake of tangible benefits to others in this world either now or in the future. We shall certainly continue to read the best of its kind, of what our time provides; but we must tirelessly criticize it according to our own principles, and not merely according to the principles admitted by the writers and by the critics who discuss it in the public press.

PAUL TILLICH,
THEOLOGY OF CULTURE

Paul Tillich (1883–1965) is an almost exact contemporary of T. S. Eliot, although his geographical move was in the opposite direction, from a Europe threatened by Hitler's Nazi Germany to the United States in 1933. Deeply influenced by the Kierkegaardian existentialist tradition and by Heidegger, Tillich is, with Karl Barth and Rudolf Bultmann, one of the most important Christian theologians of the twentieth century. In his rewriting of Christian theology in existentialist terms, Tillich emphasized the crucial role of culture and the arts, whether "secular" or "religious," and gave a central position to the symbol as the vehicle that acts between God and human beings.

The excerpt here is from his late work *Theology of Culture* (1959).

From Theology of Culture,
"Protestantism and Artistic Style"

Every work of art shows three elements: subject matter, form, style. The subject matter is potentially identical with everything which can be received by the human mind in sensory images. It is in no way limited by other qualities like good or bad, beautiful or ugly, whole or broken, human or inhuman, divine or demonic. But not every subject matter is used by every artist or artistic period. There are principles of selection dependent on form and style, the second and third elements of a work of art.

The second element is a concept which is not an ordinary one. It belongs to the structural elements of being itself and can be understood only as that which makes a thing what it is. It gives a thing its uniqueness and universality, its special place within the whole of being, its expressive power. Artistic creation is determined by the form which uses particular materials such as sounds, words, stones, colors and elevates them to a work which stands on its own. For this reason, the form is the ontologically decisive element in every artistic creation—as in any other creation. But the form itself is qualified by the third element which we call style. This term, first used to describe changing fashions in clothing, houses, gardens, etc., has been applied to the realm of artistic production universally and has even been used in relation to philosophy, politics, etc. The style qualifies the many creations of a period in a unique way. It is due to their form that they are creations. It is due to their style that they have something in common.

The problem of style is one of finding what it is that these creations of the same style have in common. To what do they all point? Deriving my answer from many analyses of style, both in art and philosophy, I would say that every style points to a self-interpretation of man, thus answering the question of the ultimate meaning of life. Whatever the subject matter which an artist chooses, however strong or weak his artistic form, he cannot help but betray by his style his own ultimate concern, as well as that of his group, and his period. He cannot escape religion even if he rejects religion, for religion is the state of being ultimately concerned. And in every style the ultimate concern of a human group or period is manifest. It is one of the most fascinating tasks to decipher the religious meaning of styles of the past such as the archaic, the classic, the naturalistic, and to discover that the same characteristics which one discovered in an artistic creation can also be found in the literature, philosophy, and morals of a period.

NATHAN A. SCOTT, JR.,
THE WILD PRAYER OF LONGING

Since his first book, *Rehearsals of Discomposure* (1952), and through a distinguished career teaching at the University of Chicago and of Virginia, Nathan A. Scott, Jr. (1925–) has been a major voice in the United States in the field of religion and literature. He was one of the first scholars systematically to draw together the study of theology and literature, consistently maintaining a close connection with questions of morality and civic virtue.

Ordained as an Episcopal priest, Scott writes within the intensity and formalism of the Christian creed. In *The Wild Prayer of Longing* (1971), a title drawn from Herod's soliloquy in W. H. Auden's poem "For the Time Being," Scott attempts to define and contextualize the all-significant concept of *figura* as a key notion in literature and religion, working via recourse to Heidegger's definition of certain figures as avatars of sacrality. Scott comments on the desacralizing of the world as an absence that must be countered by an exercise of the sacraments as sacred objects and actions.

From The Wild Prayer of Longing: Poetry and the Sacred

I begin, in the opening chapter, by recalling the account that Erich Auerbach gives in his great book *Mimesis* of the world-picture which was held by the traditional or the premodern imagination. In this connection, I stress the centrality in Auerbach's argument of the concept of figure; for, as he maintained, it was this notion which constituted the crucial theme of Western poetry and philosophy and theology in the ages prior to the advent of the modern period. The figural interpretation of reality did, of course, rest on the belief that, given its providential supervision by the divine Sovereign, history has such a unity as makes all persons and events belong essentially to one continuum; and thus any single person or event, it was felt, might be declared to be a figure of another, however great the intervening chronological distance, if the two persons or events exhibited some significant analogical relationship. But, more importantly even, figural thought took historical existence itself to be a figure of that occult reality belonging to the supernatural, for the world was conceived to be but a shadow of the Eternal. As I suggest, however, it is most especially in this crucial particular that modern mentality finds itself standing at a great remove from the figural outlook, for we do not ordinarily take the world to be a figure of anything other than or transcendent to itself. And the first chapter tries to offer some indication of how the history of poiesis in the modern period reflects this gradual decline and disintegration of the figural perspective.

Yet, once the world is "defiguralized," once it is disengaged from that occult reality of which it is presumed by the traditional imagination to be a kind of veil, must it not then become something stale and distant and nowhere "charged with the grandeur of God"? And can it thereafter be conceived in any fundamental way to be invested with holiness? This, it seems to me, is the question that increasingly haunts us, as we contemplate the possibility that l'oubli des hiérophanies (as Paul Ricoeur speaks of it) may have entailed, as its ultimate cost, the disappearance from the modern universe of any sacral dimension at all. Indeed, as I suggest, it is a prodigious kind of search for sacramental reality that accounts for one of the more interesting developments being reflected now by much of contemporary artistic life—namely, the rebirth of "savage thought" (la pensée sauvage) that follows upon the decline of the figural imagination.

NORTHROP FRYE,
THE GREAT CODE: THE BIBLE AND LITERATURE

Northrop Frye (1912–1991), like Nathan Scott, was an ordained Christian minister as well as a professor of literature. His early writings focused on such literary figures as William Blake and John Milton, as well as on the structures that underlie literary works. In The Anatomy of Criticism (1957), Frye explores four "theories" in literature—of modes, symbols, myths, and genres. His interest in myth and the creative imagination led him to consider more closely the influences of the Bible—which he considered the single most important work in all of Western literature—on literature. For him, the Bible is the key to understanding Western literature and culture, providing a structure of mythological meaning that guides our religious behavior.

The title of his work The Great Code is taken from the writings of William Blake, who maintained that "the Old and New Testaments are the Great Code of Art."

From The Great Code: The Bible and Literature

A literary approach to the Bible is not in itself illegitimate: no book could have had so specific a literary influence without itself possessing literary qualities. But the Bible is just as obviously "more" than a work of literature, whatever "more" means—I could not feel that a quantitative metaphor was much help. I have spoken of my wish to get clear of conventional aesthetic canons, but "unity" is one of those canons, and the Bible's disregard of unity is quite as impressive as its exhibition of it. Ultimately, as we should expect, the Bible evades all literary criteria. As Kierkegaard said, an apostle is not a genius— not that I ever found "genius" a very useful word either. My experience in secular literature has shown me how the formal principles of literature had been contained within literature, as the formal principles of music, embodied in sonata, fugue, or rondo, have no existence outside music. But here is a book that has had a continuously fertilizing influence on English literature from Anglo-Saxon writers to poets younger than I, and yet no one would say that the Bible "is" a work of literature. Even Blake, who went much farther than anyone else in his day in identifying religion and human creativity, did not call it that: he said "The Old and New Testaments are the Great Code of Art," a phrase I have used for my title after pondering its implications for many years. . . .

Man lives, not directly or nakedly in nature like the animals, but within a mythological universe, a body of assumptions and beliefs developed from his existential concerns. Most of this is held unconsciously, which means that our imaginations may recognize elements of it, when presented in art or literature, without consciously understanding what it is that we recognize. Practically all that we can see of this body of concern is socially conditioned and culturally inherited. Below the cultural inheritance there must be a common psychological inheritance, otherwise forms of culture and imagination outside our own traditions would not be intelligible to us. But I doubt if we can reach this common inheritance directly, by-passing the distinctive qualities in our specific culture. One of the practical functions of criticism, by which I mean the conscious organizing of a cultural tradition, is, I think, to make us more aware of our mythological conditioning.

The Bible is clearly a major element in our own imaginative tradition, whatever we may think we believe about it. It insistently raises the question: Why does this huge, sprawling, tactless book sit there inscrutably in the middle of our cultural heritage like the "great Boyg," or sphinx, in *Peer Gynt,* frustrating all our efforts to walk around it? Giambattista Vico, a thinker to whom I will refer again in a moment, worked out an elaborate theory of culture as he saw it, confining himself to secular history and avoiding the whole of the Bible. This was doubtless for prudential reasons, but there is no such excuse today for scholars who, in discussing cultural issues originally raised by the Bible and still largely informed by it, proceed as though the Bible did not exist. It seems to me that someone not a specialist in the Biblical field needs to call attention to the Bible's existence and relevance.

FURTHER READING

Arnold, Matthew. *Literature and Dogma.* London and New York: Thomas Nelson & Sons, 1873.

Ashton, Rosemary. *The German Idea: Four English Writers and the Reception of German Thought, 1800–1860.* Cambridge and New York: Cambridge University Press, 1980.

Eliot, T. S. *Notes towards a Definition of Culture.* London: Faber & Faber, 1948.

Frye, Northrop. *The Double Vision: Language and Meaning in Religion.* Toronto: University of Toronto Press, 1991.

Hesla, David H. "Religion and Literature: The Second Stage." *Journal of the American Academy of Religion* 46:181–92.

Livingston, James C. *Matthew Arnold and Christianity: His Religious Prose Writings.* Columbia: University of South Carolina Press, 1986.

Malantschuk, Gregor. *Kierkegaard's Thought.* Edited and translated by Howard V. Hong and Edna H. Hong. Princeton, N.J.: Princeton University Press, 1971.

Poole, Roger, and Henrik Stangerup, eds. *The Laughter Is on My Side: An Imaginative Introduction to Kierkegaard.* Princeton, N.J.: Princeton University Press, 1989.

Prickett, Stephen. *Romanticism and Religion: The Tradition of Coleridge and Wordsworth in the Victorian Church.* Cambridge and New York: Cambridge University Press, 1976.

Prickett, Stephen, and Robert Barnes. *The Bible.* Cambridge and New York: Cambridge University Press, 1991.

Reardon, Bernard M. G. *Religion in the Age of Romanticism: Studies in Early Nineteenth-Century Thought.* Cambridge and New York: Cambridge University Press, 1985.

Scott, Nathan A., Jr. *The Broken Center: Studies in the Theological Horizon of Modern Literature.* New Haven, Conn.: Yale University Press, 1966.

Tillich, Paul. *The Courage to Be.* New Haven, Conn.: Yale University Press, 1952.

———. "Existential Aspects of Modern Art." In *Christianity and the Existentialists,* edited by Carl Michalson, 128–47. New York: Charles Scribner's Sons, 1956.

2
The Exploration
of Origins

In the exploration of origins there must always be reached a point beyond which the logic of pursuit collapses. We might, for example, begin from the premise that God made the world "out of nothing" (*ex nihilo*). But then, who made God, or where did God come from? Or if we begin, as in the ancient Mesopotamian myths, with a watery chaos from which the first gods come into existence, then where did the watery chaos come from and by whose agency? Precisely because the question of origins and creation defies logic, it becomes a matter for the poets and, perhaps, later the theologians, as in the book of Genesis. In the selection of texts that make up this chapter, we see a variety of poetic narratives concerned with this matter.

The first striking thing to notice is the similarity between texts of such diverse culture and authorship. It would be hard to find texts further apart than Genesis and the *Popol Vuh* ("The Book of the Community"), the one a sophisticated priestly document of the Ancient Near East, the other a relatively recently written version of an ancient oral tradition from a lost people of Central America. This suggests that the human imagination is a remarkably coherent, universal function. Images and narratives written to provide a response to the most fundamental and inescapable of human questions—Where does it all come from? And how did we begin?—seem to be extremely tenacious and insistent. What is also interesting is the *literary* quality of these accounts. Emerging themselves from earlier oral traditions, these written texts seem almost to *form* a moment of creation: which comes first—the story or the act? Are we looking here, in these ancient texts, at a moment of creation itself in the history of the human mind and imagination?

In some ways, the exercise engaged in by the writers of the first three chapters of Genesis is not so far removed from the scientific inquiries of people like the mathematician Stephen Hawking in his celebrated book *A Brief History of Time* (1988), or Joseph Addison in the eighteenth century, celebrating the harmony of creation as evidence of the divinity of its creator. Science and religion meet in the myths of time and space and the concern for the origins of being. For to understand the opening chapter of the book of Genesis one must realize that this is not a mere myth or fairy story but a statement of doctrine which is the result of centuries of reflection and earlier transmission. This is how things were thought to have been in a world in which God was an integral and unquestioned part.

These stories of creation are ways of explaining how things came to be as they are. In a sense, they are more about the time now than the time "in the beginning." The opening verses of John's Gospel bring Genesis into the Hellenic world of reason, relating the language of the creation story to the Christian experience of Jesus within contemporary Greek thought.

Every age and culture has to return to the exploration of origins and retell the tale in its own way. The excerpts in this chapter could be expanded almost *ad infinitum*, but what is remarkable is how closely related all this poetic, theological, philosophical material would seem to be. In the first few pages of Ovid's *Metamorphoses* we encounter a story of a flood that comes as a punishment from the gods and covers the whole earth except the peak of one mountain—Parnassus—on which one righteous man, Deucalion, and his wife Pyrrha land and are preserved. The story mirrors almost exactly the narrative of Noah, in Genesis 6–7, and his landing on Mount Ararat. Another even more ancient version can be found in the Mesopotamian *Epic of Gilgamesh,* one of the most ancient of all texts dating from some fifteen hundred years before the great epics of the Greek Homer. Behind all these stories lies the exploration of human wickedness and how that affects human relationships with God or the gods.

As people have considered the nature of the origin of all things as a means of explaining how things are in the present time, so, inevitably, the problem of suffering and evil together with the question of who is responsible for them, quickly arises. The Hebrew Bible explores this through a narrative, the great story of Adam and Eve and the Fall, a theme taken up in the seventeenth century by the poet John Milton in perhaps the greatest of all English epic poems, *Paradise Lost.* Reprinted here is a lesser-known retelling of the story by Mark Twain, a humorous revisiting of Genesis which, among other things, glances at another origin—that of language. While still in Paradise (in a North American setting that features Niagara Falls), Adam comments on the "new creature" (Eve) and her ability to give names to things and places with a sense that the word and the thing are entirely harmonious—an experience that we have lost as we struggle to express ourselves and feel less than confident that our words accurately refer to and say what we intend. D. J. Enright, a more recent poet, has pursued the same theme in his poetic sequence *Paradise Illustrated* (1978), not included in this volume.

In the Iroquois creation story "The Woman Who Fell from the Sky," we have a more modern version of the process that almost certainly happened to the earliest stories in the Bible, in which an oral tradition is eventually written down and becomes a text. Another remarkable feature of this creation story is the tree, which is here literally a tree of life, since the woman is made pregnant by its blossom. Yet this tree is reminiscent of not only the tree of life that stands in the center of the Garden of Eden (Gen. 2:9) but also the Viking World Tree, Yggdrasil, which joins the home of the gods with the world of human beings. In this Iroquois story the woman falls through the hole left by the uprooted tree to the "shining blue world below," while in Norse myth the man and woman who will repopulate the world after the doom of the gods emerge out of Yggsdrasil.

D. H. Lawrence's *The Man Who Died* takes another view of our mortal condition, in an eclectic revisiting of the Christian theme of life after death, beginning with a (re)birth into a world of pain and solitariness. Lawrence, who had lost his own Christian faith, deliberately draws together different literatures and mythologies to refashion his own story. And so we need to remember the *literary* nature of these stories of origins and explorations of the human condition. Images and narratives cohere across huge expanses of time and place, in different cultures and systems of belief. When scientists today consider the boundaries of the universe and propose theories of its beginning, the theories they produce have a curious similarity to the most ancient of stories and poems.

As we read the Bible, we should not dismiss too quickly the wisdom of its greatest early poets, for we find it interleaved in poetry and narrative in a continuous tradition to our own time. (Hollywood knows that it is always a safe bet to return to the myths of origins and the fall from innocence to sin.) Nor, as we attend theologically to these narratives of the creative acts of God, should we forget that they lie at the heart of the Western tradition of literature—a reminder of the central importance of the study of literature and religion.

THE BOOK OF GENESIS

At the beginning of the Bible, as one might expect, there is a story about the creation of the world. The famous words begin the Bible, "In the beginning when God created the heavens and the earth . . . " These words, as we will see in other excerpts, are reinterpreted in a variety of ways within the context of other creation stories. Furthermore, it is not entirely clear which creation stories came first. Many claim that the ancient Near Eastern myths found in the *Enuma Elish* actually predate the story found in the Bible, but no one can speculate very far on how particular myths originated or spread in a primarily oral context. Here, as elsewhere, the creation story is bound up with the creation of the story itself. Where does the story come from? How much did it borrow from the creation stories of other religions and cultures?

If we read past the first chapter of Genesis, we find that even here, in the same text, is an alternative version of the creation story. In Genesis 2, the creation seems to occur all over again, only this time things look a little different and the order of events seems to change. Finally, moving into chapter 3, we have the account of the fall of Adam and Eve, the story that is as important as the creation of the world itself for the beginnings of humanity.

Genesis 1–3

1:1 In the beginning when God created the heavens and the earth, ²the earth was a formless void and darkness covered the face of the deep, while a wind from God swept over the face of the waters. ³Then God said, "Let there be light";

and there was light. [4]And God saw that the light was good; and God separated the light from the darkness. [5]God called the light Day, and the darkness he called Night. And there was evening and there was morning, the first day.

6 And God said, "Let there be a dome in the midst of the waters, and let it separate the waters from the waters." [7]So God made the dome and separated the waters that were under the dome from the waters that were above the dome. And it was so. [8]God called the dome Sky. And there was evening and there was morning, the second day.

9 And God said, "Let the waters under the sky be gathered together into one place, and let the dry land appear." And it was so. [10]God called the dry land Earth, and the waters that were gathered together he called Seas. And God saw that it was good. [11]Then God said, "Let the earth put forth vegetation: plants yielding seed, and fruit trees of every kind on earth that bear fruit with the seed in it." And it was so. [12]The earth brought forth vegetation: plants yielding seed of every kind, and trees of every kind bearing fruit with the seed in it. And God saw that it was good. [13]And there was evening and there was morning, the third day.

14 And God said, "Let there be lights in the dome of the sky to separate the day from the night; and let them be for signs and for seasons and for days and years, [15]and let them be lights in the dome of the sky to give light upon the earth." And it was so. [16]God made the two great lights—the greater light to rule the day and the lesser light to rule the night—and the stars. [17]God set them in the dome of the sky to give light upon the earth, [18]to rule over the day and over the night, and to separate the light from the darkness. And God saw that it was good. [19]And there was evening and there was morning, the fourth day.

20 And God said, "Let the waters bring forth swarms of living creatures, and let birds fly above the earth across the dome of the sky." [21]So God created the great sea monsters and every living creature that moves, of every kind, with which the waters swarm, and every winged bird of every kind. And God saw that it was good. [22] God blessed them, saying, "Be fruitful and multiply and fill the waters in the seas, and let birds multiply on the earth." [23]And there was evening and there was morning, the fifth day.

24 And God said, "Let the earth bring forth living creatures of every kind: cattle and creeping things and wild beasts of the earth of every kind." And it was so. [25]God made the wild animals of the earth of every kind, and the cattle of every kind, and everything that creeps upon the ground of every kind. And God saw that it was good.

26 Then God said, "Let us make humankind in our image, according to our likeness; and let them have dominion over the fish of the sea, and over the birds of the air, and over the cattle, and over all the wild animals of the earth, and over every creeping thing that creeps upon the earth."

27 So God created humankind in his image,
    in the image of God he created them;
    male and female he created them.

[28]God blessed them, and God said to them, "Be fruitful and multiply, and fill the earth and subdue it; and have dominion over the fish of the sea and over

the birds of the air and over every living thing that moves upon the earth." ²⁹God said, "See, I have given you every plant yielding seed that is upon the face of all the earth, and every tree with seed in its fruit; you shall have them for food. ³⁰And to every beast of the earth, and to every bird of the air, and to everything that creeps on the earth, everything that has the breath of life, I have given every green plant for food." And it was so. ³¹God saw everything that he had made, and indeed, it was very good. And there was evening and there was morning, the sixth day.

2:1 Thus the heavens and the earth were finished, and all their multitude. ²And on the seventh day God finished the work that he had done, and he rested on the seventh day from all the work that he had done. ³So God blessed the seventh day and hallowed it, because on it God rested from all the work that he had done in creation.

4 These are the generations of the heavens and the earth when they were created.

In the day that the LORD God made the earth and the heavens, ⁵when no plant of the field was yet in the earth and no herb of the field had yet sprung up—for the LORD God had not caused it to rain upon the earth, and there was no one to till the ground; ⁶but a stream would rise from the earth, and water the whole face of the ground— ⁷then the LORD God formed man from the dust of the ground, and breathed into his nostrils the breath of life; and the man became a living being. ⁸And the LORD God planted a garden in Eden, in the east; and there he put the man whom he had formed. ⁹Out of the ground the LORD God made to grow every tree that is pleasant to the sight and good for food, the tree of life also in the midst of the garden, and the tree of the knowledge of good and evil.

10 A river flows out of Eden to water the garden, and from there it divides and becomes four branches. ¹¹The name of the first is Pishon; it is the one that flows around the whole land of Havilah, where there is gold; ¹²and the gold of that land is good; bdellium and onyx stone are there. ¹³The name of the second river is Gihon; it is the one that flows around the whole land of Cush. ¹⁴The name of the third river is Tigris, which flows east of Assyria. And the fourth river is the Euphrates.

15 The LORD God took the man and put him in the garden of Eden to till it and keep it. ¹⁶And the LORD God commanded the man, "You may freely eat of every tree of the garden; ¹⁷but of the tree of the knowledge of good and evil you shall not eat, for in the day that you eat of it you shall die."

18 Then the LORD God said, "It is not good that the man should be alone; I will make him a helper as his partner." ¹⁹So out of the ground the LORD God formed every animal of the field and every bird of the air, and brought them to the man to see what he would call them; and whatever the man called every living creature, that was its name. ²⁰The man gave names to all cattle, and to the birds of the air, and to every animal of the field; but for the man there was not found a helper as his partner. ²¹So the LORD God caused a deep sleep to fall upon the man, and he slept; then he took one of his ribs and closed up its place with flesh. ²²And the rib that the LORD God had taken from the man he made into a woman and brought her to the man. ²³Then the man said,

> "This at last is bone of my bones
> and flesh of my flesh;
> this one shall be called Woman,
> for out of Man this one was taken."

24Therefore a man leaves his father and his mother and clings to his wife, and they become one flesh. 25And the man and his wife were both naked, and were not ashamed.

3:1 Now the serpent was more crafty than any other wild animal that the LORD God had made. He said to the woman, "Did God say, 'You shall not eat from any tree in the garden'?" 2The woman said to the serpent, "We may eat of the fruit of the trees in the garden; 3but God said, 'You shall not eat of the fruit of the tree that is in the middle of the garden, nor shall you touch it, or you shall die.'" 4But the serpent said to the woman, "You will not die; 5for God knows that when you eat of it your eyes will be opened, and you will be like God, knowing good and evil." 6So when the woman saw that the tree was good for food, and that it was a delight to the eyes, and that the tree was to be desired to make one wise, she took of its fruit and ate; and she also gave some to her husband, who was with her, and he ate. 7Then the eyes of both were opened, and they knew that they were naked; and they sewed fig leaves together and made loincloths for themselves.

8 They heard the sound of the LORD God walking in the garden at the time of the evening breeze, and the man and his wife hid themselves from the presence of the LORD God among the trees of the garden. 9But the LORD God called to the man, and said to him, "Where are you?" 10He said, "I heard the sound of you in the garden, and I was afraid, because I was naked; and I hid myself." 11He said, "Who told you that you were naked? Have you eaten from the tree of which I commanded you not to eat?" 12The man said, "The woman whom you gave to be with me, she gave me fruit from the tree, and I ate." 13Then the LORD God said to the woman, "What is this that you have done?" The woman said, "The serpent tricked me, and I ate." 14The LORD God said to the serpent,

> "Because you have done this,
> cursed are you among all animals,
> and among all wild creatures;
> upon your belly you shall go,
> and dust you shall eat
> all the days of your life.
> 15I will put enmity between you and the woman,
> and between your offspring and hers;
> he will strike your head,
> and you will strike his heel."

16To the woman he said,

> "I will greatly increase your pangs in childbearing;
> in pain you shall bring forth children,
> yet your desire shall be for your husband,
> and he shall rule over you."

17And to the man he said,
>"Because you have listened to the voice of your wife,
>>and have eaten of the tree
>about which I commanded you,
>>'You shall not eat of it,'
>cursed is the ground because of you;
>>in toil you shall eat of it all the days of your life;
>18thorns and thistles it shall bring forth for you;
>>and you shall eat the plants of the field.
>19By the sweat of your face
>>you shall eat bread
>until you return to the ground,
>>for out of it you were taken;
>you are dust,
>>and to dust you shall return."

20 The man named his wife Eve, because she was the mother of all living. 21And the LORD God made garments of skins for the man and for his wife, and clothed them.

22 Then the LORD God said, "See, the man has become like one of us, knowing good and evil; and now, he might reach out his hand and take also from the tree of life, and eat, and live forever"— 23therefore the LORD God sent him forth from the garden of Eden, to till the ground from which he was taken. 24He drove out the man; and at the east of the garden of Eden he placed the cherubim, and a sword flaming and turning to guard the way to the tree of life.

THE GOSPEL OF JOHN

The Prologue to the Gospel of John (1:1–18) is excerpted here particularly because of its connection with, and self-conscious imitation of, the Hebrew creation story in the first chapters of Genesis. Here in John the reader of the "New" Testament comes upon a notion of new beginnings, or, perhaps more accurately, renewed beginnings. While the meaning of this passage of the Bible has been hotly contested throughout history, the reader may be advised of a further influence stemming from Greek thought, and that is the use of the term *logos*, usually now translated as "the word." The Gospel author here mixes Hebrew thinking about creation with Greek thinking about the *logos* (variously translated from Greek philosophy as "reason" or "ratio," or thought of as a "cosmic ordering force") and applies this mixture to Jesus the Christ. Jesus Christ becomes the incarnation of "reason," or of the "Word," and the author seems to write Jesus Christ back into the foundations of the world.

John 1:1–18

1:1 In the beginning was the Word, and the Word was with God, and the Word was God. 2He was in the beginning with God. 3All things came into being through him, and without him not one thing came into being. What has come into being ⁴in him was life, and the life was the light of all people. ⁵The light shines in the darkness, and the darkness did not overcome it.

6 There was a man sent from God, whose name was John. ⁷He came as a witness to testify to the light, so that all might believe through him. ⁸He himself was not the light, but he came to testify to the light. ⁹The true light, which enlightens everyone, was coming into the world.

10 He was in the world, and the world came into being through him; yet the world did not know him. ¹¹He came to what was his own, and his own people did not accept him. ¹²But to all who received him, who believed in his name, he gave power to become children of God, ¹³who were born, not of blood or of the will of the flesh or of the will of man, but of God.

14 And the Word became flesh and lived among us, and we have seen his glory, the glory as of a father's only son, full of grace and truth. ¹⁵(John testified to him and cried out, "This was he of whom I said, 'He who comes after me ranks ahead of me because he was before me.'") ¹⁶From his fullness we have all received, grace upon grace. ¹⁷The law indeed was given through Moses; grace and truth came through Jesus Christ. ¹⁸No one has ever seen God. It is God the only Son, who is close to the Father's heart, who has made him known.

POPOL VUH

The *Popol Vuh* (literally, "The Book of the Community") is the sacred book of the Quiché Indians and contains mythologies, history, traditions, and the origins of this particular branch of the Mayan people. The *Popol Vuh,* like some of the other ancient stories excerpted here, was originally a collection of oral stories that helped constitute the religious life of a culture. In this case the culture was that of the Quiché Maya people in Central America (primarily in what is now Guatemala), a culture that has been almost completely eliminated since the Spanish conquest of Central and South America. The original author of this book is not known, but it is believed to have been a Quiché Indian who learned to write in Latin characters after the Spanish conquest and who transcribed the Quiché language into Latinized writing.

In part one of the *Popol Vuh,* we find the story of the creation of the world. You will note similarities to other creation stories: the notion that in the beginning, "nothing existed," and that somewhere in the beginning is the necessity of language, or "the word." One key difference, though, between this account and the creation story found in the Bible is that humans in the *Popol Vuh* actually take a long time to be created. The earthly elements of sky, ground, sea, and light are created in the first chapter, but the creation of humans is an experimental process that goes through many failures. Humans are fashioned from mud, wood, and eventually come about through numerous experiments that mix earthly and divine, organic and inorganic elements. Excerpted below is the creation of the world from chapter 1.

From Popol Vuh: The Sacred Book of the Ancient Quiché Maya,

English translation by Delia Goetz and Sylvanus G. Morley, from the translation of Adrián Recinos (Norman: University of Oklahoma Press, 1950), pp. 81–84, © 1950 University of Oklahoma Press.

This is the account of how all was in suspense, all calm, in silence; all motionless, still, and the expanse of the sky was empty.

This is the first account, the first narrative. There was neither man, nor animal, birds, fishes, crabs, trees, stones, caves, ravines, grasses, nor forests; there was only the sky.

The surface of the earth had not appeared. There was only the calm sea and the great expanse of the sky.

There was nothing brought together, nothing which could make a noise, nor anything which might move, or tremble, or could make noise in the sky.

There was nothing standing; only the calm water, the placid sea, alone and tranquil. Nothing existed.

There was only immobility and silence in the darkness, in the night. Only the Creator, the Maker, Tepeu, Gucumatz, the Forefathers, were in the water surrounded with light. They were hidden under green and blue feathers, and were therefore called Gucumatz. By nature they were great sages and great thinkers. In this manner the sky existed and also the Heart of Heaven, which is the name of God and thus He is called.

Then came the word. Tepeu and Gucamatz came together in the darkness, in the night, and Tepeu and Gucumatz talked together. They talked then, discussing and deliberating; they agreed, they united their words and their thoughts.

Then while they meditated, it became clear to them that when dawn would break, man must appear. Then they planned the creation, and the growth of the trees and the thickets and the birth of life and the creation of man. Thus it was arranged in the darkness and in the night by the Heart of Heaven who is called Hurácan.

The first is called Caculhá Hurácan. The second is Chipi-Caculhá. The third is Raxa-Caculhá. And these three are the Heart of Heaven.

The Tepeu and Gucumatz came together; then they conferred about life and light, what they would do so that there would be light and dawn, who it would be who would provide food and sustenance.

Thus let it be done! Let the emptiness be filled! Let the water recede and make a void, let the earth appear and become solid; let it be done. Thus they spoke. Let there be light, let there be dawn in the sky and on the earth! There shall be neither glory nor grandeur in our creation and formation until the human being is made, man is formed. So they spoke.

Then the earth was created by them. So it was, in truth, that they created the earth. Earth! they said, and instantly it was made.

Like the mist, like a cloud, and like a cloud of dust was the creation, when the mountains appeared from the water; and instantly the mountains grew.

Only by a miracle, only by magic art were the mountains and valleys formed; and instantly the groves of cypresses and pines put forth shoots together on the surface of the earth.

And thus Gucumatz was filled with joy, and exclaimed: "Your coming has been fruitful, Heart of Heaven; and you Huracán, and you Chipi-Caculhá, Raxa-Caculhá!"

"Our work, our creation shall be finished," they answered.

First the earth was formed, the mountains and the valleys; the currents of water were divided, the rivulets were running freely between the hills, and the water was separated when the high mountains appeared.

Thus was the earth created, when it was formed by the Heart of Heaven, the Heart of Earth, as they are called who first made it fruitful, when the sky was in suspense, and the earth was submerged in the water.

So it was that they made perfect the world, when they did it after thinking and meditating upon it.

"THE WOMAN WHO FELL FROM THE SKY"

"The Woman Who Fell from the Sky" is an Iroquois creation story. What we see here, as with so many creation stories, is a myth that has passed down through centuries and finally was written down on paper sometime after European settlers came to North America. Thus, like the *Popol Vuh*, also anthologized here, it functions within this chapter's theme of "origins" in two ways. First, it deals with a creation story and thus, of course, with origins. But, second, the story itself is involved in a process of creation whereby, as Walter Ong points out, the story is changed through the translation from oral to written text. In this case, the actual function of a sacred text changed its nature within a religious community when it shifted from an oral to a written narrative.

In the beginning of this story, excerpted here, we find certain parallels with other creation stories. This may seem particularly true for those who read this out of a Judeo-Christian context. However, the differences between this text and Genesis 1–3 are significant and must also be noted.

From "The Woman Who Fell from the Sky"

Once upon a time, long ago so far, a young woman was told by her dead father to go and marry a stranger. Being a strange woman, she did as he said, not taking her mother's counsel in the matter as she should have done. She journeyed to the place where the dead father had directed her to go, and there found the man she was to marry.

Now this man was a renowned magician, a sorcerer. He heard her proposal that they marry skeptically. He said to himself, "This woman is but a girl. It would be more fitting for her to ask to be my servant rather than my wife." But he only listened silently to her, then he said, "It is well. If you can meet my tests, we will see if I will make you my wife."

He took her into his lodge and said, "Now you must grind corn." She took the corn and boiled it slightly, using wood he brought her for the fire. When the kernels were softened, she began to grind them on the grinding stone. And though there were mounds and mounds of stuff to be ground, still she was done with the task in a very short time. Seeing this, the sorcerer was amazed, but he kept silent. Instead he ordered her to remove all her clothing. When she was naked, he told her to cook the corn in the huge pot that hung over the fire. This she did, though the hot corn popped and spattered scalding, clinging mush all over her. But she did not flinch, enduring the burns with calm.

When the mush was done, the woman told the sorcerer it was ready. "Good," he said. "Now you will feed my servants." He noted that her body was covered with corn mush. Opening the door, he called in several huge beasts who ran to the woman and began to lick the mush from her body with their razor sharp tongues, leaving deep gashes where their tongues sliced her flesh. Still she did not recoil but endured the torment, not letting her face lose its look of calm composure.

Seeing this, the sorcerer let the beasts back out, then said she and he would be married, and so they were. After four nights that they spent sleeping opposite each other with the soles of their feet touching, he sent her back to her village with gifts of meat for the people. He commanded her to divide the meat evenly among all the people, and further to see to it that every lodge had its roof removed that night, as he was going to send a white corn rain among them. She did as she was told, and after the village had received its gifts, the meat and the white corn rain, she returned to her husband's lodge.

Outside his lodge there grew a tree that was always filled with blossoms so bright they gave light to his whole land. The woman loved the tree, loved to sit under it and converse with the spirits and her dead father, whom she held dear in her heart. She so loved the light tree that once, when everyone was sleeping, she lay down under it and opened her legs and her body to it. A blossom fell on her vagina then, touching her with sweetness and a certain joy. And soon after she knew she was pregnant.

About that time her husband became weak and ill. His medicine people could not heal him, but told him that his sickness was caused by his wife. He was certain they were right, for he had never met anyone so powerful as she. He feared that her power was greater than his own, for hadn't she been able to withstand his most difficult tests? "What should I do?" he asked his advisors. They did not advise him to divorce her, because that kind of separation was unknown to them. They did not advise him to kill her, because death was unknown among them. The only death that had occurred was of the woman's father, and they did not understand what had happened to him.

After deliberating on the matter for four days, the advisors told the sorcerer that he should uproot the tree of light. Then, lying beside it, he should call his wife to come and sit with him. He should by some ruse get her to fall over the edge of the hole the uprooted tree would leave, and she would fall into the void. When she had fallen, they said, he was to replace the tree and then he would recover his health and his power.

That afternoon he went outside his lodge and pulled up the tree. He peered over the edge of the hole it left, and he could see another world below. He called his wife to come and see it. When she came, he said, "Lean over the edge. You can see another world below." She knelt beside the hole and leaning over the edge, looked down. She saw darkness, and a long way below, she saw blue, a shining blue that seemed filled with promise and delight. She looked at her husband and smiled, eyes dancing with pleasure. "It looks like a beautiful place there," she said. "Who would have thought that the tree of light would be growing over such a place!"

"Yes," her husband agreed. "It surely seems beautiful there." He regarded her for a moment carefully, then said, "I wonder what it is like there. Maybe somebody could go down there and find out." Astonished, the woman looked at her husband. "But how would someone do that?"

"Jump." The husband said.

"Jump?" she asked, looking down through the opening, trying to calculate the distance. "But it is very far." "Someone of your courage could do it," he said. "You could jump. Become the wind or a petal from this tree." He indicated the tree lying fallen next to them. "A petal could fall, gently, on the wind it would be carried. You could be a petal in the wind. You could be a butterfly, a downgliding bright bird."

She gazed for a long time at the shining blue below her. "I could jump like that. I could float downward. I could fall into the shining blue world below us."

"Yes," he said. "You could."

For another long moment she knelt gazing downward, then taking a deep breath she stood, and flexing her knees and raising her arms high over her head she leaned into the opening and dove through. For some time the sorcerer watched her body as it fell downward through the dark, toward the blue. "She jumped," he finally said to the council as they made their way slowly toward him. "She's gone." And they raised the tree and placed it back firmly in its place, covering the opening to the other world with its roots.

OVID,
METAMORPHOSES

The Latin poet Ovid (43 B.C.E–18 C.E.) has been enormously influential on Western literature as a guide to Greek mythology and Roman legend, and his *Metamorphoses* influenced, among others, Chaucer, Spenser, and Shakespeare.

The *Metamorphoses* (literally, "transformation") is a collection, in verse hexameters in fifteen books, of some two hundred and fifty stories from ancient mythology. Like the Hebrew Bible, it begins with an account of the origin of the world from a chaos of elements ("everything gets in the way of everything else") and their transformation into an ordered whole out of which emerges a continuous narrative of the four ages of the world, from gold to silver, to bronze and finally to iron, and the emergence of wickedness and conflict. Notice the distinctions between the all-governing gods and the creator, who is "a natural force of a higher kind." The account of the flood sent by Neptune at the angry calling of his brother god Jupiter, is highly reminiscent of Genesis 6–7. Ovid ends his epic with an account of the reign of the emperor Augustus, who shares with the god Jupiter the control of earth and heaven.

From Chaos Transformed into the Ordered Universe, *in* Metamorphoses

My purpose is to tell of bodies which have been transformed into shapes of a different kind. You heavenly powers, since you were responsible for those changes, as for all else, look favourably on my attempts, and spin an unbroken thread of verse, from the earliest beginnings of the world, down to my own times.

Before there was any earth or sea, before the canopy of heaven stretched overhead, Nature presented the same aspect the world over, that to which men have given the name of Chaos. This was a shapeless uncoordinated mass, nothing but a weight of lifeless matter, whose ill-assorted elements were indiscriminately heaped together in one place. There was no sun, in those days, to provide the world with light, no crescent moon ever filling out her horns: the earth was not poised in the enveloping air, balanced there by its own weight, nor did the sea stretch out its arms along the margins of the shores. Although the elements of land and air and sea were there, the earth had no firmness, the water no fluidity, there was no brightness in the sky. Nothing had any lasting shape, but everything got in the way of everything else; for, within that one body, cold warred with hot, moist with dry, soft with hard, and light with heavy.

This strife was finally resolved by a god, a natural force of a higher kind, who separated the earth from heaven, and the waters from the earth, and set the clear air apart from the cloudy atmosphere. When he had freed these elements, sorting them out from the heap where they had lain, indistinguishable from one another, he bound them fast, each in its separate place, forming a harmonious union. The fiery aether, which has no weight, formed the vault of heaven, flashing upwards to take its place in the highest sphere. The air, next to it in lightness, occupied the neighbouring regions. Earth, heavier than these, attracted to itself the grosser elements, and sank down under its own weight, while the encircling sea took possession of the last place of all, and held the solid earth in its embrace. In this way the god, whichever of the gods it was, set the chaotic mass in order, and, after dividing it up, arranged it in its constituent parts.

When this was done, his first care was to shape the earth into a great ball, so that it might be the same in all directions. After that, he commanded the seas to spread out this way and that, to swell into waves under the influence of the rushing winds, and to pour themselves around earth's shores. Springs, too, he created, and great pools and lakes, and confined between sloping banks the rivers which flow down from the hills and continue, each in its own channel, until they are either swallowed up by the earth itself, or reach the sea and enter its expanse of wider waters, there to wash against shores instead of banks. Then the god further ordained that earth's plains should unroll, its valleys sink down, the woods be clothed with leaves, and rocky mountain peaks rise up.

As the sky is divided into two zones on the right hand, and two on the left, with a fifth in between, hotter than any of the rest, so the world which the sky encloses was marked off in the same way, thanks to the providence of the god: he imposed the same number of zones on earth as there are in the heavens. The central zone is so hot as to be uninhabitable, while two others are covered in deep snow: but between these extremes he set two zones to which he gave a temperate climate, compounded of heat and cold.

Over all these regions hangs the air, as much heavier than the fiery aether as it is lighter than earth or water. To the air the god assigned mists and clouds, and thunder that was destined to cause human hearts to tremble: here too he placed the thunderbolts, and winds that strike out lightnings from the clouds. Nor did the builder of the world allow the winds, any more than the rest, to roam at will throughout the air—they can scarcely be prevented from tearing the world apart, even as it is, although each blows in a different direction: so violent is the strife between brothers. The East wind withdrew to the lands of the dawn, to the kingdoms of Arabia and Persia, and to the mountain ridges that lie close to the sun's morning rays. The West, and the shores which are warmed by the setting sun, are subject to Zephyr. Boreas, who makes men shudder with his chill breath, invaded Scythia and the North, while the lands opposite to those are continually drenched with rain and clouds, brought by the South wind.

Above all these, the god set the clear aether that has no weight, and is untainted by any earthly particles.

No sooner were all things separated in this way, and confined within definite limits, than the stars which had long been buried in darkness and obscurity began to blaze forth all through the sky. So that every region should have its appropriate inhabitants, stars and divine forms occupied the heavens, the waters afforded a home to gleaming fishes, earth harboured wild beasts, and the yielding air welcomed the birds.

There was as yet no animal which was more akin to the gods than these, none more capable of intelligence, none that could be master over all the rest. It was at this point that man was born: either the Creator, who was responsible for this better world, made him from divine seed, or else Prometheus, son of Iapetus, took the new-made earth which, only recently separated from the lofty aether, still retained some elements related to those of heaven and, mixing it with rainwater, fashioned it into the image of the all-governing gods. Whereas other animals hang their heads and look at the ground, he made man stand erect, bidding him look up to heaven, and lift his head to the stars. So the earth, which had been rough and formless, was moulded into the shape of man, a creature till then unknown. . . .

Nor was Jupiter's anger satisfied with the resources of his own realm of heaven: his brother Neptune, the god of the sea, lent him the assistance of his waves. He sent forth a summons to the rivers, and when they entered their king's home: "No time now for long exhortations!" he cried. "Exert your strength to the utmost: that is what we need. Fling wide your homes, withdraw all barriers, and give free course to your waters." These were his orders. The rivers returned to their homes and, opening up the mouths of their springs, went rushing to the sea in frenzied torrents. . . .

Some tried to escape by climbing to the hilltops, others, sitting in their curved boats, plied the oars where lately they had been ploughing; some sailed over cornlands, over the submerged roofs of their homes, while some found fish in the topmost branches of the elms. At times it happened that they dropped anchor in green meadows, sometimes the curved keels grazed vineyards that lay beneath them. Where lately sinewy goats cropped the grass, now ugly seals disported themselves. The Nereids wondered to see groves and towns and houses under the water; dolphins took possession of the woods, and dashed against high branches, shaking the oak trees as they knocked against them. Wolves swam among the flocks, and the waves supported tawny lions, and tigers too. The lightning stroke of his strong tusk was of no use, then, to the wild boar, nor his swift legs to the stag—both alike were swept away. Wandering birds searched long for some land where they might rest, till their wings grew weary and they fell into the sea. The ocean, all restraints removed, overwhelmed the hills, and waves were washing the mountain peaks, a sight never seen before. The greater part of the human race was swallowed up by the waters: those whom the sea spared died from lack of food, overcome by long-continued famine.

There is a land, Phocis, which separates the fields of Boeotia from those of Oeta. It was a fertile spot while it was land, but now it had become part of the sea, a broad stretch of waters, suddenly formed. In that region a high mountain, called Parnassus, raises twin summits to the stars, and its ridges pierce the clouds. When the waters had covered all the rest of the earth, the little boat which carried Deucalion and his wife ran aground here. Of all the men who ever lived, Deucalion was the best and the most upright, no woman ever showed more reverence for the gods than Pyrrha, his wife. Their first action was to offer prayers to the Corycian nymphs, to the deities of the mountain, and to Themis, the goddess who foretold the future from its oracular shrine.

Now Jupiter saw the earth all covered with standing waters. He perceived that one alone survived of so many thousand men, one only of so many thousand women, and he knew that both were guiltless, both true worshippers of god. So, with the help of the North wind he drove away the storm clouds and, scattering the veils of mist, displayed heaven to earth and earth to heaven. The sea was no longer angry, for the ruler of ocean soothed the waves, laying aside his trident. Then he called to the sea-god Triton, who rose from the deep, his shoulders covered with clustering shellfish. Neptune bade him blow on his echoing conch shell, and recall waves and rivers by his signal. He lifted his hollow trumpet, a coiling instrument which broadens out in circling spirals from its base. When he blows upon it in mid-ocean, its notes fill the furthest shores of east and west. So now, too, the god put it to his lips which were all damp from his dripping beard, and blew it, sending forth the signal for retreat as he had been bidden. The sound was heard by all the waters that covered earth and sea, and all the waves which heard it were checked in their course. The sea had shores once more, the swollen rivers were contained within their own channels, the floods sank down, and hills were seen to emerge. Earth rose up, its lands advancing as the waves retreated, and after a long interval the woods displayed their treetops uncovered, the mud left behind still clinging to their leaves.

MARK TWAIN,
EXTRACTS FROM ADAM'S DIARY

Mark Twain, the pen name for Samuel L. Clemens (1836–1910), was one of the most famous and popular American writers. Twain shaped the American experience as much as did Emerson or Edwards. Best known for *Huckleberry Finn* and *Tom Sawyer*, Twain also wrote journalism and fiction of strong wit and critical satire. Reared in the Midwest, Twain was brought up attending Sunday school, and this early religious education helped form some of the characters in his stories. Religion became a target for his satire, as did politics and society in general. He believed that humans tended too much toward superstition, and the effect of religion was, on the whole, detrimental to the good of humanity.

Excerpts here are from *Extracts from Adam's Diary* (1904), which was written under the name of Mark Twain, and which carries the note, "Translated from the original manuscript." While it is a humorous look at the story of Adam and Eve (set not in the Garden of Eden, but at Niagara Falls), it also describes something of the way Twain saw the relationship between men and women. The character of Eve was meant as a tribute to his recently deceased wife, Olivia. Adam's bemused, half-exasperated observations about conjugal life in the garden foreshadow the pain and pleasure of life after the Fall. The *Extracts* also highlights the struggle for language in the beginning.

From Extracts from Adam's Diary

Monday
This new creature with the long hair is a good deal in the way. It is always hanging around and following me about. I don't like this; I am not used to company. I wish it would stay with the other animals. . . . Cloudy today, wind in the east; think we shall have rain. . . . *We?* Where did I get that word? . . . I remember now—the new creature uses it.

Tuesday
Been examining the great waterfall. It is the finest thing on the estate, I think. The new creature calls it Niagara Falls—why, I am sure I do not know. Says it *looks* like Niagara Falls. That is not a reason; it is mere waywardness and imbecility. I get no chance to name anything myself. The new creature names everything that comes along, before I can get in a protest. And always that same pretext is offered—it *looks* like the thing. There is the dodo, for instance. Says the moment one looks at it one sees at a glance that it "looks like a dodo." It will have to keep that name, no doubt. It wearies me to fret about it, and it does no good, anyway. Dodo! It looks no more like a dodo than I do. . . .

Wednesday

I have had a variegated time. I escaped that night, and rode a horse all night as fast as he could go, hoping to get clear out of the Park and hide in some other country before the trouble should begin; but it was not to be. About an hour after sunup, as I was riding through a flowery plain where thousands of animals were grazing, slumbering, or playing with each other, according to their wont; all of a sudden they broke into a tempest of frightful noises, and in one moment the plain was in a frantic commotion and every beast was destroying its neighbor. I knew what it meant—Eve had eaten that fruit, and death was come into the world. . . . The tigers ate my horse, paying no attention when I ordered them to desist, and they would even have eaten me if I had stayed—which I didn't, but went away in much haste. . . . I found this place, outside the Park, and was fairly comfortable for a few days, but she has found me out. Found me out, and has named the place Tonawanda—says it *looks* like that. In fact, I was not sorry she came, for there are but meagre pickings here, and she brought some of those apples. I was obliged to eat them, I was so hungry. It was against my principles, but I find that principles have no real force except when one is well fed. . . . She came curtained in boughs and bunches of leaves, and when I asked her what she meant by such nonsense, and snatched them away and threw them down, she tittered and blushed. I had never seen a person titter and blush before, and to me it seemed unbecoming and idiotic. She said I would soon know how it was myself. This was correct. Hungry as I was, I laid down the apple half eaten—certainly the best one I ever saw, considering the lateness of the season—and arrayed myself in the discarded boughs and branches, and then spoke to her with some severity and ordered her to go and get some more and not make such a spectacle of herself. She did it, and after this we crept down to where the wild beast battle had been, and collected some skins, and I made her patch together a couple of suits proper for public occasions. They are uncomfortable, it is true, but stylish, and that is the main point about clothes. . . . I find she is a good deal of a companion. I see I should be lonesome and depressed without her, now that I have lost my property. Another thing, she says it is ordered that we work for our living hereafter. She will be useful. I will superintend. . . .

Ten Years Later

They are boys; we found it out long ago. It was their coming in that small, immature shape that puzzled us; we were not used to it. There are some girls now. Abel is a good boy, but if Cain had stayed a bear it would have improved him. After all these years, I see that I was mistaken about Eve in the beginning; it is better to live outside the Garden with her than inside it without her. At first I thought she talked too much; but now I should be sorry to have that voice fall silent and pass out of my life. Blessed be the chestnut that brought us near together and taught me to know the goodness of her heart and the sweetness of her spirit!

THE END

JOSEPH ADDISION,
"ODE"

Joseph Addision (1672–1719) was once described as "the first Victorian." In this formal poem, still sometimes sung in churches as a hymn, Addison describes the formal harmony of creation as evidence of the divine nature of its origin. The theology behind this poem is known as "deist," that is, a natural religion that denies the doctrine of special revelation, and argues that God, having created the universe, has finished his task. From the initial moment, the natural order continues (like clockwork) without further divine intervention.

"Ode"

> The spacious firmament on high
> With all the blue ethereal sky,
> And spangled heavens, a shining frame,
> Their great original proclaim:
> The unwearied sun, from day to day,
> Does his creator's power display,
> And publishes to every land
> The work of an almighty hand.
>
> Soon as the evening shades prevail,
> The moon takes up the wondrous tale,
> And nightly to the listening earth
> Repeats the story of her birth:
> Whilst all the stars that round her burn,
> And all the planets in their turn,
> Confirm the tidings as they roll,
> And spread the truth from pole to pole.
>
> What though, in solemn silence, all
> Move around the dark, terrestrial ball?
> What though nor real voice nor sound
> Amid their radiant orbs be found?
> In reason's ear they all rejoice,
> And utter forth a glorious voice,
> For ever singing, as they shine,
> "The hand that made us is divine."

D. H. LAWRENCE,
"THE MAN WHO DIED"

D. H. Lawrence (1885–1930) remains one of the most widely read English novelists of the twentieth century. Best known, perhaps, for his novels *The Rainbow* (1915), *Women in Love* (1920), and *Lady Chatterley's Lover* (1928), with their frank sexuality and involvement with the physical world of nature, Lawrence excelled as a writer of short stories and in his imaginative treatment of religious subjects.

"The Man Who Died" was published in 1929 under the title "The Escaped Cock." It mixes Christian themes of resurrection with the mystery religions of Isis in Egypt. In the passage here, "the peasant" is awakened to the world by the crowing of the escaped cockerel. The narrative is reminiscent of the story of the raising of Lazarus from the tomb (John 11:1–44), a return from death to the world that had already been left. It raises acutely the question of the nature of resurrection or even, perhaps, birth itself into a world of pain and loneliness.

From "The Man Who Died"

At the same time, at the same hour before dawn, on the same morning, a man awoke from a long sleep in which he was tied up. He woke numb and cold, inside a carved hole in the rock. Through all the long sleep his body had been full of hurt, and it was still full of hurt. He did not open his eyes. Yet he knew that he was awake, and numb, and cold, and rigid, and full of hurt, and tied up. His face was banded with cold bands, his legs were bandaged together. Only his hands were loose.

He could move if he wanted: he knew that. But he had no want. Who would want to come back from the dead? A deep, deep nausea stirred in him, at the premonition of movement. He resented already the fact of the strange, incalculable moving that had already taken place in him: the moving back into consciousness. He had not wished it. He had wanted to stay outside, in the place where even memory is stone dead.

But now, something had returned to him, like a returned letter, and in that return he lay overcome with a sense of nausea. Yet suddenly his hands moved. They lifted up, cold, heavy and sore. Yet they lifted up, to drag away the cloth from his face, and push at the shoulder-bands. Then they fell again, cold, heavy, numb, and sick with having moved even so much, unspeakably unwilling to move further.

With his face cleared and his shoulders free, he lapsed again, and lay dead, resting on the cold nullity of being dead. It was the most desirable. And almost, he had it complete: the utter cold nullity of being outside.

Yet when he was most nearly gone, suddenly, driven by an ache at the wrists, his hands rose and began pushing at the bandages of his knees, his feet began to stir, even while his breast lay cold and dead still.

And at last, the eyes opened. On to the dark. The same dark! Yet perhaps there was a pale chink, of the all-disturbing light, prising open the pure dark. He could not lift his head. The eyes closed. And again it was finished.

Then suddenly he leaned up, and the great world reeled. Bandages fell away. And narrow walls of rock closed upon him, and gave the new anguish of imprisonment. There were chinks of light. With a wave of strength that came from revulsion, he leaned forward, in that narrow well of rock, and leaned frail hands on the rock near the chinks of light.

Strength came from somewhere, from revulsion; there was a crash and a wave of light, and the dead man was crouching in his lair, facing the animal onrush of light. Yet it was hardly dawn. And the strange, piercing keenness of daybreak's sharp breath was on him. It meant full awakening.

Slowly, slowly he crept down from the cell of rock with the caution of the bitterly wounded. Bandages and linen and perfume fell away, and he crouched on the ground against the wall of rock, to recover oblivion. But he saw his hurt feet touching the earth again, with unspeakable pain, the earth they had meant to touch no more, and he saw his thin legs that had died, and pain unknowable, pain like utter bodily disillusion, filled him so full that he stood up, with one torn hand on the ledge of the tomb.

To be back! To be back again, after all that! He saw the linen swathing-bands fallen round his dead feet, and stooping, he picked them up, folded them, and laid them back in the rocky cavity from which he had emerged. Then he took the perfumed linen sheet, wrapped it round him as a mantle, and turned away, to the wanness of the chill dawn.

He was alone; and having died, was even beyond loneliness.

WALTER ONG,
THE PRESENCE OF THE WORD

Walter (Jackson) Ong (b. 1912) is a Jesuit scholar, born in Kansas City, who became interested in anthropological findings about the differences between cultures that are primarily oral and those that are primarily written or printed. Drawing on the work of Jack Goody, Eric Havelock, Lurria, Marshall McLuhan, and others, Ong helped instigate a reinterpretation of religion through categories of orality and literacy. The work he borrowed from anthropologists was taken up by others within religious studies and has been applied to biblical interpretation and studies of religion in general.

Ong's key point is that the very content of information changes when it is transmitted in a different medium, in part, because different media rely on different senses, such as the physical sense of touch, sight, or hearing. Various cultural communications stress different senses, constructing what Ong calls a "sensorium." Therefore, oral stories that were told within a religious communal setting were fundamentally changed when they were later written down (oftentimes by literate, colonial powers overtaking an oral culture). He argues that the dynamic force of religion itself lost some of its potency when it was put into print, which Ong sees as a delimiting and solidifying medium. In the passages below, some of the implications of the shift from oral language to written texts are noted for their effects on religion.

From The Presence of the Word

The question of the sensorium in the Christian economy of revelation is particularly fascinating because of the primacy which this economy accords to the word of God and thus in some mysterious way to sound itself, a primacy already suggested in the Old Testament pre-Christian tradition. Many religions make much of the word of God or of gods, or simply of the word as a source of wisdom. But the distinctively personal cast of the relationship between man and God in the Hebreo-Christian tradition heightens from the earliest Old Testament times the importance of the word as the focus of personal communication. God calls to Abraham, "Abraham!" and Abraham answers "Here I am" (Gen. 22:1). A similar thing happens to Jacob, who is called by an angel of God (later recognized to be God himself), "Jacob!" and who likewise answers, "Here I am" (Gen. 31:11). As Erich Auerbach has made clear in the first chapter of his *Mimesis*, this direct and unexplained confrontation—a verbal assault on a given person by God—is not the sort of thing one meets with in Greek or other nonbiblical tradition. God's word impinges on the human person as a two-edged sword. . . .

The New Testament Gospel or Good News about the Word is itself likewise tied to the spoken word of man. For it is the business of those who know this truth to make it known to all other men by use of the word in preaching, where the human word exists in a mysterious connection with the divine. The Christian Church is thus inevitably a missionary Church, committed to sharing its good news with all men, driven by the Word to maximum communication, and in all this, through the personal contacts effected most basically by the spoken word. *Fides ex auditu,* "faith comes through hearing," we read in the Epistle to the Romans (10:17).

But the word of God in both Old and New Testament is also involved in writing, and thus in man's shift from a primitive oral-aural culture to one organized through a more visualist sensorium. In the scriptural account the Old Testament public revelation was first given to the ancient Hebrews, one of the peoples actually possessing the alphabet, at a time when the alphabet was new and rare. Jesus himself, the Word of God, could read and write, as we know from several incidents in the New Testament, although sometimes his opponents were nonplussed as to how he had learned to do so: "How does this man know letters without having studied them?" (John 7:15). Gradually through its history the Hebrew people had become more and more a people of the book, the Law and the Prophets, and the Christians if anything were a people of the book even more decisively. Their glory in their unity, and their shame when they fell out among themselves, had often to do with what they made of the Holy Scriptures. Nevertheless, despite this addiction to literacy, the spoken word retains always for the Christian some special value. In Catholicism this is manifest by, among other things, devotion to nonwritten tradition as well as to the Scriptures. In Protestantism it is manifest by a special stress on preaching the word of God, a stress of course not unknown in Catholicism and growing stronger in Catholic circles today, though less uniquely dominant there. . . .

But the study of the word is a complex matter. In our own day the word takes on a seemingly limitless number of new forms. Long given visual extension by writing and print, it is now given artificial oral-aural public presence through the electronic media of radio and tapes and loudspeakers. It is projected on television with special visual accompaniment, not only dancing men but also dancing cigarettes and bars of soap, such as could not be realized without this or other spatial media. It is towed visibly through the skies behind aircraft and bounced invisibly off satellites.

In this milieu the question of man's relation to the word of God or to the bearing of the term "word" becomes of crucial importance. Could the cry of Nietzsche's madman, "God is dead," derive from the fact that He cannot be readily found by the old signs in the newly organized sensorium where the word stands in such different relationship to the total complex of awarenesses by which man earlier situated himself in his life world? Could the late Martin Buber's more sensitive suggestion that this is an age in which God is "silent" reflect the same state of affairs? Could it be that God is not silent but that man is relatively deaf, his sensorium adjusted to the post-Newtonian silent universe?

If so, the situation is not hopeless. If we have moved far from the original culture in which the word acquired its basic meaning, yet we still do use the word, we still talk. How much is the word the same and how much different? To understand ourselves and the religious question as it exists in the modern world, we have somehow to understand man's past in which the word existed in a sensorium by now grown utterly strange to us. What was the word like to men of old, more particularly to men before the word was put into writing? The past is, after all, ourselves, and it is our future. Our possibilities themselves are what they are because of what we have been.

FURTHER READING

"The Babylonian Creation." In *Poems of Heaven and Hell from Ancient Mesopotamia.* Translated by N. K. Sanders. London: Penguin Classics, 1971.

Barnes, Julian. *A History of the World in 10 1/2 Chapters.* New York: Jonathan Cape, 1989.

Enright, D. J. *Paradise Illustrated* (1978). In *Collected Poems.* Oxford: Oxford University Press, 1987.

The Epic of Gilgamesh: An English Version. 2d ed. Translated by N. K. Sanders. London: Penguin Classics, 1972.

Levinas, Emmanuel. "And God Created Woman." In *Nine Talmudic Readings.* Translated by Annete Aronowicz. Bloomington: Indiana University Press, 1994.

Margenau, Henri, and Roy Abraham Varghese, eds. *Cosmos, Bios, Theos: Scientists Reflect on Science, God, and the Origins of the Universe, Life, and Homo Sapiens.* La Salle, Ill.: Open Court, 1992.

Scholem, Gershom. *Kabbalah.* Jerusalem: Keter Publishing, 1974; New York: New American Library/Penguin, 1978.

Sproul, Barbara C. *Primal Myths: Creating the World.* San Francisco: Harper & Row, 1979.

3

The Interpretive Tradition
of Literature and Religion

This chapter is concerned with both the origin of texts, particularly the texts of the Bible, and the development of the interpretation and continuity of those texts through a tradition that stretches back across more than two millennia in the Western tradition. It is a highly complex and often technical tradition, which can hardly be dealt with adequately here, and we concentrate on a few central themes: word, text, imagination, and reading. It is also a tradition that supports the remarkable continuities underlying the contemporary interdiscipline and is characterized by a consistent literary-religious interaction.

Time and again, various efforts to articulate religious and theological concerns have stimulated literary expression and prompted forms of literary interpretation. Thus the interplay of priestly and prophetic writing in the Hebrew Bible generated poetry and narrative that have profoundly influenced Western literature to the present day, while interpretive traditions of mishnah and midrash have guided or even determined the way in which these texts are read, never more so than in our own time. Through early Christian scholars such as Augustine of Hippo, methods of interpretation and the use of allegory and typology were developed from the Hebrew writers of the Bible itself, and these have reached us through medieval and Renaissance traditions.

We look briefly at the disciplines of contemplation and meditation in women writers like Hildegard of Bingen and Teresa of Avila and then move through the Protestant Reformation with the *Table Talk* of Martin Luther, and finally to the modern period with the Danish philosopher Søren Kierkegaard.

The excerpts begin with three biblical passages. The origin of the term "song of ascents," which prefaces Psalm 130 and fourteen other psalms, is unclear. It may refer to the "ascending" of the exiles from their Babylonian captivity. In the Christian tradition, Psalm 130 is one of the Penitential Psalms of the ancient church. It was a favorite of Martin Luther's and expresses a remarkably colloquial conversation with God in terms of highly poetic imagery. Such closeness to the Divine is characteristic also of the prophetic writings, exemplified here by chapter 3 of the book of Ezekiel. In the opening verse, the "text" of the Word of God is described as a scroll that is to be eaten—literally digested. Throughout the Bible, the physical presence of the "word" is powerfully felt, not merely as a cerebral event to be understood, but also to be taken into the body physically, while the utterances of the prophet are dictated directly by God himself to the judgment of those who choose either to hear or not to hear.

Revelation, the last book of the New Testament, continues this ancient prophetic tradition, as the visionary writer also eats the scroll given to him by the angel, though now its honey sweetness (Ezek. 3:3; Rev. 10:9) becomes bitter as it enters the body.

As we move into the literature of the church fathers, we find Saint Augustine (more often referred to as Augustine of Hippo in contemporary theology), in his great work *The City of God* (*De Civitate Dei*), addressing the nature of God's "speech" and how it is to be interpreted by mere humans with their limited languages. Although God's speech is beyond our describing, we may grasp it "with our inward ears." For Augustine, this means that theological constructions such as the Trinity become the human referents for divine words, enabling us to interpret indirectly the language of God in the Bible. In the writings of the medieval nun, scholar, and musician Hildegard of Bingen, the notion of the Word of God is first associated (as in the Fourth Gospel) with the incarnate Christ himself, prefigured in the Old Testament and "declared" in the New. According to Hildegard, God speaks in three divisions—law, grace, and the exposition of scripture—but she acknowledges, like Augustine, that our knowledge of God's glory can never be direct, but only indirect, by interpretation and study of the "wisdom of the doctors."

One persistent tradition of spirituality and spiritual writing is the mystical, which, though often highly figurative in its literary forms, celebrates a direct relationship with God through ecstatic experiences. The result has frequently been poetry of the highest order, such as that of the Spanish mystical theologian John of the Cross (1542–1591). A Carmelite friar, John knew personally Teresa of Avila, whose contemplative life inspired in her ecstatic experiences of the Divine. The English poet Richard Crashaw (1612–1649) wrote of her in his great "Hymn to Sainte Teresa," describing in her the qualities of "the eagle and the dove."

The writings of Martin Luther mark a turning point in the history of Christian interpretation of scripture. Luther placed unique emphasis on the power of the scriptural word apart from the authority of the church as an institution (*sola scriptura*) and the ability of each individual reader of the Bible to encounter God. This understanding of the power of the text inspired translations of the Bible into readable vernaculars so that, as the English archbishop Cranmer wrote in 1539, "folk should not lack the fruit of reading." For the first time, perhaps, reading and understanding the Bible became a common task.

Within the traditions of Lutheranism, Søren Kierkegaard (see above, chapter 1) recognized that the man who read the great story of the sacrifice of Isaac in Genesis 22 might not be a "thinker [and] he felt no need of getting beyond faith." Entering into the experience of the biblical narrative, Kierkegaard's reader "was not a learned exegete," and with him we enter the world of contemporary existentialist thought. Kierkegaard's readings of Genesis 22, with their attempts to fill in and complete the spare biblical narrative, attracted the close attention of the novelist Franz Kafka, as well as the later commentator on Kierkegaard, Jacques Derrida, who is of Jewish extraction. Derrida's *The Gift of Death* combines literalist readings within the traditions of Protestant hermeneutics ("Abraham doesn't speak in figures, fables, parables, metaphors, or enigmas") with the subtleties of ancient Jewish reading practices that combined overlapping methods of interpretation and met the original text with imaginative readings that are literary texts in their own right.

We include the Jewish novelist Isaac Bashevis Singer among our group of interpreters, as a writer of narratives that, in a sense, continue the biblical tradition itself. The interpretive tradition begins within the Bible and includes a long line of creative writers—the critic and the poet/writer cannot be finally distinguished, which is why the study of religion and literature is so important. This chapter ends, therefore, with a brief passage from the contemporary French philosopher and critic Paul Ricoeur, which stresses the close and continuing relationship between the Bible and the "productive imagination."

PSALM 130,
EZEKIEL 3, REVELATION 10

The scriptures lie at the heart and foundation of the faith of both Israel and the Christian church and are the key to the interpretive traditions to which they give rise. In many different ways they explore the experience of call and response—the word and the demands that it makes on the listener in terms of comprehension and subsequent action. How then do we as readers understand and act on the texts that we read?

Within the Hebrew Bible, the need to find ways of distinguishing between true and false prophecy is recognized—the legitimate and the false word, in texts that weave together different strands; the priestly; the prophetic; and so on. The scriptures profess a different understanding of "inspiration" from that of classical Greece, which understood human words to be inspired. The Jews understood the Torah to represent God's own words, so that interpretation involves the human attempt to grasp nothing less than the word of God.

The literature of the Bible challenges us with texts of power that work through strong, sometimes violent, images, testing our intellects and our imaginations.

Psalm 130

A Song of Ascents.

    ¹Out of the depths I cry to you, O LORD.
    ² Lord, hear my voice!

Let your ears be attentive
  to the voice of my supplications!

³If you, O LORD, should mark iniquities,
  Lord, who could stand?

⁴But there is forgiveness with you,
  so that you may be revered.

⁵I wait for the LORD, my soul waits,
  and in his word I hope;
⁶my soul waits for the Lord
  more than those who watch for the morning,
  more than those who watch for the morning.

⁷O Israel, hope in the LORD!
  For with the LORD there is steadfast love,
  and with him is great power to redeem.
⁸It is he who will redeem Israel
  from all its iniquities.

Ezekiel 3

1 He said to me, O mortal, eat what is offered to you; eat this scroll, and go, speak to the house of Israel. ²So I opened my mouth, and he gave me the scroll to eat. ³He said to me, Mortal, eat this scroll that I give you and fill your stomach with it. Then I ate it; and it was in my mouth as sweet as honey.

4 He said to me, Mortal, go to the house of Israel and speak my very words to them. ⁵For you are not sent to a people of obscure speech and difficult language, but to the house of Israel— ⁶not to many peoples of obscure speech and difficult language, whose words you cannot understand. Surely, if I sent you to them, they would listen to you. ⁷But the house of Israel will not listen to you, for they are not willing to listen to me; because all the house of Israel have a hard forehead and a stubborn heart. ⁸See, I have made your face hard against their faces, and your forehead hard against their foreheads. ⁹Like the hardest stone, harder than flint, I have made your forehead; do not fear them or be dismayed at their looks, for they are a rebellious house. ¹⁰He said to me: Mortal, all my words that I shall speak to you receive in your heart and hear with your ears; ¹¹then go to the exiles, to your people, and speak to them. Say to them, "Thus says the Lord GOD"; whether they hear or refuse to hear.

12 Then the spirit lifted me up, and as the glory of the LORD rose from its place, I heard behind me the sound of loud rumbling; ¹³it was the sound of the wings of the living creatures brushing against one another, and the sound of the wheels beside them, that sounded like a loud rumbling. ¹⁴The spirit lifted me up and bore me away; I went in bitterness in the heat of my spirit, the hand of the LORD being strong upon me. ¹⁵I came to the exiles at Tel-abib, who lived by the river Chebar. And I sat there among them, stunned, for seven days.

16 At the end of seven days, the word of the LORD came to me: [17]Mortal, I have made you a sentinel for the house of Israel; whenever you hear a word from my mouth, you shall give them warning from me. [18]If I say to the wicked, "You shall surely die," and you give them no warning, or speak to warn the wicked from their wicked way, in order to save their life, those wicked persons shall die for their iniquity; but their blood I will require at your hand. [19]But if you warn the wicked, and they do not turn from their wickedness, or from their wicked way, they shall die for their iniquity; but you will have saved your life. [20]Again, if the righteous turn from their righteousness and commit iniquity, and I lay a stumbling block before them, they shall die; because you have not warned them, they shall die for their sin, and their righteous deeds that they have done shall not be remembered; but their blood I will require at your hand. [21]If, however, you warn the righteous not to sin, and they do not sin, they shall surely live, because they took warning; and you will have saved your life.

22 Then the hand of the LORD was upon me there; and he said to me, Rise up, go out into the valley, and there I will speak with you. [23]So I rose up and went out into the valley; and the glory of the LORD stood there, like the glory that I had seen by the river Chebar; and I fell on my face. [24]The spirit entered into me, and set me on my feet; and he spoke with me and said to me: Go, shut yourself inside your house. [25]As for you, mortal, cords shall be placed on you, and you shall be bound with them, so that you cannot go out among the people; [26]and I will make your tongue cling to the roof of your mouth, so that you shall be speechless and unable to reprove them; for they are a rebellious house. [27]But when I speak with you, I will open your mouth, and you shall say to them, "Thus says the Lord GOD"; let those who will hear, hear; and let those who refuse to hear, refuse; for they are a rebellious house.

Revelation 10

1 And I saw another mighty angel coming down from heaven, wrapped in a cloud, with a rainbow over his head; his face was like the sun, and his legs like pillars of fire. [2]He held a little scroll open in his hand. Setting his right foot on the sea and his left foot on the land, [3]he gave a great shout, like a lion roaring. And when he shouted, the seven thunders sounded. [4]And when the seven thunders had sounded, I was about to write, but I heard a voice from heaven saying, "Seal up what the seven thunders have said, and do not write it down." [5]Then the angel whom I saw standing on the sea and on the land

> raised his right hand to heaven
> [6]and swore by him who lives forever and ever,

who created heaven and what is in it, the earth and what is in it, and the sea and what is in it: "There will be no more delay, [7]but in the days when the seventh angel is to blow his trumpet, the mystery of God will be fulfilled, as he announced to his servants the prophets."

8 Then the voice that I had heard from heaven spoke to me again, saying, "Go, take the scroll that is open in the hand of the angel who is standing on

the sea and on the land." [9]So I went to the angel and told him to give me the little scroll; and he said to me, "Take it, and eat; it will be bitter to your stomach, but sweet as honey in your mouth." [10]So I took the little scroll from the hand of the angel and ate it; it was sweet as honey in my mouth, but when I had eaten it, my stomach was made bitter.

11 Then they said to me, "You must prophesy again about many peoples and nations and languages and kings."

AUGUSTINE OF HIPPO,
THE CITY OF GOD

Augustine of Hippo (354–430 C.E.) is perhaps the greatest of the teachers of the early Western church. Trained in classical rhetoric, he developed a systematic hermeneutics in his work *De Doctrina Christiana* (*On Christian Doctrine*) based upon a theory of signs—in Greek, *semeia*, from which we derive the term "semiotics." Augustine insisted on the unity of scripture, which permitted the the more obscure parts of the Bible to be understood through those which are clearer. Furthermore, he recognized that there may be various ways of reading one passage, avoiding the trap of assuming that there is just one definitive meaning to be sought out. His interpretive efforts are always driven by the practical demands of his work as a bishop and teacher in the church, as is evident in the passage below from his greatest work, *De Civitate Dei* (*The City of God*). Within the biblical tradition itself, his concern is to understand the manner of God's speech and our understanding of it, linking both Old and New Testaments with the Christian doctrine of the Trinity.

From The City of God,
Book 16, Chapter 6

There is another passage which might have been interpreted with reference to the angels; it is the place where, at the creation of man God said, "Let US make man," instead of "Let me make man." However, since this is followed by "in our image," and since it is unthinkable that we should believe man to have been made in the image of the angels, or that the angels and God have the same image, the plural here is correctly understood to refer to the Trinity. Nevertheless, the Trinity is one God, and therefore even after the words "let us make" the narrative proceeds: "And God made man in the image of God." It does not say, "The Gods made" or "in the image of the Gods."

Now the passage we are discussing might also be understood as referring to the Trinity, as if the Father said to the Son and the Holy Spirit, "Come, let us go down and bring confusion on their speech," if there had been anything to prevent our understanding this in reference to the angels. But it is more appropriate that the angels should "come" to God with holy movements, that is to say, with reverent thoughts; for it is with reverent thoughts that they consult the changeless Truth, as the law which is established eternally in that heavenly court of theirs. For they themselves are not the truth for themselves; they are partakers of the creative Truth, and move towards it, as to the fountain of life, to receive from it what they do not possess of themselves. And this movement of theirs is a stable movement, by which they approach without withdrawing.

And God does not speak to the angels in the same way as we speak to one another, or to God, or to the angels, or as the angels speak to us. He speaks in his own fashion, which is beyond our describing. But his speech is explained to us in our fashion. God's speech, to be sure, is on a higher plane; it precedes his action as the changeless reason of the action itself; and his speaking has no sound, no transitory noise; it has a power that persists for eternity and operates in time. It is with this speech that he addresses the holy angels, whereas he speaks to us, who are situated far off, in a different way. And yet, when we also grasp something of this kind of speech with our inward ears, we come close to the angels. Therefore I do not have to be continually explaining about God's acts of speaking in this present work. For unchanging Truth either speaks by itself, in a way we cannot explain, to the minds of rational creatures, or it speaks through a mutable creature, either to our spirit by spiritual images, or to our physical sense by physical voices.

Certainly the words, "And from now on they will not fail to achieve anything they try to do," were not put as an assertion but as a question. This is frequently the way men express a threat, as when a speaker says,

> Shall they not take up arms and then pursue
> From the whole city?

Accordingly, the passage quoted must be interpreted as if God said, "Will not they fail to achieve everything they try to do?" The quotation as given would not in itself suggest a threat. But I have added the particle—*ne,* for the benefit of the slow-witted, to read *nonne,* since a tone of voice cannot be indicated in writing.

We now see that from those three men, Noah's sons, seventy-three nations—or rather seventy-two, as a calculation will show—and as many languages came into being on the earth, and by their increase they filled even the islands. However, the number of nations increased at a greater rate than the languages. For even in Africa we know of many barbarous nations using only one language.

HILDEGARD OF BINGEN, *SCIVIAS*

Hildegard of Bingen (1098–1179) founded a Benedictine community at Bingen, near the Rhine River in what is now Germany. Hildegard has recently become the object of renewed interest, particularly because of her writings, which emphasize the human (and female) body in the spiritual life, and her music. She had interests in and wrote about medicine, politics, theology, as well as music and drama. In contrast, however, to the individuality of other mystics, Hildegard stressed communal prayer and wrote about political and liturgical reform. And while she has often been considered a mystic, her writings were more about doctrine than union with God. She wrote as an interpreter of texts and doctrine rather than as a relayer of personal experience.

The *Scivias* (shortened from the Latin *Scito Vias Domini*, which translates, "Know the ways of the Lord") was based on a series of visions that Hildegard experienced, but that nonetheless display a thoroughly rational exercise of interpretation, chiefly through allegory. In fact, the three parts of the *Scivias* took over ten years to write. The *Scivias* is significant because it combines a personal visionary experience with intellectual thought and theology. The book is divided into three parts which tell of creation, redemption, and sanctification. The excerpt below is from the "fourth vision" of part 3, entitled "The Pillar of the Word of God." Here, as in all the visions, Hildegard begins with a description of the vision, and then moves to interpret the vision phrase by phrase, supporting her interpretation through doctrine and scripture.

From Scivias

And then, beyond the tower of anticipation of God's will, one cubit past the corner that faces the North, attached to the outside of the shining part of the main wall of the Building, I saw a pillar the color of steel, most dreadful to behold, and so big and tall that I could not form an idea of its measurements. And the pillar was divided from bottom to top into three sides, with edges sharp as a sword; the first edge faced the East, the second the North and the third the South, and the latter was somewhat merged with the outside wall of the building. . . .

And the third edge, facing the South, was broad and wide in the middle, but thinner and narrower at the bottom and top, like a bow drawn and ready to shoot arrows. And at the top of the pillar I saw a light so bright that human tongue cannot describe it; and in this light appeared a dove, with a gold ray coming out of its mouth, which shed brilliant light on the pillar. . . .

1 The austerity of the Law
was sweetened by the Incarnation of the Word

The Word of God, by Whom all things were made, was Himself begotten before time in the heart of the Father; but afterward, near the end of time, as the Old Testament saints had predicted, he became incarnate of the Virgin. And, assuming humanity, He did nor forsake Deity; but, being one and true God with the Father and the Holy Spirit, he sweetened the world with His sweetness and illumined it with the brilliance of His glory.

Hence, *the pillar you see beyond the tower of anticipation of God's will* designates the ineffable mystery of the Word of God; for in that true Word, the Son of God, all the justice of the New and Old Testaments is fulfilled. This justice was opened to believers for their salvation by divine inspiration, when the

Son of the Supreme Father deigned to become incarnate of the Sweet Virgin; and the virtues showed themselves to be powerful in the anticipation of God's will, which was the beginning of the circumcision. Then the mystery of the Word of God was also declared in strict justice by the voice of the patriarchs and prophets, who foretold that He would be manifest in justice and godly deeds and great severity, doing the justice of God and leaving no injustice free to evade the commands of the Law. . . .

5 The Word of God has three divisions:
Law, Grace and exposition of scripture

And the pillar *is divided from bottom to top into three sides, with edges sharp as a sword;* which is to say that the strength of the Word of God as pre-figured in the Old Testament and declared in the New, circling and turning in grace, showed in the Holy Spirit three points of division. These were the old Law, the new Grace, and the exposition of the faithful doctors; and by these the holy person does what is just from the beginning, starting with the good and moving upward to end with the perfect. For all that is just was, is and will be forever in the simple Deity, which is in all things; and no power can stand firm in malice, if He wills to conquer it by the glory of His loving kindness.

6 The knowledge of Law,
the work of the Gospel and the wisdom of the doctors

The first edge faces the East, which signifies the start of the knowledge of God through the divine Law, before the perfect day of justice. *The second looks up to the North,* for after this good and chosen work was started there came the gospel of My Son and the other precepts of Me, the Father, which rose up against the North where injustice originated. *And the third faces the South, and is somewhat merged with the outside wall of the building.* This is to say that when the works of justice had been confirmed, there came the profound and rich Wisdom of the principal doctors, who through the fire of the Holy Spirit made known what was obscure in the Law and the prophets, and showed their fruition in the Gospels. Thus they made these things fruitful to the understanding; they touched on the outward content of the Scriptures in the work of the Father's goodness, and sweetly ruminated on their mystical significance. . . .

14 God shows people the mysteries
of the Son of God by foreshadowing

But at the top of the pillar you see a light so bright that human tongue cannot describe it. This is to say that the Heavenly Father, in His highest and deepest mysteries, made known the mystery of His Son, Who shines in His Father with glorious light, in which there appears all the justice of the giving of the Law and the New Testament. And the latter *is of such clarity and brilliance of wisdom that it is not possible for any earthly person to express it in words,* as long as he is in corruptible flesh.

And in this light appears a dove, with a gold ray coming out of its mouth, which sheds brilliant light on the pillar; for in the heart of the radiant Father, in the brilliance of the light of the Son of God, burns the Holy Spirit, Who comes from on high and declares the mysteries of the Son of the Most High to redeem the people seduced by the ancient serpent. And so the Holy Spirit inspires all the commandments and all the new testimonies, giving before the Incarnation of the Lord the law of His glorious mysteries, and then showing the same glory in the Incarnation itself. And the Spirit's inspiration is a golden splendor and a high and excellent illumination, and by this outpouring It makes known, as was said, the mystical secrets of God's Only-Begotten to the ancient heralds who showed the Son of God through types and marvelled at His coming from the Father and His miraculously arising in the dawn of the perpetual Virgin. And thus the Spirit in Its power fused the Old Testament and the Gospels into one spiritual seed, from which grew all justice.

And so you cannot contemplate the divine glory because of the immense power of Divinity; no mortal can see it except those to whom I will to fore-shadow it. Therefore take care not to presume rashly to look at what is divine, as the trembling that seizes you shows.

TERESA OF AVILA,
THE INTERIOR CASTLE

Teresa of Avila (1515–1582) spent her entire life in the central region of Spain. At twenty-one she became a Carmelite nun and, as a Carmelite, came to understand that the relationship with God is a relationship in and through Christ, a relationship thought of as a "spiritual marriage." The Carmelite life was one of deep contemplation and prayer, and its goal was to achieve a mystical union with God. At the same time, due to the order's emphasis on the mediation of Christ and its belief in Christ's full humanity, Teresa did not live an abstract "nonearthly" existence but lived fully with other humans here on earth. She exerted a strong influence on the overall state of contemplative life in Spain, and on the life of another well-known Spanish mystic, John of the Cross.

True unity with God is only possible when the mystic is able to go beyond her own senses, feelings, and knowledge, for God is beyond human life. Thus, the mystic must take on a mode of nothingness, moving away from her own human abilities and allowing God to act. Yet, paradoxically, we are given this most interior union through language, and Teresa wrote several well-known books. *The Interior Castle* was written when she was sixty-two and is perhaps her greatest expression of the mystical life with God. Telling the reader to "consider our soul to be like a castle made entirely out of a dia-mond or of very clear crystal, in which there are many rooms," *The Interior Castle* is the description of an inward journey to union with God. In this cas-tle are seven "dwelling places," each one being a deeper move inward. As would be expected, as Teresa moves inward, her description must rely more and more heavily on metaphor and rich imaginative language.

From The Interior Castle, *"The Seven Dwelling Places"*

The soul always remains with its God in that center. Let us say that the union is like the joining of two wax candles to such an extent that the flame coming from them is but one, or that the wick, the flame, and the wax are all one. But afterward one candle can be easily separated from the other and there are two candles; the same holds for the wick. In the spiritual marriage the union is like what we have when rain falls from the sky into a river or fount; all is water, for the rain that fell from heaven cannot be divided or separated from the water of the river. Or it is like what we have when a little stream enters the sea, there is no means of separating the two. Or, like the bright light entering a room through two different windows; although the streams of light are separate when entering the room, they become one.

5. Perhaps this is what Saint Paul means in saying *He that is joined or united to the Lord becomes one spirit with him,* and is referring to this sovereign marriage, presupposing that His Majesty has brought the soul to it through union. And he also says: *For me to live is Christ, and to die is gain.* The soul as well, I think, can say these words now because this state is the place where the little butterfly we mentioned dies, and with the greatest joy because its life is now Christ.

6. And that its life is Christ is understood better, with the passing of time, by the effects this life has. Through some secret aspirations the soul understands clearly that it is God who gives life to our soul. These aspirations come very, very often in such a living way that they can in no way be doubted. The soul feels them very clearly even though they are indescribable. But the feeling is so powerful that sometimes the soul cannot avoid the loving expressions they cause, such as: O Life of my life! Sustenance that sustains me! and things of this sort. For from those divine breasts where it seems God is always sustaining the soul there flow streams of milk bringing comfort to all the people of the castle. It seems the Lord desires that in some manner these others in the castle may enjoy the great deal the soul is enjoying and that from that full-flowing river, where this tiny fount is swallowed up, a spurt of that water will sometimes be directed toward the sustenance of those who in corporeal things must serve these two who are wed. Just as a distracted person would feel this water if he were suddenly bathed in it, and would be unable to avoid feeling it, so are these operations recognized, and even with greater certitude. For just as a great gush of water could not reach us if it didn't have a source, as I have said, so it is understood clearly that there is Someone in the interior depths who shoots these arrows and gives life to this life, and that there is a Sun in the interior of the soul from which a brilliant light proceeds and is sent to the faculties. The soul, as I have said, does not move from that center nor is its peace lost; for the very One who gave peace to the apostles when they were together can give it to the soul.

7. It has occurred to me that this greeting of the Lord must have amounted to much more than is apparent from its sound, as well as our Lord's words to the glorious Magdalene that she go in peace. Since the Lord's words are effected in us as deeds, they must have worked in those souls already disposed

in such a manner that everything corporeal in them was taken away and they were left in pure spirit. Thus the soul could be joined in this heavenly union with the uncreated spirit. For it is very certain that in emptying ourselves of all that is creature and detaching ourselves from it for the love of God, the same Lord will fill us with Himself. And thus, while Jesus our Lord was once praying for His apostles—I don't remember where—He said that they were one with the Father and with Him, just as Jesus Christ our Lord is in the Father and the Father is in Him. I don't know what greater love there can be than this. And all of us are included here, for His Majesty said: *I ask not only for them but for all those who also will believe in me;* and He says: *I am in them.*

8. O God help me, how true these words are! And how well they are understood by the soul who is in this prayer and sees for itself. How well we would all understand them if it were not for our own fault, since the words of Jesus Christ, our King and Lord, cannot fail. But since we fail by not disposing ourselves and turning away from all that can hinder this light, we do not see ourselves in this mirror that we contemplate, where our image is engraved.

MARTIN LUTHER,
TABLE TALK

Martin Luther (1483–1546) intended to pursue a legal career in his home of Thuringia (in Germany) until a lightning bolt literally struck him, after which he vowed to become a monk. Luther's key theological concern, perhaps fueled by his legal training, was how a person could be considered "holy" in the face of a righteous God. The pursuit of this concern brought him to accept a stance that was in contradistinction to the received medieval thought of the church. Luther determined through his reading of the scriptures that it is only through God's grace that humans can be made righteous, and no amount of works can earn God's justification. With this determination, Luther unwittingly set the wheels in motion for the Protestant Reformation, causing theological and military battles in Europe over the following centuries (which continue in many ways to be fought today).

As a result of the Reformation, the monastery Luther originally joined was turned into something of a "guest house" for relatives, students, and others who needed a place to stay. During this time, afternoon supper became a place where colleagues and visitors would eat and talk with Luther. Eventually these conversations were recorded by various persons who took part, and they were published as a part of Luther's complete works. The two excerpts below begin to show some of Luther's views about how to approach the scriptures. At the same time the passages here show some of his playfulness.

From Table Talk

I wonder whether Peter, Paul, Moses, and all the saints fully and thoroughly understood a single word of God so that they had nothing more to learn from it, for the understanding of God is beyond measure. To be sure, the saints understood the Word of God and could also speak about it, but their practice did not keep pace with it. Here one forever remains a learner. The scholastics illustrated this with a ball which only at one point touches the table on which it rests, although the whole weight of the ball is supported by the table.

Though I am a great doctor, I haven't yet progressed beyond the instruction of children in the Ten Commandments, the Creed, and the Lord's Prayer. I still learn and pray these every day with my Hans and my little Lena. Who understands in all of its ramifications even the opening words, "Our Father who art in heaven"? For if I understood these words in faith—that the God who holds heaven and earth in his hand is my Father—I would conclude that therefore I am Lord of heaven and earth, therefore Christ is my brother, therefore all things are mine, Gabriel is my servant, Raphael is my coachman, and all the other angels are ministering spirits sent forth by my Father in heaven to serve me in all my necessities, lest I strike my foot against a stone. In order that this faith should not remain untested, my Father comes along and allows me to be thrown into prison or to be drowned in water. Then it will finally become apparent how well we understand these words. Our faith wavers. Our weakness gives rise to the question, "Who knows if it is true?" So this one word "your" or "our" is the most difficult of all in the whole Scripture. It's like the word "your" in the first commandment, "I am the Lord your God" [Ex. 20:2]. . . .

Surely a great light has gone up, for we understand both the words and the content [of the scriptures] according to the testimony of the ancient writers. None of the sophists was able to expound the passage, "He who through faith is righteous shall live" [Rom. 1:17], for they interpreted "righteous" and "righteousness" differently. Except only for Augustine, there was great blindness among the fathers. After the Holy Scriptures, Augustine should especially be read, for he had keen judgment. However, if we turn from the Bible to the commentaries of the fathers, our study will be bottomless.

Consequently this is the best advice, that one should draw from the source and diligently read the Bible. For a man who knows the text is also an extraordinary theologian. One passage or one text from the Bible is worth more than the glosses of four writers who aren't reliable and thorough. Suppose I take the text, "Everything created by God is good" [1 Tim. 4:4]; food, marriage, etc., are created by God; therefore [they are good], etc. The glosses contradict this; Bernard, Dominic, and Basil wrote and acted otherwise. But the text itself overcomes the glosses. The dear fathers were held in high esteem; meanwhile what they did to the Bible was wrong. Ambrose and Basil were quite dull, and Gregory Nazianzen was accused of writing nothing honestly about God in his poetry and songs.

The Holy Spirit doesn't let himself be bound by words but makes the content known. This once happened to me when with the help of certain men I concentrated on a Greek form. Because I insisted on definitions, I said nothing about the matter and couldn't tell about the function, use, or utility of the thing about which I spoke.

SØREN KIERKEGAARD,
FEAR AND TREMBLING

Kierkegaard's extraordinary reading of Genesis 22, the story of God's command to Abraham to sacrifice his son Isaac, or rather the reading of his pseudonymous author Johannes de Silentio, makes the crucial distinction between the ethical and the religious in the narrative. As he puts it, "The ethical expression for what Abraham did is that he meant to murder Isaac; the religious expression is that he meant to sacrifice Isaac." Identifying Abraham as "the knight of faith," he exposes the "prodigious paradox" of faith, necessitating his highly rhetorical literary mode of irony in his reading of scripture. Reading Kierkegaard in 1913, Franz Kafka remarked: "He doesn't see the ordinary man . . . and paints this monstrous Abraham in the clouds." Neither Kierkegaard nor Kafka can avoid seeing something of themselves in the biblical figure of the father who is seemingly prepared to sacrifice (or murder) the beloved son.

From Fear and Trembling

Once upon a time there was a man who as a child had heard the beautiful story about how God tempted Abraham, and how he endured temptation, kept the faith, and a second time received again a son contrary to expectation. When the child became older he read the same story with even greater admiration, for life had separated what was united in the pious simplicity of the child. The older he became, the more frequently his mind reverted to that story, his enthusiasm became greater and greater, and yet he was less and less able to understand the story. At last in his interest for that he forgot everything else; his soul had only one wish, to see Abraham, one longing, to have been witness to that event. His desire was not to behold the beautiful countries of the Orient, or the earthly glory of the Promised Land, or that Godfearing couple whose old age God had blessed, or the venerable figure of the aged patriarch, or the vigorous young manhood of Isaac whom God had bestowed upon Abraham—he saw no reason why the same thing might not have taken place on a barren heath in Denmark. His yearning was to accompany them on the three days' journey when Abraham rode with sorrow before him and with Isaac by his side. His only wish was to be present at the time when Abraham lifted up his eyes and saw Mount Moriah afar off, at the time when he left the asses behind and went alone with Isaac up unto the mountain; for what his mind was intent upon was not the ingenious web of imagination but the shudder of thought.

That man was not a thinker, he felt no need of getting beyond faith; he deemed it the most glorious thing to be remembered as the father of it, an enviable lot to possess it, even though no one else were to know it.

That man was not a learned exegete, he didn't know Hebrew, if he had known Hebrew, he perhaps would easily have understood the story and Abraham. . . .

"And God tempted Abraham and said unto him, Take Isaac, thine only son, whom thou lovest, and get thee into the land of Moriah, and offer him there for a burnt offering upon the mountain which I will show thee."

It was early in the morning, Abraham arose betimes, he had the asses saddled, left his tent, and Isaac with him, but Sarah looked out of the window after them until they had passed down the valley and she could see them no more. They rode in silence for three days. On the morning of the fourth day Abraham said never a word, but he lifted up his eyes and saw Mount Moriah afar off. He left the young men behind and went on alone with Isaac beside him up to the mountain. But Abraham said to himself, "I will not conceal from Isaac whither this course leads him." He stood still, he laid his hand upon the head of Isaac in benediction, and Isaac bowed to receive the blessing. And Abraham's face was fatherliness, his look was mild, his speech encouraging. But Isaac was unable to understand him, his soul could not be exalted; he embraced Abraham's knees, he fell at his feet imploringly, he begged for his young life, for the fair hope of his future, he called to mind the joy in Abraham's house, he called to mind the sorrow and loneliness. Then Abraham lifted up the boy, he walked with him by his side, and his talk was full of comfort and exhortation. But Isaac could not understand him. He climbed Mount Moriah, but Isaac understood him not. Then for an instant he turned away from him, and when Isaac again saw Abraham's face it was changed, his glance was wild, his form was horror. He seized Isaac by the throat, threw him to the ground, and said, "Stupid boy, dost thou then suppose that I am thy father? I am an idolater. Dost thou suppose that this is God's bidding? No, it is my desire." Then Isaac trembled and cried out in his terror, "O God in heaven, have compassion upon me. God of Abraham, have compassion upon me. If I have no father upon earth, be Thou my father!" But Abraham in a low voice said to himself, "O Lord in heaven, I thank Thee. After all it is better for him to believe that I am a monster, rather than that he should lose faith in Thee."

JACQUES DERRIDA,
THE GIFT OF DEATH

Jacques Derrida, Directeur d'études at the Ecole des Hautes Etudes en Sciences Sociales in Paris, has been the foremost exponent of deconstruction since the publication of his book *Of Grammatology* in 1967. Intensely aware of his background in Hasidic Judaism, his writings embrace a wide range of disciplines and have become increasingly concerned with the religious and theological implications of his understanding of texts and the processes of reading.

In his work *Donner la mort* (*The Gift of Death*), Derrida continues the discussion of Genesis 22 begun by Kierkegaard. He engages with the biblical text not simply as interpretation but in a literary conversation that explores the grounds of faith as both traditional and radical, returning to the ancient themes of historicity and story reminiscent of D. F. Strauss (see above, chapter 1) and the whole course of biblical interpretation through the past 150 years.

From The Gift of Death

Abraham doesn't speak in figures, fables, parables, metaphors, ellipses, or enigmas. His irony is meta-rhetorical. If he knew what was going to happen, if for example God had charged him with the mission of leading Isaac onto the mountain so that He could strike him with lightning, then he would have been right to have recourse to enigmatic language. But the problem is precisely that he doesn't know. Not that that makes him hesitate, however. His nonknowledge doesn't in any way suspend his own decision, which remains resolute. The knight of faith must not hesitate. . . .

Abraham's decision is absolutely responsible because it answers for itself before the absolute other. Paradoxically it is also irresponsible because it is guided neither by reason nor by an ethics justifiable before men or before the law of some universal tribunal. Everything points to the fact that one is unable to be responsible at the same time before the other and before others, before the others of the other. If God is completely other, the figure or name of the wholly other, then every other (one) is every (bit) other. *Tout autre est tout autre.* This formula disturbs Kierkegaard's discourse on one level while at the same time reinforcing its most extreme ramification. It implies that God, as the wholly other, is to be found everywhere there is something of the wholly other. And since each of us, everyone else, each other is infinitely other in its absolute singularity, inaccessible, solitary, transcendent, nonmanifest, originarily nonpresent to my *ego* (as Husserl would say of the *alter ego* that can never be originarily present to my consciousness and that I can apprehend only through what he calls *appresentation* and *analogy*), then what can be said about Abraham's relation to God can be said about my relation without relation to *every other* (*one*) *as every* (*bit*) *other* [*tout autre comme tout autre*], in particular my relation to my neighbor or my loved ones who are as inaccessible to me, as secret and transcendent as Jahweh. Every other (in the sense of each other) is every bit other (absolutely other). From this point of view what *Fear and Trembling* says about the sacrifice of Isaac is the truth. Translated into this extraordinary story, the truth is shown to possess the very structure of what occurs every day. Through its paradox it speaks of the responsibility required at every moment for every man and every woman. At the same time, there is no longer any ethical generality that does not fall prey to the paradox of Abraham. At the instant of every decision and through the relation to *every other* (*one*) *as every* (*bit*) *other,* every one else asks us at every moment to behave like knights of faith. Perhaps that displaces a certain emphasis of Kierkegaard's discourse: the absolute uniqueness of Jahweh doesn't tolerate analogy; we are not all Abrahams, Isaacs, or Sarahs either. We are not Jahweh. But what seems thus to universalize or disseminate the exception or the extraordinary by imposing a supplementary complication upon ethical generality, that very thing ensures that Kierkegaard's text gains added force. It speaks to us of the paradoxical truth of our responsibility and of our relation to *the gift of death* of each instant. Furthermore, it explains to us its own status, namely its ability to be read by all at the very moment when it is speaking to us of secrets in secret, of intelligibility and absolute undecipherability. It stands for Jews, Christians, Muslims, but also for everyone else, for every other in its relation to the wholly other. We no longer know who is called Abraham, and he can no longer even tell us.

ISAAC BASHEVIS SINGER,
"JACHID AND JECHIDAH"

Isaac Bashevis Singer (1904–1991) was born in Poland into an Orthodox Jewish family. He moved to the United States but continued to write in Yiddish. All of his novels and short stories have now been translated into English. Bashevis Singer combines a history of Polish Jewish life with a "Christianized" Western European tradition. This combination affects not only the content of the stories (a mix, he describes, of "mysticism, deism, and skepticism") but also the style (a rhythmic flow of Yiddish oral stories mixed with the written philosophy of Spinoza and Schopenhauer). This combination is also affected by the literal extermination of centuries of Polish Jewish life by the Nazis. In this aftermath, Bashevis Singer writes of a God who exists in the world, but such existence does not mean that God will necessarily act in the world. God does act, but so does evil, and in any situation there is no guarantee that good will win out over evil.

Short Friday is a collection of short stories published in 1964 that describe the interactions between good and evil in a variety of particular circumstances. "Jachid and Jechidah" is told from the perspective of two "souls" in a Platonic heaven where souls preexist human life on earth. These two souls believe that souls evolve, that they are not created, and that there is no such thing as free will. For their blasphemy they are sentenced to death, which means earth.

From "Jachid and Jechidah"

In a prison where souls bound for Sheol—Earth they call it there—await destruction, there hovered the female soul Jechidah. Souls forget their origin. Purah, the Angel of Forgetfulness, he who dissipates God's light and conceals His face, holds dominion everywhere beyond the Godhead. Jechidah, unmindful of her descent from the Throne of Glory, had sinned. Her jealousy had caused much trouble in the world where she dwelled. She had suspected all female angels of having affairs with her lover Jachid, had not only blasphemed God but even denied him. Souls, she said, were not created but had evolved out of nothing: they had neither mission nor purpose. Although the authorities were extremely patient and forgiving, Jechidah was finally sentenced to death. The judge fixed the moment of her descent to that cemetery called Earth.

The attorney for Jechidah appealed to the Superior Court of Heaven, even presented a petition to Metatron, the Lord of the Face. But Jechidah was so filled with sin and so impenitent that no power could save her. The attendants seized her, tore her from Jachid, clipped her wings, cut her hair, and clothed her in a long white shroud. She was no longer allowed to hear the music of the spheres, to smell the perfumes of Paradise and to meditate on the secrets of the Torah, which sustain the soul. She could no longer bathe in the wells of balsam oil. In the prison cell, the darkness of the nether world already surrounded her. But her greatest torment was her longing for Jachid. She could no longer reach him telepathically. Nor could she send a message to him, all of her servants having been taken away. Only the fear of death was left to Jechidah.

Death was no rare occurrence where Jechidah lived but it befell only vulgar, exhausted spirits. Exactly what happened to the dead, Jechidah did not know. She was convinced that when a soul descended to Earth it was to extinction, even though the pious maintained that a spark of life remained. A dead soul immediately began to rot and was soon covered with a slimy stuff called semen. Then a grave digger put it into a womb where it turned into some sort of fungus and was henceforth known as a child. Later on, began the tortures of Gehenna: birth, growth, toil. For according to the morality books, death was not the final stage. Purified, the soul returned to its source. But what evidence was there for such beliefs? So far as Jechidah knew, no one had ever returned from Earth. The enlightened Jechidah believed that the soul rots for a short time and then disintegrates into a darkness of no return.

Now the moment had come when Jechidah must die, must sink to Earth. Soon, the Angel of Death would appear with his fiery sword and thousand eyes.

At first Jechidah had wept incessantly, but then her tears had ceased. Awake or asleep she never stopped thinking of Jachid. Where was he? What was he doing? Whom was he with? Jechidah was well aware he would not mourn for her forever. He was surrounded by beautiful females, sacred beasts, angels, seraphim, cherubs, ayralim, each one with powers of seduction. How long could someone like Jachid curb his desires? He, like she, was an unbeliever. It was he who had taught her that spirits were not created, but were products of evolution. Jachid did not acknowledge free will, nor believe in ultimate good and evil. What would restrain him? Most certainly he already lay in the lap of some other divinity, telling those stories about himself he had already told Jechidah.

But what could she do? In this dungeon all contact with the mansions ceased. All doors were closed: neither mercy, nor beauty entered here. The one way from this prison led down to Earth, and to the horrors called flesh, blood, marrow, nerves, and breath. The God-fearing angels promised resurrection. They preached that the soul did not linger forever on Earth, but that after it had endured its punishment, it returned to the Higher Sphere. But Jechidah, being a modernist, regarded all of this as superstition. How would a soul free itself from the corruption of the body? It was scientifically impossible. Resurrection was a dream, a silly comfort of primitive and frightened souls.

PAUL RICOEUR,
"THE BIBLE AND THE IMAGINATION"

Paul Ricoeur's contemporary philosophical hermeneutics continues to embrace a huge variety of issues and disciplines and returns insistently to questions of the sacred and to the mystery and power of religious language. In the excerpt below, Ricoeur insists on the centrality of "the imagination at work in the biblical text" and the necessity of an interpretive tradition that acknowledges this.

Ricoeur's long career has patiently focused on theological questions, yet with a critical skepticism that keeps alive the debates about the nature of God begun in the pages of the Bible itself. He balances the poetic with the philosophical, and while acknowledging the transformative potential of sacred literature, affirms in his book *Soi-même comme un autre* (*Oneself as Another*, 1990) that "all my philosophical work, leads to a type of philosophy from which the actual mention of God is absent and in which the question of God, as a philosophical question, itself remains in a suspension that could be called agnostic." Such faith and skepticism together has always characterized the field of literature and religion.

From "The Bible and the Imagination"

Now turning to my other pole, the Bible, I would like in this essay to begin investigating two traits of reading that correspond to the two traits of the imagination just spoken of. As one part of this investigation, I would like to consider the act of reading as a dynamic activity that is not confined to repeating significations fixed forever, but which takes place as a prolonging of the itineraries of meaning opened up by the work of interpretation. Through this first trait, the act of reading accords with the idea of a norm-governed productivity to the extent that it may be said to be guided by a productive imagination at work in the text itself. Beyond this, I would like to see in the reading of a text such as the Bible a creative operation unceasingly employed in decontextualizing its meaning and recontextualizing it in today's *Sitz im Leben*. Through this second trait, the act of reading realizes the union of fiction and redescription that characterizes the imagination in the most pregnant sense of this term.

So this is the first presupposition of this essay, to seek *in* reading itself the key to the heuristic functioning of the productive imagination.

This presupposition, at first glance, may seem to set aside another way of approaching our subject that would consist in exploring the work of the imagination after reading, either as a personal form of the imagination (I have in mind Dorothee Sölle's fine little book *Imagination et Obéissance*) or as a collective form of the imagination (as in works on the relations between faith, ideology, and utopia, which I consider to be equally important). By placing myself at the very heart of the act of reading, I am hoping to place myself at the starting point of the trajectory that unfolds itself into the individual and social forms of the imagination. In this sense, my approach does not exclude this other wholly different approach but leads to it.

. . . Within the vast domain of the form of the imagination at work in the biblical text, I propose to limit myself to one particular category of texts, the narrative texts. My reasons for this choice are as follows.

First, beginning from the side of a theory of fiction, I observe that we possess a general theory of narratives, coming from literary semiotics, which may allow us to give a concrete meaning to the twofold idea of a rule-governed creation and a heuristic model. On the one hand, narratives may be seen as a remarkable example of rule-governed invention to the extent that their submission to narrative codes testifies to the encoded character of their invention, and where their abundance attests to the ludic character of this rule-governed generation. On the other hand, narratives offer a remarkable example of the conjunction between fiction and redescription. Narratives, in virtue of their form, are all fictions. And yet it is through these fictions that we give a narrative form to our experience, be it individual or communal. Stephen Crites, in a noteworthy essay, has even spoken of "the narrative quality of experience" and shown how narrative provides a discursive articulation explicitly applicable to the narrative forms of lived experience.

Next, placing myself on the side of the biblical text, I can hardly be contradicted if I recall that there the narrative kernels occupy a central place and play an exceptional role from the election of Abraham to the anointing of David by way of the exodus, and from the narratives of the life and teaching of Jesus to those of the Acts of the Apostles by way of the accounts of the passion. Whatever may be the destiny of those narrative theologies that some thinkers are attempting to elaborate, these narratives may be for us a favorable occasion for making our first presupposition more precise; I mean that the act of reading should be seen as the meeting point of the itineraries of meaning offered by the text as a production of fiction (in the sense given above) and the free course (*parcours*) of meaning brought about by the reader seeking "to apply" the text to life. My second presupposition, therefore, will be that it is within the structure of the narrative itself that we can best apprehend this intersection between the text and life that engenders the imagination according to the Bible.

FURTHER READING

Augustine of Hippo. *Confessions* (c. 400 C.E.).

Adam, A. K. M. *What Is Postmodern Biblical Criticism?* Minneapolis: Fortress Press, 1995.

Bruns, Gerald L. *Hermeneutics Ancient and Modern.* New Haven, Conn.: Yale University Press, 1992.

Flanagan, Sabina. *Hildegard of Bingen: A Visionary Life.* London and New York: Routledge, 1989.

Jeanrond, Werner G. *Theological Hermeneutics: Development and Significance.* New York: Crossroad, 1991.

Klemm, David E. *Hermeneutical Inquiry.* Vol. 1: *The Interpretation of Texts;* vol. 2: *The Interpretation of Existence,* 43 and 44 in the American Academy of Religion's Studies in Religion Series. Atlanta: Scholars Press, 1986.

McKnight, Edgar V. *The Bible and the Reader: An Introduction to Literary Criticism.* Philadelphia: Fortress Press, 1985.

Petroff, Elizabeth, ed. *Medieval Women's Visionary Literature.* New York: Oxford University Press, 1986.

Ricoeur, Paul. *Essays on Biblical Interpretation.* Edited and with an introduction by Lewis S. Mudge. Philadelphia: Fortress Press, 1980.

Robbins, Jill. *Prodigal Son/Elder Brother: Interpretation and Alterity in Augustine, Petrarch, Kafka, Levinas.* Chicago: University of Chicago Press, 1991.

Rosenberg, David, ed. *Congregation: Contemporary Writers Read the Jewish Bible.* San Diego: Harcourt Brace Jovanovich, 1987.

4

The Language
and Literature of Worship

This chapter focuses on the kinds of texts that have been employed in worship or acts of devotion, private or public. Beginning, again, with the Bible, they include literature from liturgy, drama, ritual chant, devotion, prayer, and sermon. A number of these texts would not normally be read as "literature" (for example, those from liturgies) but they contain poetry and prose of the highest order and have been enormously influential because of their ancient and public use. The word "liturgy" derives from a Greek word that means "public service" and, by extension, "worship of the gods." We include examples from both Jewish and Christian liturgies that owe much to these ancient writings. These prayers are a form of poetry, part of which is intended to be recited by a whole congregation, and thus have a powerful rhythm. As acts of "remembrance" (in Greek, *anamnesis*), they link worship and doctrines of atonement with the themes of creation and fall, discussed in chapter 2, above. Liturgy is also dramatic, accompanied by actions as in a play; indeed, the great European traditions of medieval and Renaissance drama emerged directly out of the liturgy of the church, specifically the services of Holy Week and Easter as they rehearsed the events of the passion and resurrection of Jesus.

Wole Soyinka's "translation" of the ancient Greek tragedy *The Bacchae of Euripides* is a fascinating example of the way in which literature draws eclectically upon different traditions and cultures and uses powerful stories and myths from one to explore situations in another. Moreover, in his description of his version of the play as "a communion rite," Soyinka daringly links the imagery of the Dionysiac religion with the Christian Eucharist, or Communion, in the blood of the "sacrificed" Pentheus, whose body has been broken in a "fraction" (in Greek, *sparagmos*) like the "host" of the Eucharist that is found to be not blood but wine. The extract should be read alongside the accounts in the Gospels of Matthew and Luke of the Last Supper of Jesus and his disciples, where Jesus' "blood of the covenant" is likened to the wine of the Passover supper. Euripides' original Theban play about exile, insanity, and the limitations of human reason, dating from 405 B.C.E., is linked by Soyinka with his own modern Nigeria, from which he was exiled for a time.

There is, thus, an extraordinary series of connections between the first three excerpts in this chapter. With the *Prasna Upanishad* we move into a quite different tradition and language of meditation, though the connection between the spirituality of the *Upanishads* and the New Testament are remarkable, particularly in their sense of oneness and wholeness.

This literary "holism" has links in the European tradition with Thomas Merton's celebration of nature and art in William Blake, the subject of his master's thesis before he became a Trappist monk. For Merton, Blake's poetry in works like *Songs of Innocence and Experience* (1795) looks toward a harmony between nature and human experience which he identifies as "mystical experience," a drawing together of the natural and the supernatural. This poetic expression of the highest religious feeling looks back to a venerable tradition of Christian mysticism, represented here in an excerpt from the medieval English anchoress or hermit Dame Julian of Norwich. Her visions of Divine Love express a direct experience of God which is articulated in highly poetic language that both meditates on Christian doctrine and, at the same time, voices a freedom of image and metaphor beyond the limits of orthodox theology. In her "poetry" she is able to describe Christ as a Mother who feeds her with the food of the Blessed Sacrament of Communion as a human mother suckles her child.

The two British poets John Donne and George Herbert are almost contemporaries and share many of the same "metaphysical" poetic characteristics. Donne's great sonnet "Batter my heart, three-personed God" is a powerful example of the relationship between the Christian and God, which can only be explored through a highly rhetorical and contradictory language that draws upon a wide and eclectic range of images that look back, ultimately, to the Bible itself. It is permeated with Donne's Protestant theology with its sense of human unworthiness and the freedom granted by God's grace. Herbert's poetry, too, though rooted in Anglican worship, is highly eclectic, drawing theological reflection into the very heart of human life and experience. In both these poets we see literature taking up and energizing the material of the faith of the biblical and Christian tradition with a sometimes shocking freedom of expression that allows us to explore the drama of the human encounter with the divine, the sense of human limit, and the world as shot through with the sacred.

This dimension of shock in literature is present also in the last two selections, which are examples of sermons, not as preached in church or chapel, but in the pages of works of fiction. Father Mapple's sermon in Herman Melville's novel *Moby Dick* (1851) is set within one of the greatest of all fictional accounts of the symbolic conflict between man and his fate. Melville's Captain Ahab declares that "all visible objects are but as pasteboard masks," and his allegory relentlessly explores concepts of good and evil in the pursuit of the great white whale. Father Mapple's sermon is rooted in the great maritime story of the biblical Jonah and his encounter with an ancestor of Moby Dick—a story of God's pursuit, preaching, and salvation. The language of the sermon, with its address to Mapple's "shipmates," links the Bible with myths and the immediate experience of the seafolk of New Bedford, literature drawing all together in a seamless web of poetry that ends with the question, full of biblical resonances: "for what is man that he should live out the lifetime of his God?" (Compare "What is man that thou art mindful of him, and the son of man that thou dost care for him?" Ps. 8:4, RSV.)

John Updike's novel *A Month of Sundays* is structured on a series of Sunday sermons, excerpted below. Serious, yet highly comic, as explorations of a clerical life struggling with the "temptations of the flesh," these sermons remain founded on biblical texts and themes. The Reverend Thomas Marshfield roots his sermons (which are less "preached" than meditative) on the "drama of the Bible" as still intrinsic to his experience of modern America. What makes them so disturbing is that they are very good sermons, in the traditional sense, though "preached" by the libertine antihero of the novel. Thus literature can take the stuff of theology and its traditions and resituate them in new and disturbing contexts, shedding new light and uprooting old assumptions.

MATTHEW 26:17–29; LUKE 22:7–23

There is a close connection between the New Testament accounts of the Last Supper and the structure and language of the early Christian liturgies. Indeed, it is probable that by the time the Gospels were written, their words embodied already existing liturgies and forms of worship in the church. The words ascribed to Jesus are to be seen as part of a performance.

The basic shape of the Christian Eucharist is here present in the fourfold action of taking the bread, blessing, breaking, and giving. Furthermore, the language is shaped into a *parallelism* (a crucial element of Hebrew poetry) as the action with the bread is repeated in the action with the wine.

There are four accounts of this event in the New Testament in Mark, Matthew, Luke, and Paul's first letter to the Corinthians. (The Fourth Gospel, John, stands apart as a separate narrative.) They fall into two pairs, Mark and Matthew forming the first. Thus, the two versions excerpted here represent both forms of this ancient narrative.

Matthew 26:17–29

17 On the first day of Unleavened Bread the disciples came to Jesus, saying, "Where do you want us to make the preparations for you to eat the Passover?" [18]He said, "Go into the city to a certain man, and say to him, 'The Teacher says, My time is near; I will keep the Passover at your house with my disciples.'" [19]So the disciples did as Jesus had directed them, and they prepared the Passover meal.

20 When it was evening, he took his place with the twelve; [21]and while they were eating, he said, "Truly, I tell you, one of you will betray me." [22]And they became greatly distressed, and began to say to him one after another, "Surely not I, Lord?" [23]He answered, "The one who has dipped his hand into the bowl with me will betray me. [24]The Son of Man goes as it is written of him, but woe to that one by whom the Son of Man is betrayed! It would have been

better for that one not to have been born." [25]Judas, who betrayed him, said, "Surely not I, Rabbi?" He replied, "You have said so."

26 While they were eating, Jesus took a loaf of bread, and after blessing it he broke it, gave it to the disciples, and said, "Take, eat; this is my body." [27]Then he took a cup, and after giving thanks he gave it to them, saying, "Drink from it, all of you; [28]for this is my blood of the covenant, which is poured out for many for the forgiveness of sins. [29]I tell you, I will never again drink of this fruit of the vine until that day when I drink it new with you in my Father's kingdom."

Luke 22:7–23

7 Then came the day of Unleavened Bread, on which the Passover lamb had to be sacrificed. [8]So Jesus sent Peter and John, saying, "Go and prepare the Passover meal for us that we may eat it." [9]They asked him, "Where do you want us to make preparations for it?" [10]"Listen," he said to them, "when you have entered the city, a man carrying a jar of water will meet you; follow him into the house he enters [11]and say to the owner of the house, 'The teacher asks you, "Where is the guest room, where I may eat the Passover with my disciples?"' [12]He will show you a large room upstairs, already furnished. Make preparations for us there." [13]So they went and found everything as he had told them; and they prepared the Passover meal.

14 When the hour came, he took his place at the table, and the apostles with him [15]He said to them, "I have eagerly desired to eat this Passover with you before I suffer; [16]for I tell you, I will not eat it until it is fulfilled in the kingdom of God." [17]Then he took a cup, and after giving thanks he said, "Take this and divide it among yourselves; [18]for I tell you that from now on I will not drink of the fruit of the vine until the kingdom of God comes." [19]Then he took a loaf of bread, and when he had given thanks, he broke it and gave it to them, saying, "This is my body, which is given for you. Do this in remembrance of me." [20]And he did the same with the cup after supper, saying, "This cup that is poured out for you is the new covenant in my blood. [21]But see, the one who betrays me is with me, and his hand is on the table. [22]For the Son of Man is going as it has been determined, but woe to that one by whom he is betrayed!" [23]Then they began to ask one another which one of them it could be who would do this.

WOLE SOYINKA, *THE BACCHAE OF EURIPIDES: A COMMUNION RITE*

Wole Soyinka (b. 1934) was born in Nigeria but has been exiled from his country on several occasions due to his continued political activism against the government there. Since his release from prison in Nigeria in the 1960s, Soyinka has worked in Europe and America, where he has produced plays, written novels and poetry, and published the notes he wrote during his experience as a political prisoner. In 1986 he became the first African to be awarded the Nobel Prize for Literature. Yet he has recently been again exiled from Nigeria for four years and only returned in October 1998.

Throughout all of Soyinka's writing there is a strong blending of the social and the spiritual, politics and ritual. In the early 1970s he adapted Euripides' play *The Bacchae*. While using Euripides' version as a guide, Soyinka essentially rewrites the Greek play and infuses Dionysos's character with West African religious sensibilities. Nietzsche and others have pointed out the relationship between Dionysos and Christ and have shown the influences of the latter character on the former. Soyinka's *Bacchae*, however, approaches Dionysos through another syncretic move by conflating Dionysos with the Yoruba god of iron and war, Ogun, who Soyinka shows to be Dionysos's "twin brother." In this rewriting, Soyinka emphasizes the liberating possibilities of the Dionysos/Ogun/Christ character, and in so doing he winds up altering the famous ending of Euripides. Soyinka subtitles his version "a communion rite" and sees his ending as "a new resolution in the symbolic extension of ritual powers" (from the introduction). Excerpted below is the opening scene, which places Dionysos in the midst of the downtrodden and excluded, and the final scene, which turns the famous Greek play in an entirely new direction.

From The Bacchae of Euripides: A Communion Rite

(Opening Scene)

To one side, a road dips steeply into lower background, lined by the bodies of crucified slaves mostly in the skeletal stage. The procession that comes later along this road appears to rise almost from the bowels of earth. The tomb of Semele, smoking slightly, is to one side, behind the shoulder of this rise. Green vines cling to its charred ruins.

In the foreground, the main gate to the palace of Pentheus. Further down and into the wings, a lean-to built against the wall, a threshing-floor. A cloud of chaff, and through it, dim figures of slaves flailing and treading. A smell and sweat of harvest. Ripeness. A spotlight reveals Dionysos just behind the rise, within the tomb of Semele. He is a being of calm rugged strength, of a rugged beauty, not of effeminate prettiness. Relaxed, as becomes divine self-assurance but equally tensed as if for action, an arrow drawn in readiness for flight.

DIONYSOS: Thebes taints me with bastardy. I am turned into an alien, some foreign outgrowth of her habitual tyranny. My followers daily pay forfeit for their faith. Thebes blasphemes against me, makes a scapegoat of a god.

It is time to state my patrimony—even here in Thebes.

I am the gentle, jealous joy. Vengeful and kind. An essence that will not exclude, nor be excluded. If you are Man or Woman, I am Dionysos. Accept.

A seed of Zeus was sown in Semele my mother earth, here on this spot. It has burgeoned through the cragged rocks of far Afghanistan, burst the banks of

fertile Tmolus, sprung oases through the red-eyed sands of Arabia, flow-
ered in hill and gorge of dark Ethiopia. It pounds in the blood and breasts
of my wild-haired women, long companions on this journey home through
Phrygia and the isles of Crete. It beats on the walls of Thebes, bringing
vengeance on all who deny my holy origin and call my mother—slut.
[*He looks down on the clouds of smoke wrapped round his feet, rising from
the tomb. He scuffs the ground with a foot, scattering ashes and sparks.*]
Something lives yet, there is smoke among the rubble. Live embers. The
phoenix rises and that is life—wings from cooling cinders, tendrils from
putrefaction, motion from what was petrified. . . . There are green vines
on the slag of mill. Mine.
As on the mountain slopes, clustering and swelling. They flush, they flood
the long-parched throats of men and release their joy. This sacrament of
earth is life. Dionysos.
[*From the direction of the "crucifixion slope" comes a new sound, a liturgical drone—lead and refrain—a dull, thin monotone, still at some distance.
A Herdsman carrying a jar darts across the stage to the threshers. Dionysos
stands still, statuesque.*]
. . .

(Final Scene)

KADMOS: Now look up at the face you've set
upon that wall. Whose head is it?

AGAVE: Whose . . . ? [*violently.*] It's a lion!
It's . . . I . . . think . . .

KADMOS: Look at it. Look directly at it.

AGAVE: No. What is it? First tell me what it is.

KADMOS: You must look. Look closely and carefully.
[*She brings herself to obey him.*]

AGAVE: Oh. Another slave? But why did I nail it
right over the entrance?

KADMOS: Closer. Move closer. Go right up to it.
[*She moves closer until she is standing almost directly under it, looking
up. She stiffens suddenly, her body shudders and she whirls round
screaming.*]

AGAVE: Bring him down! Bring him down! Bring him . . .
[*Kadmos has moved closer, and she collapses into his shoulders sobbing.*]

KADMOS [*to the Slaves*]: Bring down the head. . . .

TIRESIAS: What is it Kadmos? What is it?

KADMOS: Again blood Tiresias. Nothing but blood.

TIRESIAS [*He feels his way nearer the fount. A spray hits him and he holds out a hand, catches some of the fluid and sniffs. Tastes it.*]:
No. It's wine.

JEWISH AND CHRISTIAN PRAYERS

Liturgy—the words and forms of religious worship—and literature have never been far apart. In most great religious traditions of the world, the practices of worship in hymns, prayers, blessings, and so on have been at the center of life and culture both consciously and unconsciously.

Behind traditions of Christian worship lie the Jewish temple and synagogue, their worship in turn inextricably linked with the literature of the Hebrew Bible. We find in the excerpts below rhythms, images, and themes that have permeated English literature. The three great topics of Jewish prayer—creation, revelation, and redemption—continue to haunt Western traditions of writings and poetry even where these have abandoned "religion" in more "secular" ages.

The 1662 Anglican *Book of Common Prayer* stands beside the King James Version of the Bible as one of the great monuments of English literature, its influence spreading worldwide and far beyond the limits of the church, which continues to use it regularly more than three hundred years after its inception. The language of the *Book of Common Prayer* is enriched by two of the greatest unacknowledged poets of the English language, Miles Coverdale, who translated the Psalter, and Archbishop Thomas Cranmer. The excerpt below is from the eucharistic rite, the Order for Holy Communion.

From Prayers of the Eucharist:
Early and Reformed, *"Jewish Prayers"*

a. Blessing for food

Blessing of him who nourishes
Blessed are you, Lord our God, King of the universe, for you nourish us and the whole world with goodness, grace, kindness, and mercy.

Blessed are you, Lord, for you nourish the universe.

Blessing for the land
We will give thanks to you, Lord our God, because you have given us for our inheritance a desirable land, good and wide, the covenant and the law, life and food.

(*On the feasts of* Hanukkah *and* Purim, *here follows an embolism.*)

And for all these things we give you thanks and bless your name for ever and beyond.

Blessed are you, Lord, for the land and for food.

Blessing for Jerusalem

Have mercy, Lord our God, on us your people Israel, and your city Jerusalem, on your sanctuary and your dwelling place, on Zion, the habitation of your glory, and the great and holy house over which your name is invoked. Restore the kingdom of the house of David to its place in our days, and speedily build Jerusalem.

(*On the feast of* Passover, *here follows this embolism:*

Our God and God of our fathers, may there arise in your sight, and come, and be present, and be regarded, and be pleasing, and be heard, and be visited, and be remembered, our remembrance and our visitation, and the remembrance of our fathers, and the remembrance of the Messiah, the son of your servant David, and the remembrance of Jerusalem, the city of your holiness, and the remembrance of all your people, the house of Israel: for escape, for prosperity, for grace, and for loving-kindness and mercy, for life and for peace, on this day of the Feast of Unleavened Bread. Remember us on this day, Lord our God, for prosperity, and visit us on it for blessing, and save us on it for life. And by the word of salvation and mercy spare us, and grant us grace, and have mercy on us, and save us: for our eyes look to you, for you, O God, are a gracious and merciful king.)

Blessed are you, Lord, for you build Jerusalem. Amen.

[*Blessing of the good and beneficent*

Blessed are you, Lord our God, King of the universe, God, our father, our king, our creator, our redeemer, good and beneficent king, who day by day is concerned to benefit us in many ways, and himself will increase us for ever in grace and kindness and spirit and mercy and every good thing.]

b. The Passover Haggadah
At the elevation of the cup:

Wherefore we ought to celebrate, praise, glorify, magnify, exalt, honor, bless, extol, and proclaim him victor, who did all these signs among our fathers and among us: he brought us out of slavery into freedom, from sorrow to joy, from mourning to a feastday, from darkness into a great light, from purchase to ransom. Let us therefore say before him, "Hallelujah."

c. The Yotser

May you be blessed, our rock, our king, our redeemer, who creates the saints. May your name be glorified for ever, our king, who makes the angels. Your angels stand over the world and proclaim aloud, in fear, with one voice the great words of the living God and king of the universe. All beloved, all the chosen, all powers; and all (men) do the will of their creator in fear and trembling, and all open their mouths in holiness and purity, singing melodiously, and bless and glorify and magnify and adore the holy king, the name of God, mighty king, great and terrible: holy is he. And all, one from another, take upon them the yoke of the heavenly kingdom and give each other in turn to proclaim the holy creator with a quiet mind, a bright tongue, and a holy gentleness, all with one mind answering and saying in fear:

Holy, holy, holy (is the) Lord of hosts; the whole earth is full of his glory.

And the wheels and the holy living creatures raise themselves with great thunder, give glory from the other side and say:

Blessed be the glory of the Lord from his place . . .

d. Attah konanta

You founded the world in the beginning; you established the globe, and made the universe, and molded the creatures.

When you saw the empty void, the darkness, and the spirit on the face of the deep, you scattered the blackness and aroused the light.

He fell away from your word and was expelled from Eden; and you did not destroy him, because he was the workmanship of your hands.

From The Book of Common Prayer,
*"The Order for the Administration of the
Lord's Supper or Holy Communion"*

Lift up your hearts.
Answer: We lift them up unto the Lord.
Priest: Let us give thanks unto our Lord God.
Answer: It is meet and right so to do.

Then shall the Priest turn to the Lord's Table, and say:

It is very meet, right, and our bounden duty, that we should at all times, and in all places, give thanks unto thee, O Lord, holy Father, almighty, everlasting God.

Here shall follow the proper Preface, according to the time, if there be any specially appointed: or else immediately shall follow:

Therefore with angels and archangels, and with all the company of heaven, we laud and magnify thy glorious Name, evermore praising thee, and saying, Holy, holy, holy, Lord God of hosts, heaven and earth are full of thy glory: Glory be to thee, O Lord most High. Amen.

PROPER PREFACES

Upon Christmas Day, and seven days after.
   Because thou didst give Jesus Christ . . .

Upon Easter Day, and seven days after.
    But chiefly are we bound to praise thee . . .
Upon Ascension Day, and seven days after.
    Through thy most dearly beloved Son Jesus Christ our Lord . . .
Upon Whitsunday, and six days after.
    Through Jesus Christ our Lord; according . . .
Upon the Feast of Trinity only.
    Who art one God, one Lord . . .
After each of which Prefaces shall immediately be sung or said:
    Therefore with Angels and Archangels . . .

Then shall the Priest, kneeling down at the Lord's Table, say in the name of all them that shall receive the Communion this prayer following.

We do not presume . . . and he in us. Amen.

When the Priest, standing before the Table, hath so ordered the Bread and Wine, that he may with the more readiness and decency break the Bread before the people, and take the Cup into his hands, he shall say the Prayer of Consecration, as followeth:

Almighty God, our heavenly Father, who of thy tender mercy didst give thine only Son Jesus Christ to suffer death upon the Cross for our redemption; who made there (by his one oblation of himself once offered) a full, perfect, and sufficient sacrifice, oblation, and satisfaction, for the sins of the whole world; and did institute, and in his holy Gospel command us to continue, a perpetual memory of that his precious death, until his coming again;

    Hear us, O merciful Father, we most humbly beseech thee; and grant that we receiving these thy creatures of bread and wine, according to thy Son our Savior Jesus Christ's holy institution, in remembrance of his death and passion, may be partakers of his most blessed Body and Blood: who in the same night that he was betrayed, took Bread; and, when he had given thanks, he brake it, and gave it to his disciples, saying, Take, eat; this is my Body which is given for you: Do this in remembrance of me. Likewise after supper he took the Cup; and, when he had given thanks, he gave it to them, saying, Drink ye all of this; for this is my Blood of the New Testament, which is shed for you and for many for the remission of sins: Do this, as oft as ye shall drink it, in remembrance of me. *Amen.*

PRASNA UPANISHAD

The earliest of the *Upanishads,* sacred to the Hindu tradition, were written in Sanskrit sometime between 800 and 400 B.C.E. In many ways they are similar to the New Testament in their insistence on unity with the divine and the presence of the most High within us. The *Bhagavad Gita* could be considered an *Upanishad.*

The excerpt printed here is from the "fifth question" in the *Prasna Upanishad* and is a meditation on the syllable OM, by which the mind is concentrated on the Divine. Elsewhere, in the *Svetasvatara Upanishad*, the OM of Brahman is the love of God.

From Prasna Upanishad,
"Fifth Question"

Then Saibya Satyakama asked: Master, that man who until the end of his life rests on OM his meditation, where does he go after life?

The sage replied: The Word OM, O Satyakama, is the transcendent and the immanent Brahman, the Spirit Supreme. With the help of this sacred Word the wise attains the one or the other.

OM, or AUM, has three sounds. He who rests on the first his meditation is illumined thereby and after death returns speedily to this world of men led by the harmonies of the *Rig Veda*. Remaining here in steadiness, purity, and truth he attains greatness.

And if he rests his mind in meditation on the first two sounds, he is led by the harmonies of the *Yajur Veda* to the regions of the moon. After enjoying their heavenly joys, he returns to earth again.

But if, with the three sounds of the eternal OM, he places his mind in meditation upon the Supreme Spirit, he comes to the regions of light of the sun. There he becomes free from all evil, even as a snake sheds its old skin, and with the harmonies of the *Sama Veda* he goes to the heaven of Brahma wherefrom he can behold the Spirit that dwells in the city of the human body and which is above the highest life. There are two verses that say:

"The three sounds not in union lead again to life that dies; but the wise who merge them into a harmony of union in outer, inner and middle actions becomes steady: he trembles no more."

With the harmonies of the *Rig Veda* unto this world of man, and with those of the *Yajur Veda* to the middle heavenly regions; but, with the help of OM, the sage goes to those regions that the seers know in the harmonies of the *Sama Veda*. There he finds the peace of the Supreme Spirit where there is no dissolution or death and where there is no fear.

JULIAN OF NORWICH,
REVELATIONS OF DIVINE LOVE

Julian of Norwich (1342–1416) lived as a recluse, shutting herself away from normal social life in order to devote herself to prayer. She was one of a good number of recluses in fourteenth-century England, though perhaps one of the two or three most famous. In 1373, she claims to have experienced a series of "showings," or revelations, which she then wrote down and which were later collected under the title *Revelations of Divine Love*.

Revelations reveals her theology to be a theology of love, a love that saves and a love that unites. With this perspective she moves to a poetically reinterpreted view of the Holy Trinity, in which the Godhead takes on many forms, one of which is that of "Maker, Keeper, and Lover" (*Revelations*, chapter 5). Later in *Revelations*, Julian goes on to consider the motherhood of God. The excerpts here focus on her writing about the loving motherhood of God.

From Revelations of Divine Love

I saw the blessed Trinity working. I saw that there were these three attributes: fatherhood, motherhood, and lordship—all in one God. In the almighty Father we have been sustained and blessed with regard to our created natural being from before all time. By the skill and wisdom of the Second Person we are sustained, restored, and saved with regard to our sensual nature, for he is our Mother, Brother, and Saviour. In our good Lord the Holy Spirit we have, after our life and hardship is over, that reward and rest which surpasses for ever any and everything we can possibly desire—such is his abounding grace and magnificent courtesy.

Our life too is threefold. In the first stage we have our being, in the second our growing, and in the third our perfection. The first is nature, the second mercy, and the third grace. For the first I realized that the great power of the Trinity is our Father, the deep wisdom our Mother, and the great love our Lord. All this we have by nature and in our created and essential being. Moreover I saw that the Second Person who is our Mother with regard to our essential nature, that same dear Person has become our Mother in the matter of our sensual nature. We are God's creation twice: essential being and sensual nature. Our being is that higher part which we have in our Father, God almighty, and the Second Person of the Trinity is Mother of this basic nature, providing the substance in which we are rooted and grounded. But He is our Mother also in mercy, since he has taken our sensual nature upon himself. Thus "our Mother" describes the different ways in which he works, ways which are separate to us, but held together in him. In our Mother, Christ, we grow and develop; in his mercy he reforms and restores us; through his passion, death, and resurrection he has united us to our being. So does our Mother work in mercy for all his children who respond to him and obey him. . . .

Thus in our Father, God almighty, we have our being. In our merciful Mother we have reformation and renewal, and our separate parts are integrated into perfect man. In yielding to the gracious impulse of the Holy Spirit we are made perfect. Our essence is in our Father, God almighty, and in our Mother, God all-wise, and in our Lord the Holy Spirit, God all-good. Our essential nature is entire in each Person of the Trinity, who is one God. Our sensual nature is in the Second Person alone, Jesus Christ. In Him is the Father too, and the Holy Spirit. In and by him have we been taken out of hell with a strong arm; and out of earth's wretchedness have been wonderfully raised to heaven, and united, most blessedly, to him who is our true being. And we have developed in spiritual wealth and character through all Christ's virtues, and by the gracious work of the Holy Spirit.

A mother's is the most intimate, willing, and dependable of all services, because it is the truest of all. None has been able to fulfil it properly but Christ, and he alone can. We know that our own mother's bearing of us was a bearing to pain and death, but what does Jesus, our true Mother, do? Why, he, All-love, bears us to joy and eternal life! Blessings on him! Thus he carries us within himself in love. And he is in labour until the time has fully come for him to suffer the sharpest pangs and most appalling pain possible—and in the end he dies. And not even when this is over, and we ourselves have been born to eternal bliss, is his marvellous love completely satisfied. This he shows in that overwhelming word of love, "If I could possibly have suffered more, indeed I would have done so."

He might die no more, but that does not stop him working, for he needs to feed us . . . it is an obligation of his dear, motherly, love. The human mother will suckle her child with her own milk, but our beloved Mother, Jesus, feeds us with himself, and, with the most tender courtesy, does it by means of the Blessed Sacrament, the precious food of all true life. And he keeps us going through his mercy and grace by all the sacraments. This is what he meant when he said, "It is I whom Holy Church preaches and teaches." In other words, "All the health and life of sacraments, all the virtue and grace of my word, all the goodness laid up for you in Holy Church—it is I." The human mother may put her child tenderly to her breast, but our tender Mother Jesus simply leads us into his blessed breast through his open side, and there gives us a glimpse of the Godhead and heavenly joy—the inner certainty of eternal bliss. The tenth revelation showed this, and said as much with that word, "See how I love you," as looking into his side he rejoiced.

THOMAS MERTON,
THE SEVEN STOREY MOUNTAIN

Thomas Merton (1915–1968) was born in France, educated in England, and spent most of his adult life in the United States. Much of his youth was spent traveling and partying, even as he maintained a keen interest in English literature. By his mid-twenties, and while a graduate student and part-time lecturer at Columbia University, his restless lifestyle began to grow tiresome to him and Merton turned to other ways of life. He converted to Catholicism and at twenty-six joined a Trappist monastery in Kentucky, where he would spend almost all the rest of his life. At the same time, the "conversion" was not a simple one-time occurrence, but was something Merton understood to be a lifelong ordeal, having a great deal to do with one's everyday life.

As a Trappist monk, Merton continually struggled with his own aptitude as a writer, especially as the difficulties of maintaining such a habit conflicted with his life as a monk. He found some resolution to this conflict by writing about his life as a monk. In 1948 he published his massive autobiography, *The Seven Storey Mountain*, which takes its name from Dante's "Purgatory" in the *Divine Comedy*. The book became a best-seller, was translated into many languages, and set Merton on a path as a writer and a monk. In the excerpt below, Merton reflects back on his master's thesis (from his position as a monk some years later) and finds an important relation between aesthetics and mystical experience.

From The Seven Storey Mountain

The subject I had finally chosen was "Nature and Art in William Blake." I did not realize how providential a subject it actually was! What it amounted to was a study of Blake's reaction against every kind of literalism and naturalism and narrow, classical realism in art, because of his own ideal which was essentially mystical and supernatural. In other words, the topic, if I treated it at all sensibly, could not help but cure me of all the naturalism and materialism in my own philosophy, besides resolving all the inconsistencies and self-contradictions that had persisted in my mind for years, without my being able to explain them.

After all, from my very childhood, I had understood that the artistic experience, at its highest, was actually a natural analogue of mystical experience. It produced a kind of intuitive perception of reality through a sort of affective identification with the object contemplated—the kind of perception that the Thomists call "connatural." This means simply a knowledge that comes about as it were by the identification of natures: in the way that a chaste man understands the nature of chastity because of the very fact that his soul is full of it— it is a part of his own nature, since habit is second nature. Non-connatural knowledge of chastity should be that of a philosopher who, to borrow the language of the *Imitation,* would be able to define it, but would not possess it.

I had learned from my own father that it was almost blasphemy to regard the function of art as merely to reproduce some kind of a sensible pleasure or, at best, to stir up the emotions to a transitory thrill. I had always understood that art was contemplation, and that it involved the action of the highest faculties of man.

When I was once able to discover the key to Blake, in his rebellion against literalism and naturalism in art, I saw that his Prophetic Books and the rest of his verse at large represented a rebellion against naturalism in the moral order as well.

What a revelation that was! For at sixteen I had imagined that Blake, like the other romantics, was glorifying passion, natural energy, for their own sake. Far from it! What he was glorifying was the transfiguration of man's natural love, his natural powers, in the refining fires of mystical experience: and that, in itself, implied an arduous and total purification, by faith and love and desire, from all the petty materialistic and commonplace and earthly ideals of his rationalistic friends.

Blake, in his sweeping consistency, had developed a moral insight that cut through all the false distinctions of a worldly and interested morality. That was why he saw that, in the legislation of men, some evils had been set up as standards of right by which other evils were to be condemned: and the norms of pride or greed had been established in the judgement seat, to pronounce a crushing and inhuman indictment against all the normal healthy strivings of human nature. Love was outlawed, and became lust, pity was swallowed up in cruelty, and so Blake knew how:

> The harlot's cry from street to street
> Shall weave old England's winding-sheet.

I had heard that cry and that echo. I had seen that winding sheet. But I had understood nothing of all that. I had tried to resolve it into a matter of socio-logical laws, of economic forces. If I had been able to listen to Blake in those old days, he would have told me that sociology and economics, divorced from faith and charity, become nothing but the chains of his aged, icy demon Urizen! But now, reading Maritain, in connection with Blake, I saw all these difficulties and contradictions disappear.

I, who had always been anti-naturalistic in art, had been a pure naturalist in the moral order. No wonder my soul was sick and torn apart: but now the bleeding wound was drawn together by the notion of Christian virtue, ordered to the Union of the soul with God. . . .

By the time I was ready to begin the actual writing of my thesis, that is, around the beginning of September 1938, the groundwork of conversion was more or less complete. And how easily and sweetly it had all been done, with all the external graces that had been arranged, along my path, by the kind Prov-idence of God! It had taken little more than a year and a half, counting from the time I read Gilson's *The Spirit of Medieval Philosophy,* to bring me up from an "atheist"—as I considered myself—to one who accepted all the full range and possibilities of religious experience right up to the highest degree of glory.

JOHN DONNE,
"BATTER MY HEART, THREE-PERSONED GOD"

John Donne (1572–1631) was an English poet who studied law and the-ology. After having traveled a good deal and being considered something of a rogue, Donne eventually converted from Catholicism to Anglicanism, was ordained into the Anglican church, and later became Dean of St. Paul's Cathedral in London. Along with others of the time like Herbert and Vaughan, Donne was considered a "metaphysical" poet. Metaphysical poetry is the type of poetry that T. S. Eliot was to say gets "into the cerebral cortex, the nervous system, and the digestive tracts."

Donne's earlier love poems, full of strong sexual innuendo, later shifted into love poetry about God. In all of this was the use of "conceit," a poetical device that suggests a comparison between two things (the reader must "concede" a likeness) even while the reader remains strongly conscious that the two things are dissimilar. The poem excerpted below was part of Donne's later "Holy Sonnets," and in it strong similarities are suggested between the besieging of a fortress, a rape, and an overpower-ing love of God.

Donne meditates dramatically on Christian doctrine, beginning with a reference to the Trinity and proceeding with a series of powerful images in which each word literally batters the reader in a description of warfare and struggle, dramatizing the believer's battle with God. He draws also upon the language of his earlier love poems to describe the drama of God's con-quest of the heart, soul, and mind.

"Batter my heart, three-personed God"

Batter my heart, three-personed God; for, you
As yet but knock, breathe, shine, and seek to mend;
That I may rise, and stand, o'erthrow me, and bend
Your force, to break, blow, burn, and make me new.
I, like an usurped town, to another due,
Labour to admit you, but oh, to no end,
Reason your viceroy in me, me should defend,
But is captived, and proves weak or untrue,
Yet dearly I love you, and would be loved fain,
But am betrothed unto your enemy,
Divorce me, untie, or break that knot again,
Take me to you, imprison me, for I
Except you enthral me, never shall be free,
Nor ever chaste, except you ravish me.

GEORGE HERBERT, "LOVE"

George Herbert (1593–1633) was born to an aristocratic English family but abandoned a career as a courtier and diplomat to become an Anglican priest and vicar of a small country parish in the south of England. His elegant, deceptively simple poetry is steeped in Christian doctrines and, above all, in the language and liturgy of the Anglican *Book of Common Prayer*, which was largely the work of Archbishop Thomas Cranmer in the sixteenth century.

In the poem below, perhaps the best known of all his writings, Herbert draws on the imagery of the Eucharist or service of Holy Communion as it is found in the Anglican rite, and combines this with images of the countryside inn, welcoming the weary traveler, but also, and more daringly, the quite explicit sexual imagery of particularly the first verse. Here, "Love" is seen as a seductive woman encouraging her shy lover. The three levels work together to form a most remarkable and coherent unity, expressive also of the theology of the Reformation, which emphasizes human unworthiness in the face of God's redeeming grace in the Lord.

"Love"

Love bade me welcome: yet my soul drew back,
    Guiltie of dust and sinne.
But quick-ey'd Love, observing me grow slack
    From my first entrance in,
Drew nearer to me, sweetly questioning,
    If I lack'd anything.

A guest, I answer'd, worthy to be here:
  Love said, you shall be he.
I the unkinde, ungratefull? Ah my deare,
  I cannot look on thee.
Love took my hand, and smiling did reply,
  Who made the eyes but I?

Truth, Lord, but I have marr'd them: let my shame
  Go where it doth deserve.
And know you not, sayes Love, who bore the blame?
  My deare, then I will serve
You must sit down, sayes Love, and taste my meat:
  So I did sit and eat.

HERMAN MELVILLE,
MOBY DICK: OR THE WHALE

Herman Melville (1819–1891) grew up in New York City and spent several of his early years as a merchant seaman and teller of stories. When he turned to writing down his stories of the sea, he was almost instantly successful. At the age of thirty-two he published what is perhaps his greatest work, *Moby Dick: Or the Whale.* A master of realistic narrative and of a rich, rhythmical, almost liturgical prose, Melville offers his reader a mixture of psychological and religious searching which looks back from its very first sentence ("Call me Ishmael") to the Bible itself. He has had an enormous influence on the literature of the twentieth century.

The excerpt here is from the last part of a sermon given by Father Mapple in the town of New Bedford, where the novel's narrator, Ishmael, is attending chapel.

From Moby Dick: Or The Whale

"Shipmates, I do not place Jonah before you to be copied for his sin but I do place him before you as a model for repentance. Sin not; but if you do, take heed to repent of it like Jonah."

While he was speaking these words, the howling of the shrieking, slanting storm without seemed to add new power to the preacher, who, when describing Jonah's sea-storm, seemed tossed by a storm himself. His deep chest heaved as with a ground swell: his tossed arms seemed the warring elements at work; and the thunders that rolled away from off his swarthy brow, and the light leaping from his eye, made all his simple hearers look on him with a quick fear that was strange to them.

There now came a lull in his look, as he silently turned over the leaves of the book once more; and, at last, standing motionless with closed eyes, for the moment, seemed communing with God and himself.

But again he leaned over towards the people, and bowing his head lowly, with an aspect of the deepest yet manliest humility, he spake these words:

"Shipmates, God has laid one hand upon you; both his hands press upon me. I have read ye by what murky light may be mine the lesson that Jonah teaches to all sinners; and therefore to ye, and still more to me, for I am a greater sinner than ye. And now how gladly would I come down from this mast-head and sit on the hatches there where you sit, and listen as you listen, while some of you reads *me* that other and more awful lesson which Jonah teaches to *me,* as a pilot of the living God. How being an anointed pilot-prophet, or speaker of true things, and bidden by the Lord to sound those unwelcome truths in the ears of a wicked Ninevah, Jonah, appalled at the hostility he should raise, fled from his mission, and sought to escape his duty and his God by taking ship at Joppa. But God is everywhere; Tarshish he never reached. As we have seen, God came upon him in the whale, and swallowed him down to living gulfs of doom, and with swift slantings tore him along 'into the midst of the seas,' where the eddying depths sucked him ten thousand fathoms down, and 'the weeds were wrapped about his head,' and all the watery world of woe bowled over him. Yet even then beyond the reach of any plummet—'out of the belly of hell'—when the whale grounded upon the ocean's utmost bones, even then, God heard the engulphed, repenting prophet when he cried. Then God spake unto the fish; and from the shuddering cold and blackness of the sea, the whale come breeching up towards the warm and pleasant sun, and all the delights of air and earth; and 'vomited out Jonah upon the dry land', when the word of the Lord came a second time; and Jonah, bruised and beaten—his ears, like two sea-shells, still multitudinously murmuring of the ocean—Jonah did the Almighty's bidding. And what was that, shipmates? To preach the Truth to the face of Falsehood! That was it!

"This, shipmates, this is that other lesson; and woe to that pilot of the living God who slights it. Woe to him whom this world charms from Gospel duty! Woe to him who seeks to pour oil upon the waters when God has brewed them into a gale! Woe to him whose good name is more to him than goodness! Woe to him who, in this world, courts now dishonor! Woe to him who would not be true, even though to be false were salvation! Yea, woe to him who, as the great Pilot Paul has it, while preaching to others is himself a castaway!"

He drooped and fell away from himself for a moment; then lifting his face to them again, showed a deep joy in his eyes, as he cried out with a heavenly enthusiasm,—"But oh! shipmates! on the starboard hand of every woe, there is a sure delight; and higher the top of that delight, than the bottom of the woe is deep. Is not the main-truck higher than the kelson is low? Delight is to him— a far, far upward, and inward delight—who against the proud gods and commodores of this earth, ever stands forth his own inexorable self. Delight is to him whose strong arms yet support him, when the ship of this base treacherous world has gone down beneath him. Delight is to him, who gives no quarter in the truth, and kills, burns, and destroys all sin though he pluck it out from under the robes of Senators and Judges. Delight,—top-gallant delight is to him who acknowledges no law or lord, but the Lord his God, and is only a patriot to heaven. Delight is to him, whom all the waves of the billows of the seas of the boisterous mob can never shake from this sure Keel of the Ages. And eternal delight and deliciousness will be his, who coming to lay him down, can say with his final breath—O Father! —chiefly known to me by Thy Rod—mortal or immortal, here I die. I have striven to be Thine, more than to be this world's, or mine own. Yet this is nothing; I leave eternity to Thee; for what is man that he should live out the lifetime of his God?"

He said no more, but slowly waving a benediction, covered his face with his hands, and so remained kneeling, till all the people had departed, and he was left alone in the place.

JOHN UPDIKE,
A MONTH OF SUNDAYS

John Updike (b. 1932) is one of the most prolific writers in the United States. For the past four decades, he has written short stories, novels, essays, and reviews. While Updike had an early interest in theology, he majored in English at Harvard. Yet, his interest in all things theological has never ceased, and his stories are filled with priests, professors of theology, and religiously minded laypersons. He has been influenced by others whose work is excerpted in this anthology, including Paul Tillich and Søren Kierkegaard, from whom Updike understands the religious life (as with all life) to be one of struggle. Updike's characters struggle most with sex, and, relatedly, with the fact that humans have bodies and are therefore susceptible to bodily temptations.

The excerpt below comes from precisely such a struggle. *A Month of Sundays* is a novel about the Reverend Thomas Marshfield, who has been "banished" to the desert by his church for his liaisons with various women in his spiritual care. The novel is made up of thirty-one entries, written by Marshfield each day during the month of banishment. Every Sunday of the month he writes a sermon, even though it is not clear who the congregation is. The excerpt below begins with "Day 1" as an introduction to Marshfield's predicament, and then picks up from the third sermon from "Day 20."

From A Month of Sundays

Forgive me my denomination and my town; I am a Christian minister, and an American. I write these pages at some point in the time of Richard Nixon's unravelling. Though the yielding is mine, the temptation belongs to others: my keepers have set before me a sheaf of blank sheets—a month's worth, in their estimation. Sullying them is to be my sole therapy.

My bishop, bless his miter, has ordered (or, rather, offered as the alternative to the frolicsome rite of defrocking) me brought here to the desert, far from the green and crowded land where my parish, as the French so nicely put it, locates itself. The month is to be one of recuperation—as I think of it, "retraction," my condition being officially diagnosed as one of "distraction." Perhaps the opposite of "dis" is not "re" but the absence of any prefix, by which construal I am spiritual brother to those broken-boned athletes who must spend a blank month, amid white dunes and midnight dosages, in "traction." I doubt (verily, my name *is* Thomas) it will work. In *my* diagnosis I suffer from nothing less virulent than the human condition, and so would preach it. . . .

O, LORD.
Another Sunday is upon us.

Our text shall be taken from Deuteronomy, the thirty-second book: "He found him in a desert place."

Moses is speaking of Jacob, but it might well be of himself, or of a dozen other of the God-chosen men of the Old Testament. The verse continues, if failing memory serves, "He found him in a desert land, and in the waste howling wilderness; he led him about, he instructed him, he kept him as the apple of his eye." . . .

Though the drama of the Bible is islanded by history, the wilderness is always there, pre-existent and enduring. Adam and Eve are sent forth from their disobedience into it, and our Lord Jesus at the dawn of His ministry retired unto it, to be tempted of Satan. There, as Mark with his characteristic pungence tells us, He "was with the wild beasts; and the angels ministered unto Him." And for each of the forty days of His fast and vigil there, the children of Israel wandered a year of their forty in the wilderness of Sin, or Zin, or Sinai, wherein their thirst was often keen, so keen that on at least one occasion the Lord left off His fearsome chiding of His children and led Moses to the Rock of Horeb, and bid him smite, "which turned the rock into a standing water, the flint into a fountain of waters." Our soul, the Psalmist says, *thirsteth* for God—Whose doctrine, we are told elsewhere, drops as the rain, "as the small rain upon the tender herb, and as the showers upon the grass." "He leadeth me beside the still waters; He restoreth my soul"—the special world of God within the Bible is an oasis world; the world beyond, the world of the Lord's wider creation, is a desert. . . .

We all know the name Death Valley. How many of us have heard of *La Palma de la Mano de Dios?* So the Spaniards called the harshest basin of the American desert as they knew it. The Palm of God's Hand. Are we not all here, in the palm of God's hand? And do we not see, around us (with the knowledgeable guidance of our dear Ms. Prynne), the Joshua tree lifting its arms awkwardly in prayer, and hear the organ-pipe cactus thundering its transcendent hymn? What a chorale of praise floats free from the invisible teeming of desert life—the peccary and the ocelot, the horned lizard and the blacktailed jack rabbit, the kangaroo rat that needs never to drink water and the century plant that blooms but once in decades. How ingenious and penetrant is life! . . .

What lesson might we draw from this undaunted profusion? The lesson speaks itself. Live. Live, brothers, though there be naught but shame and failure to furnish forth your living. To those of you who have lost your place, I say that the elf owl makes a home in the pulp of a saguaro. To those upon whom recent events still beat down mercilessly, I say that the coyote waits out the day in the shade. To those who find no faith within themselves, I say no seed is so dry it does not hold the code of life within it, and that except a corn of wheat fall into the ground and die, it abideth alone; but if it die, it bringeth forth much fruit. Blessed, blessed are the poor in spirit.

Brothers, we have come to a tight place. Let us be, then, as the chuckwalla, who, when threatened, *runs* to a tight place, to a crevice in the burning rock of the desert. Once there, does he shrink in shame? No! He puffs himself up, inflates his self to more than half its normal size, and fills that crevice as the living soul fills the living body, and cannot be dislodged by the talon or fang of any enemy.

We *are* found in a desert place.

We *are* in God's palm.

We *are* the apple of His eye.

Let us be grateful *here,* and here rejoice. Amen.

FURTHER READING

Arias, Ricardo. *The Spanish Sacramental Plays.* Boston: Twayne Publishers, 1980.

Brook, Stella. *The Language of the Book of Common Prayer.* London: A. Deutsch, 1965.

Hardison, O. B., Jr. *Christian Rite and Drama in the Middle Ages: Essays in the Origin and Early History of Modern Drama.* Baltimore: Johns Hopkins Press, 1965.

Henn, T. R. *The Bible as Literature.* New York: Oxford University Press, 1970.

Jasper, David, and R. C. D. Jasper, eds. *Language and the Worship of the Church.* New York: St. Martin's Press, 1990.

Kort, Wesley A. *"Take, Read": Scripture, Textuality, and Cultural Practice.* University Park: Pennsylvania State University Press, 1996.

McNees, Eleanor J. *Eucharistic Poetry: The Search for Presence in the Writings of John Donne, Gerard Manley Hopkins, Dylan Thomas, and Geoffrey Hill.* Lewisburg, Pa.: Bucknell University Press, 1992.

Metzger, Marcel. *History of the Liturgy: The Major Stages.* French translation by Madeleine Baeumont. Collegeville, Minn.: Liturgical Press, 1997.

Ramsey, Ian T. *Religious Language: An Empirical Placing of Theological Phrases.* London: SCM Press, 1957.

Reynolds, Frank, and David Tracy, eds. *Discourse and Practice.* Albany: State University of New York Press, 1992.

Ross-Bryant, Lynn. *Imagination and the Life of the Spirit: An Introduction to the Study of Religion and Literature.* Missoula, Mont.: Scholars Press, 1979.

Smolarski, Dennis Chester. *Sacred Mysteries: Sacramental Principles and Liturgical Practice.* New York: Paulist Press, 1995.

Stock, R. D. *The Flutes of Dionysus: Daemonic Enthrallment in Literature.* Lincoln: University of Nebraska Press, 1989.

Thornton, Martin. *English Spirituality: An Outline of Ascetical Theology According to the English Pastoral Tradition.* London: SPCK, 1963.

5

The Literary Structures
of Religious Text Genres

This chapter examines the kinds of literature that constitute sacred texts or are written in response to sacred texts. Selections include texts that relate to the questions of theodicy—the problem of belief in an absolutely good God in a world containing evil—and the relationship between God and the sinner. Also there are texts vibrant with the powerful imagery of apocalypse, novelistic stories and parables that derive from the rabbinic traditions, and finally the central narrative of the Christian faith, the passion story, and, at its heart, the image of the cross.

We focus first upon the literary structure of these texts, and how this structure conveys religious and theological force, using texts from the Bible, and from drama, poetry, and modern fiction. Repeatedly we see biblical roots in later literature, and, in the case of the parable, how ancient literary traditions are alive and well. Next we review sacred text genres that have been incorporated into modern literature, especially into drama and prose fiction, or adapted for "secular" audiences rather than the congregations that gather in faith to celebrate the texts of the liturgy.

The biblical book of Job, one of the most ancient of Near Eastern texts, has been dated as early as 2100 B.C.E., and undoubtedly relates to even earlier texts from Mesopotamia. One of the greatest of all poems in literature, it explores the dilemma of the righteous man who is visited with apparently undeserved manifold ills. In the third chapter we have an example of the curse, as Job "curses the day of his birth." Not afraid even to curse God, Job delves into the depths of human misery in the face of apparently unwarranted ills. This material has been much drawn on in literature. For example, verses 13–14, "then should I have been at rest, with kings and counsellors of the earth," forms the epitaph for Herman Melville's Bartelby, as he lies in the prison in which he has died. Archibald MacLeish returns to the theme of the trials of Job in his Broadway play *J. B.*, while in more recent fiction, Muriel Spark has looked at the literary problem of introducing the character of God into a poem in her novel *The Only Problem* (1984), in which the central character Harvey Gotham is writing a commentary on Job and is accused of suggesting that through his treatment of the righteous Job, "God is a shit." But in response he replies to his critics that he was not talking about God as such, but "What I was talking about was a fictional character in the Book of Job, called God." The forms and structures of literature are never far from religious and theological discussion.

John Bunyan's early autobiographical book *Grace Abounding to the Chief of Sinners* also explores the question of God's treatment of his people, but this time from the personal perspective of one who, unlike Job, feels himself to be a dreadful sinner. Bunyan's book is an example of a confession, a literary form that finds its greatest early Christian expression in the *Confessions* of Augustine, Bishop of Hippo (circa 400 C.E.) and remains common in modern writers like C. S. Lewis and Thomas Merton. It has proved itself particularly appropriate to the developing genre of the novel, perhaps the greatest of all fictional "confession" narratives being James Hogg's terrifying *Confessions of a Justified Sinner* (1824).

The remaining four sections of this chapter link literary passages with examples of forms of biblical literature. The first introduces a powerful form of prophetic writing in Ezekiel, akin to the later literature of "apocalypse," a word derived from the Greek, and meaning "revelation" or "unveiling." These prophetic writings and apocalyptic literature abounded in powerful images that often clash in dramatic and strange ways in their attempts to describe visions of the Divine or the end of things. Here Ezekiel's word portrait of the chariot is traced through later literature in William Blake and Patrick White.

Next, the brief novella of Susanna from the Apocrypha is printed in full, with an "intertext" from William Shakespeare's *All's Well That Ends Well*. The dramatic and erotic qualities of the Susanna story of wickedness and justice have recommended it to countless artists and writers in the tradition, drawn to the sheer narrative power of the writing. This narrative power is never more in evidence than in the rabbinic tradition of the parable, a literary form that is used to such remarkable effect in the Gospels, the stories of which may well be attributable to Jesus himself. Because they are so well known—especially the parables in Luke's Gospel of the prodigal son and the good Samaritan—we have not reprinted them here, offering instead a *mashal,* or fable, from rabbinic literature, together with one of the greatest of modern parables, the parable of the doorkeeper from Franz Kafka's novel *The Trial.*

We finally return to perhaps the central text of the Christian scriptures, that is, the account of the crucifixion, here drawn from Mark, probably the earliest of the four canonical Gospels. The structure and stark moments of this great narrative resound through our literary traditions in many and various ways, for it is a story that plumbs the depths of human experience and emotions, from the deepest despair to extraordinary triumph, from the most profound hatred to unbounded love. Borges's revisioning of Mark's narrative is almost as elusive and paradoxical as the scriptural original.

By way of conclusion, we return to the writings of Paul Ricoeur and his brief discussion of the nature of the "sacred" text and its particular relationship with the community that reads it and grants it authority.

THE BOOK OF JOB

The book of Job is believed to be the oldest book of the Bible, yet it is remarkable for the power of its poetry, its deep feeling for nature and the human condition, and above all for its sense of the mystery of suffering. It stands beside other great works such as the Aeschylean tragedies, which it predates by many centuries. Unlike many of the other biblical books, it does not give the reader much of a sense of historical context. Rather, it tells a story that puts philosophical questions concerning evil at the forefront, and it is the first great work to examine what we now call the problem of theodicy—that is, how we can continue to believe in a loving and perfectly good God in a world full of suffering. The portrayal of the character of God as a participant in a gamble or dare, with Satan as a sort of prosecuting attorney, has been the source of much interpretive effort. Moreover, the book of Job is striking in God's refusal to confront his loyal worshiper with any kind of logic understandable in human terms.

A seemingly good and righteous man, Job suffers the loss of everything he loves and possesses except for his wife and a few friends. He is further afflicted with boils and suffers physical torments. The story progresses through Job's response (and that of his notorious "comforters") to this tragedy. While the end of the story has been read as "making everything good again," the story does not allow the pain and suffering of life—in whatever sense one can think of—to be ignored. The dead may have been "replaced" by other descendants, but they have not arisen. The excerpt begins after the initial "taking away" that Satan has committed and God permitted.

Job 3

1 After this Job opened his mouth and cursed the day of his birth. [2]Job said:
> [3]"Let the day perish in which I was born,
>> and the night that said,
>> 'A man-child is conceived.'
> [4]Let that day be darkness!
>> May God above not seek it,
>> or light shine on it.
> [5]Let gloom and deep darkness claim it.
>> Let clouds settle upon it;
>> let the blackness of the day terrify it.
> [6]That night—let thick darkness seize it!
>> let it not rejoice among the days of the year;
>> let it not come into the number of the months.
> [7]Yes, let that night be barren;
>> let no joyful cry be heard in it.
> [8]Let those curse it who curse the Sea,
>> those who are skilled to rouse up Leviathan.

⁹Let the stars of its dawn be dark;
    let it hope for light, but have none;
    may it not see the eyelids of the morning—
¹⁰because it did not shut the doors of my mother's womb,
    and hide trouble from my eyes.

¹¹"Why did I not die at birth,
    come forth from the womb and expire?
¹²Why were there knees to receive me,
    or breasts for me to suck?
¹³Now I would be lying down and quiet;
    I would be asleep; then I would be at rest
¹⁴with kings and counselors of the earth
    who rebuild ruins for themselves,
¹⁵or with princes who have gold,
    who fill their houses with silver.
¹⁶Or why was I not buried like a stillborn child,
    like an infant that never sees the light?
¹⁷There the wicked cease from troubling,
    and there the weary are at rest.
¹⁸There the prisoners are at ease together;
    they do not hear the voice of the taskmaster.
¹⁹The small and the great are there,
    and the slaves are free from their masters.

²⁰"Why is light given to one in misery,
    and life to the bitter in soul,
²¹who long for death, but it does not come,
    and dig for it more than for hidden treasures;
²²who rejoice exceedingly,
    and are glad when they find the grave?
²³Why is light given to the one who cannot see the way,
    whom God has fenced in?
²⁴For my sighing comes like my bread,
    and my groanings are poured out like water.
²⁵Truly the thing that I fear comes upon me,
    and what I dread befalls me.
²⁶I am not at ease, nor am I quiet;
    I have no rest; but trouble comes."

ARCHIBALD MACLEISH,
J. B.

Archibald MacLeish (1892–1982) won a Pulitzer Prize for his play *J. B.* (1958), which sets the theme of Job's trials within contemporary issues and idioms. Self-consciously theatrical, the play was performed on Broadway to great critical acclaim, although it has not, perhaps, weathered the passage of time well.

MacLeish's earlier drama was deeply influenced by the modernists Ezra Pound and T. S. Eliot, and his plays are highly subjective, giving voice to the hopeless individual in a chaotic and seemingly meaningless world. The ancient figure of Job then becomes an archetype, asking his primal questions about apparently unmerited suffering in the world. Theodicy (the word is derived from the title of a work by the eighteenth-century philosopher Leibniz) remains as pertinent and intractable a problem today as it was for the ancient poet of Job. Human suffering, as MacLeish's character Nickles puts it, still "throbs and thrashes with the need to know."

From J. B.

NICKLES:

He squats on the floor of the ring, contemplating the role of Job, thinking it out, miming it.

God has killed his sons . . .
        his daughters . . .
Taken his camels, oxen, sheep,
Everything he has . . .
        and left him
Sick and stricken on a dung-heap—
Not even the consciousness of crime to comfort him:
The rags of reasons . . .

MR. ZUSS: [*thundering*] God is reasons.

NICKLES: For the universe, yes. But human suffering
Throbs and thrashes with the need to know.
Job suffers. He must find his reason.
He does. He finds it. He sees God!

Nastily.

Sees Him by that icy moonlight,
By that cold dislosing eye
That stares the colour out and strews
Our lives . . .
        with light . . .
               for nothing.

NICKLES *looks up to* MR. ZUSS *for approval.*

MR. ZUSS: No!
Not Job. Not you. I wouldn't think of it.

NICKLES: [*brought up short*]

You wouldn't think of me for Job?
What would you think of?

MR. ZUSS: Oh, there's always
Someone playing Job.

NICKLES: There must be
Thousands! What's that got to do with it?
Millions and millions of mankind
Burned, crushed, broken, mutilated,
Slaughtered, and for what? For thinking!
For walking round the world in the wrong
Skin, the wrong-shaped noses, eyelids:
Living at the wrong address—
London, Berlin, Hiroshima,
Wrong night, wrong city.
There never could have been so many
Suffered more for less. But where do
I come in? . . .

MR. ZUSS *shuffles uncomfortably.*

. . . play the dung heap?

MR. ZUSS: [*putting on a long tattered vestment he has found in his cupboard*]
All we have to do is start.
Job will join us. Job will be there.

NICKLES: I know. I know. I know. I've seen him.
Job is everywhere we go, his children dead, his work for nothing,
Counting his losses, scraping his boils,
Discussing himself with his friends and physicians,
Questioning everything—the times, the stars,
His own soul. God's providence.
What do *I* play?

JOHN BUNYAN,
GRACE ABOUNDING TO THE CHIEF OF SINNERS

John Bunyan (1628–1688) is best known for his allegory *The Pilgrim's Progress* (1684), which has had a profound effect on the development of the English novel. Without formal education, Bunyan served as a soldier in Cromwell's army during the English Civil War, and later became a Nonconformist preacher, suffering frequent imprisonment for preaching without a license.

Grace Abounding (1666) is a confessional work looking back to such Christian classics as Augustine's *Confessions,* in which Augustine traces the history of his conversion and his coming to faith after a wild youth. Like *The Pilgrim's Progress, Grace Abounding* grows out of Bunyan's deep immersion in biblical literature, and in his prefatory address to his reader he says: "I have sent to you here enclosed, a drop of that honey, that I have taken out of the carcase of a lion (Judges xiv, 5–9). I have eaten thereof myself also, and am much refreshed thereby." The passage given here is from the opening pages of the book, and, while showing clearly Bunyan's Calvinist theology, bears many of the marks of imaginative writing which were to develop more fully in his later work and to bear fruit in the later English novel.

From Grace Abounding to the Chief of Sinners

1. In this my relation of the merciful working of God upon my soul, it will not be amiss if, in the first place, I do, in a few words, give you a hint of my pedigree, and manner of bringing up; that thereby the goodness and bounty of God towards me, may be the more advanced and magnified before the sons of men.

2. For my descent then, it was, as is well known by many, of a low and inconsiderable generation; my father's house being of that rank that is meanest and most despised of all the families in the land. Wherefore I have not here, as others, to boast of noble blood, or of a high-born state, according to the flesh; though, all things considered, I magnify the heavenly Majesty, for that by this door he brought me into this world, to partake of the grace and life that is in Christ by the gospel.

3. But yet, notwithstanding the meanness and inconsiderableness of my parents, it pleased God to put it into their hearts to put me to school, to learn both to read and write; the which I also attained, according to the rate of other poor men's children; though, to my shame I confess, I did soon lose that little I learned, and that even almost utterly, and that long before the Lord did work his gracious work of conversion upon my soul.

4. As for my own natural life, for the time that I was without God in the world, it was indeed according to the course of this world, and "the spirit that now worketh in the children of disobedience" (Eph. ii. 2, 3). It was my delight to be "taken captive by the devil at his will" (2 Tim. ii. 26). Being filled with all unrighteousness: the which did also so strongly work and put forth itself, both in my heart and life, and that from a child, that I had but few equals, especially considering my years, which were tender, being few, both for cursing, swearing, lying, and blaspheming the holy name of God.

5. Yea, so settled and rooted was I in these things, that they became as a second nature to me; the which, as I also have with soberness considered since, did so offend the Lord, that even in my childhood he did scare and affright me with fearful dreams, and did terrify me with dreadful visions; for often, after I had spent this and the other day in sin, I have in my bed been greatly afflicted, while asleep, with the apprehensions of devils and wicked

spirits, who still, as I then thought, laboured to draw me away with them, of which I could never be rid.

6. Also I should, at these years, be greatly afflicted and troubled with the thoughts of the day of judgment, and that both night and day, and should tremble at the thoughts of the fearful torments of hell fire; still fearing that it would be my lot to be found at last amongst those devils and hellish fiends, who are there bound down with the chains and bonds of eternal darkness, "unto the judgment of the great day."

7. These things, I say, when I was but a child but nine or ten years old, did so distress my soul, that when in the midst of my many sports and childish vanities, amidst my vain companions, I was often much cast down and afflicted in my mind therewith, yet could I not let go my sins. Yea, I was also then so overcome with despair of life and heaven, that I should often wish either that there had been no hell, or that I had been a devil—supposing they were only tormentors; that if it must needs be that I went thither, I might be rather a tormentor, than be tormented myself.

8. A while after, these terrible dreams did leave me, which also I soon forgot; for my pleasures did quickly cut off the remembrance of them, as if they had never been: wherefore, with more greediness, according to the strength of nature, I did still let loose the reins to my lusts, and delighted in all transgression against the law of God: so that, until I came to the state of marriage, I was the very ringleader of all the youth that kept me company, into all manner of vice and ungodliness.

9. Yea, such prevalency had the lusts and fruits of the flesh in this poor soul of mine, that had not a miracle of precious grace prevented, I had not only perished by the stroke of eternal justice, but had also laid myself open, even to the stroke of those laws, which bring some to disgrace and open shame before the face of the world.

10. In these days, the thoughts of religion were very grievous to me; I could neither endure it myself, nor that any other should; so that, when I have seen some read in those books that concerned Christian piety, it would be as it were a prison to me. Then I said unto God, "Depart from me, for I desire not the knowledge of thy ways" (Job xxi. 14). I was now void of all good consideration, heaven and hell were both out of sight and mind; and as for saving and damning, they were least in my thoughts. O Lord, thou knowest my life, and my ways were not hid from thee.

11. Yet this I well remember, that though I could myself sin with the greatest delight and ease, and also take pleasure in the vileness of my companions; yet, even then, if I have at any time seen wicked things, by those who professed goodness, it would make my spirit tremble. As once, above all the rest, when I was in my height of vanity, yet hearing one to swear that was reckoned for a religious man, it had so great a stroke upon my spirit, that it made my heart to ache.

12. But God did not utterly leave me, but followed me still, not now with convictions, but judgments; yet such as were mixed with mercy. For once I fell into a creek of the sea, and hardly escaped drowning. Another time I fell out of a boat into Bedford river, but mercy yet preserved me alive. Besides, another

time, being in the field with one of my companions, it chanced that an adder passed over the highway; so I, having a stick in my hand, struck her over the back; and having stunned her, I forced open her mouth with my stick, and plucked her sting out with my fingers; by which act, had not God been merciful unto me, I might, by my desperateness, have brought myself to mine end.

THE BOOK OF EZEKIEL

The prophet Ezekiel is thought to be the author of this biblical book. Jerusalem had been destroyed in 587 B.C.E., and the Israelites were taken captive and brought to Babylon where they lived for many years as exiles. The book of Ezekiel tells some of the history of that exile and of the hope that the prophet tried to inspire in the exiled people. The visions written down here are obscure at times, but they also contain messages of hope for the restoration of their nation.

Making sense of the imagery evoked in Ezekiel 1 (excerpted below) is notoriously difficult. Hebrew communities in the past even went so far as to ban the reading of the chapter until children came of age. Nonetheless, we may read it, as it says at the end of the chapter, as a description of the "Glory of the Lord," a glory that must necessarily surpass human comprehension and perception, as in the book of Job. Several symbols are given throughout the chapter, yet they do not fully correspond to anything we humans might understand. What is significant, therefore, is precisely the obscurity of the imagery and the fact that we are unable to grasp the full meaning and gain a clear vision of what the glory of the Lord is like.

Ezekiel 1

1 In the thirtieth year, in the fourth month, on the fifth day of the month, as I was among the exiles by the river Chebar, the heavens were opened, and I saw visions of God. 2On the fifth day of the month (it was the fifth year of the exile of King Jehoiachin), 3the word of the LORD came to the priest Ezekiel son of Buzi, in the land of the Chaldeans by the river Chebar; and the hand of the LORD was on him there.

4 As I looked, a stormy wind came out of the north: a great cloud with brightness around it and fire flashing forth continually, and in the middle of the fire, something like gleaming amber. 5In the middle of it was something like four living creatures. This was their appearance: they were of human form. 6Each had four faces, and each of them had four wings. 7Their legs were straight, and the soles of their feet were like the sole of a calf's foot; and they sparkled like burnished bronze. 8Under their wings on their four sides they had human hands. And the four had their faces and their wings thus: 9their wings touched one another; each of them went straight ahead, without turning as they moved. 10As for the appearance of their faces: the four had the face of a human being, the face of a lion on the right side, the face of an ox on the left side, and the face of an eagle; 11such were their faces. Their wings were

spread out above; each creature had two wings, each of which touched the wing of another, while two covered their bodies. [12]Each moved straight ahead; wherever the spirit would go, they went, without turning as they went. [13]In the middle of the living creatures there was something that looked like burning coals of fire, like torches moving to and fro among the living creatures; the fire was bright, and lightning issued from the fire. [14]The living creatures darted to and fro, like a flash of lightning.

15 As I looked at the living creatures, I saw a wheel on the earth beside the living creatures, one for each of the four of them. [16]As for the appearance of the wheels and their construction: their appearance was like the gleaming of beryl; and the four had the same form, their construction being something like a wheel within a wheel. [17]When they moved, they moved in any of the four directions without veering as they moved. [18]Their rims were tall and awesome, for the rims of all four were full of eyes all around. [19]When the living creatures moved, the wheels moved beside them; and when the living creatures rose from the earth, the wheels rose. [20]Wherever the spirit would go, they went, and the wheels rose along with them; for the spirit of the living creatures was in the wheels. [21]When they moved, the others moved; when they stopped, the others stopped; and when they rose from the earth, the wheels rose along with them; for the spirit of the living creatures was in the wheels.

22 Over the heads of the living creatures there was something like a dome, shining like crystal, spread out above their heads. [23]Under the dome their wings were stretched out straight, one toward another; and each of the creatures had two wings covering its body. [24]When they moved, I heard the sound of their wings like the sound of mighty waters, like the thunder of the Almighty, a sound of tumult like the sound of an army; when they stopped, they let down their wings. [25]And there came a voice from above the dome over their heads; when they stopped, they let down their wings.

26 And above the dome over their heads there was something like a throne, in appearance like sapphire; and seated above the likeness of a throne was something that seemed like a human form. [27]Upward from what appeared like the loins I saw something like gleaming amber, something that looked like fire enclosed all around; and downward from what looked like the loins I saw something that looked like fire, and there was a splendor all around. [28]Like the bow in a cloud on a rainy day, such was the appearance of the splendor all around. This was the appearance of the likeness of the glory of the LORD.

When I saw it, I fell on my face, and I heard the voice of someone speaking.

WILLIAM BLAKE,
"AND DID THOSE FEET IN ANCIENT TIME"

William Blake (1757–1827) was one of the greatest of English poets and artists. Like John Bunyan, he had little formal schooling, though he was for a while apprenticed as an engraver and became a student at the Royal Academy. He was deeply influenced by the mystical tradition and the apocalyptic writings of the Bible, especially Ezekiel and the book of Revelation. In the Preface to his poem *Milton* (1804), from which this excerpt is taken, he wrote: "The Stolen and Perverted Writings of Homer & Ovid, of Plato & Cicero, which all Men ought to condemn, are set up by artifice against the Sublime of the Bible."

This short poem is now familiar as a hymn and popular as a statement, perhaps, of Christ's presence in the England of the Industrial Revolution of the late eighteenth century with its "dark Satanic mills." With its mysterious contempt for history, it contains many of the great apocalyptic images that we have already encountered in Ezekiel with its chariot of fire, its bow, arrows, spear and sword, and its vision of the countenance divine — that is, Ezekiel's "appearance of the likeness of the glory of the LORD."

From the Preface to Milton *(1804)*
"And did those feet in ancient time"

And did those feet in ancient time
Walk upon England's mountains green?
And was the holy Lamb of God
On England's pleasant pastures seen?

And did the Countenance Divine
Shine forth upon our clouded hills?
And was Jerusalem builded here
Among these dark Satanic Mills?

Bring me my Bow of burning gold:
Bring me my Arrows of desire:
Bring me my Spear: O clouds unfold!
Bring me my Chariot of fire.

I will not cease from Mental Fight,
Nor shall my Sword sleep in my hand
Till we have built Jerusalem
In England's green and pleasant Land.

PATRICK WHITE,
RIDERS IN THE CHARIOT

Patrick White (1912–1990) became the first Australian to win the Nobel Prize for Literature, in 1973. He wrote poetry, drama, novels, and screenplays. Though in a very different style than Mark Twain had with the United States, White satirized Australian society. Several of his novels are based in the fictional Sydney suburb of "Sarsaparilla," a place of artificial goodness stricken with a strong undercurrent of evil.

Riders in the Chariot (1961) is set in Sarsaparilla and satirically tells of the everydayness of evil. White has been criticized for doing so, but what he shows through the novel is a connection between the atrocities that took place in Nazi Germany and that of everyday life in a banal suburb in peace-time Australia even while "the War was over, and the peace had not yet set hard" (p. 7). The novel climaxes in what was supposed to be a mock lynch-ing of the German-Jewish refugee Mordechai Himmelfarb, but instead turns into a very real crucifixion scene. The hatred and fear of outsiders in the homogeneous and "Christian" Sarsaparilla leads to the scapegoat struc-ture of sacrifice, and thus the novel mimics Christ's crucifixion (in a very different way than the Borges story) in the Gospels. As one of the charac-ters says to another, "All bad things have a family resemblance" (p. 326).

But *Riders in the Chariot* also mimics another biblical story. Reinterpreting the chariot vision from the book of Ezekiel (see p. 89), and also the chariot of Elijah and the visions of William Blake, the four main characters in the novel are linked through their own visions of chariots. It is significant that there are four characters and that there are ambiguous and divergent visions. The excerpt below tells something of Himmelfarb's vision and struggle. And while these visions suffer from a conflict of perception among the characters, the visions also serve to unify and point beyond the banal suburban life, per-haps like the prophet Ezekiel's function in exilic times in Babylon.

From Riders in the Chariot

"What is that, Mordecai? I did not know you could draw."

"I was scribbling," he said. "This, it appears, is the Chariot."

"Ah," she exclaimed, softly, withdrawing her glance; she could have lost interest. "Which chariot?" she did certainly ask, but now it might have been to humour him.

"That, I am not sure," he replied. "It is difficult to distinguish. Just when I think I have understood, I discover some fresh form—so many—streaming with implications. There is the Throne of God, for instance. That is obvious enough—all gold, and chrysoprase, and jasper. Then there is the Chariot of Redemption, much more shadowy, poignant, personal. And the faces of the riders. I cannot begin to see the expression of the faces."

All the time Reha was searching the shelves.

"This is in the old books?" she asked.

"Some of it," he admitted, "is in some."

Reha continued to explore the shelves.

She yawned. And laughed softly.

"I think I shall probably fall asleep," she said, "before I find Morike."

But took a volume.

He felt her kiss the back of his head as she left.

Or did she remain, to protect him more closely, with some secret part of her being, after the door had closed? He was never certain with Reha: to what extent perception was revealed in her words and her behaviour, or how far she had accompanied him along the inward path.

For, by now, Himmelfarb had taken the path of inwardness. He could not resist silence, and became morose on evenings when he was prevented from retreating early to his room. Reha would continue to sew, or mend. Her expression did not protest. She would smile a gentle approval—but of what, it was never made clear.

Some of the old books were full of directions which he did not dare follow, and to which he adopted a deliberately sceptical attitude, or, if it was ever necessary, one of crudest cynicism. But he did, at last, unknown, it was to be hoped, to his rational self, begin fitfully to combine and permute the Letters, even to contemplate the Names.

It was, however, the driest, the most cerebral approach—when spiritually he longed for the ascent into an ecstasy so cool and green that his own desert would drink the heavenly moisture. Still, his forehead of skin and bone continued to burn with what could have been a circlet of iron. Or sometimes he would become possessed by a rigid coldness of mind, his soul absorbed into the entity of his own upright, leather chair, his knuckles carved out of oak.

Mostly he remained at a level where, it seemed, he was inacceptable as a vessel of experience, and would fall asleep, and wake at cockcrow. But once he was roused from sleep, during the leaden hours, to identify a face. And got to his feet, to receive the messenger of light, or resist the dark dissembler. When he was transfixed by his own horror. Of his own image, but fluctuating, as though in fire or water. So that the long-awaited moment was reduced to a reflection of the self. In a distorting mirror. Who, then, could hope to be saved? Fortunately, he was prevented from shouting the blasphemies that occurred to him, because his voice had been temporarily removed. Nor could he inflict on the material forms which surrounded him, themselves the cloaks of spiritual deceit, the damage which he felt compelled to do, for his will had become entangled, and his nails were tearing on the shaggy knots. He could only struggle and sway inside the column of his body. Until he toppled forward, and was saved further anguish by hitting his head on the edge of the desk.

Reha Himmelfarb discovered her husband early that morning. He was still weak and confused, barely conscious, as if he had had a congestive attack of some kind. After recovering from her fright, during which she had tried to warm his hands with her own, and was repeatedly kissing, and crying, and breathing into his cold lips, she ran and telephoned to Dr. Vogel, who decided, after an examination, that the *Herr Dozent* was suffering from exhaustion as the result of overwork. The doctor ordered his patient to bed, and for a couple of weeks Himmelfarb saw nobody but his devoted wife. It was very delightful. She read him the whole of *Effi Briest,* and he lay with his eyes closed, barely following, yet absorbing the episodes of that touching, though slightly insipid story. Or perhaps it was his wife's voice which he appreciated most, and which, as it joined the words together with a warm and gentle precision, seemed the voice of actuality.

SUSANNA/THE BOOK OF DANIEL

The Story of Susanna appears in the Greek version of the Hebrew Bible (the Septuagint) as chapter 13 of the book of Daniel, but it is clearly a late addition to the work, and even its original language is uncertain—Greek,

Hebrew, or Aramaic. The patristic scholar Jerome (circa 342–420 C.E.) placed it among the Apocryphal writings, that is, writings outside the canon of the Bible but worthy to be read (as the Articles of the Church of England put it) "for example of life and instruction of manners."

Possibly written during the period of Babylonian exile, Susanna is an exquisite novella, perhaps the first precursor of the detective story, telling in a mere sixty-four verses a story of lust, false accusation, innocence, and deliverance through the wisdom of Daniel himself. In the Greek versions of the text, Daniel responds to the lies of each of the men with a play on words that includes both the place they claim to have seen Susanna and God's punishment (in the Oxford Study Edition/Apocrypha, an attempt is made to reproduce this effect using *"clove* tree / *cleave* in two" and *"yew* tree / *hew* you down").

Because of its subject, the book has attracted the attention of secular artists and poets, but, at the same time, from the early days of the Christian church it became symbolic of the saved soul, and representations of the story can be found among the earliest examples of Christian art in the catacombs in Rome.

Susanna

1 There was a man living in Babylon whose name was Joakim. [2]And he took a wife named Susanna, the daughter of Hilkiah, a very beautiful woman and one who feared the Lord. [3]Her parents were righteous, and had taught their daughter according to the law of Moses. [4]Joakim was very rich, and had a spacious garden adjoining his house; and the Jews used to come to him because he was the most honored of them all.

5 In that year two elders from the people were appointed as judges. Concerning them the Lord had said "Iniquity came forth from Babylon, from elders who were judges, who were supposed to govern the people." [6]These men were frequently at Joakim's house, and all who had suits at law came to them.

7 When the people departed at noon, Susanna would go into her husband's garden to walk. [8]The two elders used to see her every day, going in and walking about, and they began to desire her. [9]And they perverted their minds and turned away their eyes from looking to Heaven or remembering righteous judgments. [10]Both were overwhelmed with passion for her, but they did not tell each other of their distress, [11]for they were ashamed to disclose their lustful desire to possess her. [12]And they watched eagerly, day after day, to see her.

13 They said to each other, "Let us go home, for it is mealtime." [14]And when they went out, they parted from each other. But turning back, they met again; and when each pressed the other for the reason, they confessed their lust. And then together they arranged for a time when they could find her alone.

15 Once, while they were watching for an opportune day, she went in as before with only two maids, and wished to bathe in the garden, for it was very hot. [16]And no one was there except the two elders, who had hid themselves and were watching her. [17]She said to her maids, "Bring me oil and ointments, and shut the garden doors so that I may bathe." [18]They did as she

said, shut the garden doors, and went out by the side doors to bring what they had been commanded; and they did not see the elders, because they were hidden.

19 When the maids had gone out, the two elders rose and ran to her, and said 20"Look, the garden doors are shut, no one sees us, and we are in love with you; so give your consent, and lie with us. 21If you refuse, we will testify against you that a young man was with you, and this was why you sent your maids away."

22 Susanna sighed deeply, and said, "I am hemmed in on every side. For if I do this thing, it is death for me; and if I do not, I shall not escape your hands. 23I choose not to do it and to fall into your hands, rather than to sin in the sight of the Lord."

24 Then Susanna cried out with a loud voice, and the two elders shouted against her. 25 And one of them ran and opened the garden doors. 26When the household servants heard the shouting in the garden, they rushed in at the side door to see what had happened to her. 27And when the elders told their tale, the servants were greatly ashamed, for nothing like this had ever been said about Susanna.

28 The next day, when the people gathered at the house of her husband Joakim, the two elders came, full of their wicked plot to have Susanna put to death. 29They said before the people, "Send for Susanna, the daughter of Hilkiah, who is the wife of Joakim." 30So they sent for her. And she came, with her parents, her children, and all her kindred.

31 Now Susanna was a woman of great refinement, and beautiful in appearance. 32As she was veiled, the wicked men ordered her to be unveiled, that they might feast upon her beauty. 33But her family and friends and all who saw her wept.

34 Then the two elders stood up in the midst of the people, and laid their hands upon her head. 35And she, weeping, looked up toward heaven, for her heart trusted in the Lord. 36The elders said, "As we were walking in the garden alone, this woman came in with two maids, shut the garden doors, and dismissed the maids. 37Then a young man, who had been hidden, came to her and lay with her. 38We were in a corner of the garden, and when we saw this wickedness we ran to them. 39We saw them embracing, but we could not hold the man, for he was too strong for us, and he opened the doors and dashed out. 40So we seized this woman and asked her who the young man was, but she would not tell us. These things we testify."

41 The assembly believed them, because they were elders of the people and judges; and they condemned her to death.

42 Then Susanna cried out with a loud voice, and said, "O eternal God, who dost discern what is secret, who art aware of all things before they come to be, 43thou knowest that these men have borne false witness against me. And now I am to die! Yet I have done none of the things that they have wickedly invented against me!"

44 The Lord heard her cry. 45And as she was being led away to be put to death, God aroused the holy spirit of a young lad named Daniel; 46and he cried with a loud voice, "I am innocent of the blood of this woman."

47 All the people turned to him, and said, "What is this that you have said?" [48]Taking his stand in the midst of them, he said, "Are you such fools, you sons of Israel? Have you condemned a daughter of Israel without examination and without learning the facts? [49]Return to the place of judgment. For these men have borne false witness against her." [50]Then all the people returned in haste. And the elders said to him, "Come, sit among us and inform us, for God has given you that right." [51]And Daniel said to them, "Separate them far from each other, and I will examine them."

52 When they were separated from each other, he summoned one of them and said to him, "You old relic of wicked days, your sins have now come home, which you have committed in the past, [53]pronouncing unjust judgments, condemning the innocent and letting the guilty go free, though the Lord said, 'Do not put to death an innocent and righteous person.' [54]Now then, if you really saw her, tell me this: Under what tree did you see them being intimate with each other?" He answered, "Under a mastic tree."

55 And Daniel said, "Very well! You have lied against your own head, for the angel of God has received the sentence from God and will immediately cut you in two."

56 Then he put him aside, and commanded them to bring the other. And he said to him, "You offspring of Canaan and not of Judah, beauty has deceived you and lust has perverted your heart. [57]This is how you both have been dealing with the daughters of Israel, and they were intimate with you through fear; but a daughter of Judah would not endure your wickedness. [58]Now then, tell me: Under what tree did you catch them being intimate with each other?" He answered, "Under an evergreen oak." [59]And Daniel said to him, "Very well! You also have lied against your own head, for the angel of God is waiting with his sword to saw you in two, that he may destroy you both."

60 Then all the assembly shouted loudly and blessed God, who saves those who hope in him. [61]And they rose against the two elders, for out of their own mouths Daniel had convicted them of bearing false witness; [62]and they did to them as they had wickedly planned to do to their neighbor; acting in accordance with the law of Moses, they put them to death. Thus innocent blood was saved that day.

63 And Hilkiah and his wife praised God for their daughter Susanna, and so did Joakim her husband and all her kindred, because nothing shameful was found in her. [64]And from that day onward Daniel had a great reputation among the people.

WILLIAM SHAKESPEARE,
ALL'S WELL THAT ENDS WELL

The excerpt below from William Shakespeare's play *All's Well That Ends Well* is within a long literary tradition of writing on the story of Susanna. There are two main themes drawn from it—the first of Susanna as the beautiful young innocent falsely accused. The second, which Shakespeare (1564–1616) uses here in the speech of the young Helena to the ailing King of

France, focuses on Daniel as the clever young judge. One should also note that the speech of Helena clearly suggests that Shakespeare is using the popular Geneva Bible (the first mass-produced Bible to appear in English), which refers to Daniel as a "young child" in its translation of the Susanna story.

From All's Well That Ends Well
Act 2, Scene 1

> *King.* I cannot give thee less, to be called grateful . . .
> Thou thought'st to help me, and such thanks I give
> As one near death to those that wish him live:
> But what at full I know, thou know'st no part,
> I knowing all my peril, thou no art.
> *Helena.* What I can do can do no hurt to try,
> Since you set up your rest 'gainst remedy:
> He that of greatest works is finisher,
> Oft does them by the weakest minister:
> So holy writ in babes hath judgement shown,
> When judges have been babes; great floods have flown
> From simple sources; and great seas have dried
> When miracles have by the greatest been denied.
> Oft expectation fails, and most oft there
> Where most it promises; and oft it hits,
> Where hope is coldest, and despair most fits.

THE PARABLE OF SIMEON AND BAR KAPPARA

The parable of Simeon and Bar Kappara tells us a great deal about the society and table manners of the rabbis in Palestine of the third century C.E. Common in rabbinic literature, such parabolic narratives are called *meshalim* (singular—*mashal*) and may be found throughout the Hebrew Bible, influencing the great and familiar parables of the Gospels in the New Testament.

This is a story about storytelling and its power to affect the way in which we behave. It works indirectly and by allusion, leaving the reader to work out a solution to its meaning. In other words, the *mashal* explains little and demands much. It is an ancient form of literature extending back to the beginnings of Near Eastern literature, and in the work of modern writers like Kierkegaard, Kafka, and Borges it continues to flourish in the literature of our own time.

The Parable of Simeon and Bar Kappara

Simeon, the son of Rabbi [Judah], prepared a [wedding] banquet for his son. He went and invited all the sages, but he forgot to invite Bar Kappara, who thereupon went and wrote on the door of R. Simeon's house: After rejoicing is death. So what value is there to rejoicing?

Who did this to me? R. Simeon asked. Is there anyone we did not invite?

One of his men told him: Bar Kappara. You forgot to invite Bar Kappara.

R. Simeon said: To invite him now would be unseemly. So he went and made a second banquet, and he invited all the sages, and he invited Bar Kappara as well. But at every course that was brought before the guests Bar Kappara recited three hundred fox-fables, and the guests didn't even taste the dishes before they grew cold. The dishes were removed from the tables just as they had been brought in.

R. Simeon asked his servant: Why are the dishes all coming back untouched?

The servant replied: There is an old man sitting there. At every course he tells fables until the dishes grow cold, and no one eats.

R. Simeon went up to Bar Kappara: What did I do to make you ruin my banquet?

Bar Kappara answered: What do I need your banquet for? Didn't Solomon say, "What real value is there for a man in all the gains he makes beneath the sun?" (Eccles. 1:3). And what is written after that verse? "One generation goes, another comes, but the earth remains the same forever" (1:4).

FRANZ KAFKA,
THE TRIAL

Kafka's parable "Before the Law," sometimes known as the parable of the doorkeeper, forms part of the chapter "In the Cathedral" in Kafka's novel *The Trial* (1925). Born a German-speaking Jew in Prague in 1883, Kafka wrote within the traditions of Jewish midrash, his novels and stories exchanging what has been called "appallingly violent tradings with the Jewish Scriptures" (Valentine Cunningham, *In the Reading Gaol* [1994], p. 386). These writings are enigmatic and often surreal, and in them are found lonely individuals, perplexed and frequently overwhelmed by a mysterious sense of guilt, as we see in the famous opening sentence of *The Trial*. "Someone must have been telling lies about Joseph K., for without having done anything wrong he was arrested one fine morning."

The parable here is to be found toward the end of the novel, and is spoken by a priest in conversation with Joseph K. It might be suggested that the story deliberately evades interpretation, as in the great tradition of rabbinic parables. After the priest has finished, K. concludes that the doorkeeper has deluded the man, but the priest denies that there is any delusion in the narrative. The listener, he says, must have absolute respect for the words of the story.

From The Trial,
"Before the Law"

. . . before the Law stands a door-keeper on guard. To this door-keeper there comes a man from the country who begs for admittance to the Law. But the door-keeper says that he cannot admit the man at the moment. The man, on reflection, asks if he will be allowed, then, to enter later. "It is possible," answers the door-keeper, "but not at this moment." Since the door leading into the Law stands open as usual and the door-keeper steps to one side, the man bends down to peer through the entrance. When the door-keeper sees that, he laughs and says: "If you are so strongly tempted, try to get in without my permission. But note that I am powerful. And I am only the lowest door-keeper. From hall to hall, keepers stand at every door, one more powerful than the other. Even the third of these has an aspect that even I cannot bear to look at." These are difficulties which the man from the country has not expected to meet, the Law, he thinks, should be accessible to every man and at all times, and when he looks more closely at the door-keeper in his furred robe, with his huge pointed nose and long thin, Tartar beard, he decides that he had better wait until he gets permission to enter. The door-keeper gives him a stool and lets him sit down at the side of the door. There he sits waiting for days and years. He makes many attempts to be allowed in and wearies the door-keeper with his importunity. The door-keeper often engages him in brief conversation, asking him about his home and about other matters, but the questions are put quite impersonally, as great men put questions, and always conclude with the statement that the man cannot be allowed to enter yet. The man, who has equipped himself with many things for his journey, parts with all he has, however valuable, in the hope of bribing the door-keeper. The door-keeper accepts it all, saying, however, as he takes each gift: "I take this only to keep you from feeling that you have left something undone." During all these long years the man watches the door-keeper almost incessantly. He forgets about the other door-keepers, and this one seems to him the only barrier between himself and the Law. In the first years he curses his evil fate aloud; later, as he grows old, he only mutters to himself. He grows childish, and since in his prolonged watch he has learned to know even the fleas in the door-keeper's fur collar, he begs the very fleas to help him and to persuade the door-keeper to change his mind. Finally his eyes grow dim and he does not know whether the world is really darkening around him or whether his eyes are only deceiving him. But in the darkness he can now perceive a radiance that streams immortally from the door of the Law. Now his life is drawing to a close. Before he dies, all that he has experienced during the whole time of his sojourn condenses in his mind into one question, which he has never yet put to the door-keeper. He beckons the door-keeper, since he can no longer raise his stiffening body. The door-keeper has to bend far down to hear him, for the difference in size between them has increased very much to the man's disadvantage. "What do you want to know now?" asks the door-keeper, "you are insatiable." "Everyone strives to attain the Law," answers the man, "how does it come about, then, that in all these years no one has come seeking admittance but me?" The door-keeper perceives that the man is at the end of his strength and his hearing is failing, so he bellows in his ear: "No one but you could gain admittance through this door, since this door was intended only for you. I am now going to shut it."

THE GOSPEL OF MARK

The story of Christ's crucifixion is the climax of the passion narratives of the Gospels, and it lies at the heart of the Christian faith. The version in Mark's Gospel is the shortest and the most disturbing of all, for there is little in the narrative to soften the sense of cruelty and extreme agony of this most excruciating form of execution.

Not only is the cross the most important Christian symbol, representing the death Jesus Christ necessarily experienced before his resurrection, but it is repeatedly reconstructed in art and literature from innumerable perspectives. Only one example from modern fiction by Jorge Luis Borges is given here—but we could have equally used texts from the medieval English miracle plays to other modern rehearsals of the crucifixion in novels such as Herman Melville's *Billy Budd, Sailor* (1891) to Nikos Kazantzakis's notorious *The Last Temptation of Christ* (1960).

Mark 15:21–32

21 They compelled a passer-by, who was coming in from the country, to carry his cross; it was Simon of Cyrene, the father of Alexander and Rufus. [22]Then they brought Jesus to the place called Golgotha (which means the place of a skull). [23]And they offered him wine mixed with myrrh; but he did not take it. [24]And they crucified him, and divided his clothes among them, casting lots to decide what each should take.

25 It was nine o'clock in the morning when they crucified him. [26]The inscription of the charge against him read, "The King of the Jews." [27]And with him they crucified two bandits, one on his right and one on his left. [29]Those who passed by derided him, shaking their heads and saying, "Aha! You who would destroy the temple and build it in three days, [30]save yourself, and come down from the cross!" [31]In the same way the chief priests, along with the scribes, were also mocking him among themselves and saying, "He saved others; he cannot save himself. [32]Let the Messiah, the King of Israel, come down from the cross now, so that we may see and believe." Those who were crucified with him also taunted him.

JORGE LUIS BORGES, "THE GOSPEL ACCORDING TO MARK"

Jorge Luis Borges (1899–1986) was born in Argentina and has had a tremendous literary influence throughout South and North America and Europe. He writes poetry and essays but is perhaps best known in the English-speaking world for his short stories. Borges typically combines difficult philosophical ideas about space, time, and existence and weaves them into fabulous otherworldly tales.

From Doctor Brodie's Report,
"The Gospel According to Mark"

These events took place at La Colorada ranch, in the southern part of the township of Junin, during the last days of March, 1928. The protagonist was a medical student named Baltasar Espinosa. We may describe him, for now, as one of the common run of young men from Buenos Aires, with nothing more noteworthy about him than an almost unlimited kindness and a capacity for public speaking that had earned him several prizes at the English school in Ramos Mejia. He did not like arguing, and preferred having his listener rather than himself in the right. Although he was fascinated by the probabilities of chance in any game he played, he was a bad player because it gave him no pleasure to win. His wide intelligence was undirected; at the age of thirty-three he still lacked credit for graduation, by one course—the course to which he was most drawn. His father, who was a freethinker (like all the gentlemen of his day), had introduced him to the lessons of Herbert Spencer, but his mother, before leaving on a trip for Montevideo, once asked him to say the Lord's Prayer and make the sign of the cross every night. Through the years, he had never gone back on that promise. . . .

One morning at daybreak, thunder woke him. Outside, the wind was rocking the Australian pines. Listening to the first heavy drops of rain, Espinosa thanked God. All at once, cold air rolled in. That afternoon, the Salado overflowed its banks. . . .

Exploring the house, still hemmed in by the watery waste, Espinosa came across an English Bible. Among the blank pages at the end, the Guthries—such was their original name—had left a handwritten record of their lineage. They were natives of Inverness; had reached the New World, no doubt as common laborers, in the early part of the nineteenth century; and had intermarried with indians. The chronicle broke off sometime during the eighteen-seventies, when they no longer knew how to write. After a few generations, they had forgotten English; their Spanish, at the time Espinosa knew them, gave them trouble. They lacked any religious faith, but there survived in their blood, like faint tracks, the rigid fanaticism of the Calvinist and the superstitions of the pampa Indian. Espinosa later told them of his find, but they barely took notice.

Leafing through the volume, his fingers opened it at the beginning of the Gospel according to St. Mark. As an exercise in translation, and maybe to find out whether the Gutres understood any of it, Espinosa decided to begin reading them that text after their evening meal. It surprised him that they listened attentively, absorbed. Maybe the gold letters on the cover lent the book authority. It's still there in their blood, Espinosa thought. It also occurred to him that the generations of men, throughout recorded time, have always told and retold two stories—that of a lost ship which searches the Mediterranean seas for a dearly loved island, and that of a god who is crucified on Golgotha. Remembering his lessons in elocution from his schooldays in Ramos Mejia, Espinosa got to his feet when he came to the parables. . . .

101

Having finished the Gospel according to St. Mark, he wanted to read another of the three Gospels that remained, but the father asked him to repeat the one he had just read, so that they could understand it better. Espinosa felt that they were like children, to whom repetition is more pleasing than variations or novelty. That night—this is not to be wondered at— he dreamed of the Flood; the hammer blows of the building of the Ark woke him up, and he thought that perhaps they were thunder. In fact, the rain, which had let up, started again. The cold was bitter. The Gutres had told him that the storm had damaged the roof of the tool shed, and that they would show it to him when the beams were fixed. No longer a stranger now, he was treated by them with special attention, almost to the point of spoiling him. None of them liked coffee, but for him there was always a small cup into which they heaped sugar.

The new storm had broken out on a Tuesday. Thursday night, Espinosa was awakened by a soft knock at his door, which—just in case—he always kept locked. He got out of bed and opened it; there was the girl. In the dark he could hardly make her out, but by her footsteps he could tell she was barefoot, and moments later, in bed, that she must have come all the way from the other end of the house naked. She did not embrace him or speak a single word; she lay beside him, trembling. It was the first time she had known a man. When she left, she did not kiss him; Espinosa realized that he didn't even know her name. For some reason that he did not want to pry into, he made up his mind that upon returning to Buenos Aires he would tell no one about what had taken place.

The next day began like the previous ones, except that the father spoke to Espinosa and asked him if Christ had let Himself be killed so as to save all other men on earth. Espinosa, who was a freethinker but who felt committed to what he had read to the Gutres, answered, "Yes, to save everyone from Hell."

Gutre then asked, "What's Hell?"

"A place under the ground where souls burn and burn."

"And the Roman soldiers who hammered in the nails—were they saved, too?"

"Yes," said Espinosa, whose theology was rather dim.

All along, he was afraid that the foreman might ask him about what had gone on the night before with his daughter. After lunch, they asked him to read the last chapters over again.

Espinosa slept a long nap that afternoon. It was a light sleep, disturbed by persistent hammering and by vague premonitions. Toward evening, he got up and went out onto the gallery. He said, as if thinking aloud, "The waters have dropped. It won't be long now."

"It won't be long now," Gutre repeated, like an echo.

The three had been following him. Bowing their knees to the stone pavement, they asked his blessing. Then they mocked at him, spat on him, and shoved him toward the back part of the house. The girl wept. Espinosa understood what awaited him on the other side of the door. When they opened it, he saw a patch of sky. A bird sang out. A goldfinch, he thought. The shed was without a roof; they had pulled down the beams to make the cross.

PAUL RICOEUR,
"THE 'SACRED' TEXT AND THE COMMUNITY"

In this passage, Paul Ricoeur (see also above, chapter 3) meditates on the nature of sacrality and the sacred text. In this chapter we have concentrated on various structures of religious, or sacred, texts—dealing with theodicy, the confessional, the poetic and apocalyptic, and different forms of narrative. In his conclusion, Ricoeur reminds us of the central importance of the subject of chapter 4, above—that is, the liturgical and the text in the context of worship.

But his crucial point is his discrimination between the sacred text and the critical act. The Christian tradition and, in different ways, Judaism have always engaged in acts of critical reading and interpretation of their scriptures. The Bible has always been, in every sense of the word, a translated book, as the Qur'an is not for the Muslim. If such activity is indeed a kind of desacralization, then the literary task is all the more important. For we have placed beside texts of scripture literary *intertexts* that do not purport to interpret or criticize, but engage in conversations with the Bible, claiming their own independence without attacking scripture with the instruments of critical inquiry.

This is why the business of religion and literature is so important, for it treats the sacred text with the utmost respect, even while it makes enormous claims for those later texts which converse and even "play" with the sacred in acts of literary community.

From "The 'Sacred' Text and the Community"

I am intrigued by the question of the response of the community whose text has been "critically edited." Of course when this is done, it no longer is a sacred text, because it is no longer the text that the community has always regarded as sacred; it is a scholars' text. So, in a sense, there can be no such thing as the critical editing of sacred texts. It is true that, in the early history of the church, there were many communities, each with its own sacred text, and the church attempted to bring them together, to produce one sacred text. So there is the history of the canon, and therefore there is not "the" sacred text. But nevertheless, the critical act that we are committing is quite different from this gathering of texts from the Coptic and so on, when the community constituted its canon. The kind of biblical criticism that began in the eighteenth and nineteenth centuries was of quite a different nature, because now we may get texts that are not texts of *any* community, except perhaps of the community of the academic world.

Maybe in the case of Christianity there is no sacred text, because it is not the text that is sacred but the one about which it is spoken. For instance, there is no privilege of the language in which it was said for the first time; it is completely indifferent whether we read it in Greek or Hebrew or Aramaic, and so on. There is already something that allows the critical act; the critical act is not forbidden by the nature of the text, because it is not a sacred text in the sense in which the Qur'an is sacred (for a Muslim would say that to read the Qur'an in English is not to read the Qur'an; one must read it in Arabic). But in Christianity, translation is quite possible, for the Septuagint is a kind of desacralization of the original language, once one has admitted that the Bible could be set in Greek. And a certain critical activity was implied in this act of translation. Jerome was, for his time, a critical mind. . . .

In Christianity there is a polarity of proclamation and manifestation, which Mircea Eliade does not recognize in his homogeneous concept of manifestation, epiphany, and so forth. I wonder whether there is not also, in the Hebraic and Christian traditions, a polarity of another kind, the charismatic, which is linked to language. For us, manifestation is not by necessity linked to language. The word "sacred" belongs to the side of manifestation, not to the side of proclamation, because many things may be sacred without being a text: a tree may be sacred, water may be sacred, and we read in Eliade that it is the cosmos that is sacred. And therefore if there is only the word to mediate this sacredness, it is precisely because it mediates something that is not of the nature of the word but of the nature of appearance. The manifestation is not verbal by origin. But I think that there is something specific in the Hebraic and Christian traditions that gives a kind of privilege to the word. You have the tradition that the word was created by the word; in the switch from the first narrative of creation to the second, God not only does but says. The notion of sacred text may have been alien to the Hebraic and pre-Christian tradition. We apply a category that belongs to this sacrality that is cosmic and then that is condensed, as it were, in a book and that thus changes its function as it becomes fundamental without being sacred. What Eliade shows is that the polarity sacred/profane is absolutely primitive in relation to this: this water is sacred but not that water; this tree and not that tree.

I wonder whether it does not belong to the nature of proclamation to be always brought back from the written to the oral; and it is the function of preaching to reverse the relation from written to spoken. In that sense preaching is more fundamental to Hebrew and Christian tradition because of the nature of the text that has to be reconverted to word, in contrast with scripture; and therefore it is a kind of desacralization of the written as such, by the return to the spoken word. This is the impact of the fixation of liturgy, for in Christianity the liturgical kernel represents the Eucharist, as a kind of text that tells the story of the Last Supper; and it becomes a sacred text because it founds a sacred act, which is the Eucharist. What was the influence of the Eucharist in the sacralization of the text? For the word "sacrifice" used in this connection has to do with the sacred act.

I was very reluctant to use the word "sacred' in my essay on revelation. I had to fight very hard to say finally what I believe, what I think, when I use the word "revelation." But to an extent I am prepared to say that I recognize something *revealing* that is not frozen in any ultimate or immutable text. Because the process of revelation is a permanent process of opening something that is closed, of making manifest something that was hidden. Revelation is a historical process, but the notion of sacred text is something antihistorical. I am frightened by this word "sacred."

FURTHER READING

Anderson, David. *The Passion of Man in Gospel and Literature*. London: Bible Reading Fellowship, 1980.

Bloom, Harold. *Ruin the Sacred Truths: Poetry and Belief from the Bible to the Present*. Cambridge, Mass.: Harvard University Press, 1989.

Borges, Jorge Luis. *Labyrinths: Selected Stories and Other Writings*. Edited by Donald A.Yates and James E. Irby. Preface by André Maurois. New York: New Directions, 1964.

Collmer, Robert G., ed. *Bunyan in Our Time*. Kent, Ohio: Kent State University Press, 1989.

Crossan, John Dominic. *In Parables: The Challenge of the Historical Jesus* (1973). Sonoma, Calif.: Polebridge Press, 1992.

Deleuze, Gilles, and Félix Guattari. *Kafka: Toward a Minor Literature*. Translated by Dana Polan. Foreword by Reda Bensmaia. Minneapolis: University of Minnesota Press, 1986.

Farrer, Austin. *Love Almighty and Ills Unlimited*. London: Collins, 1966.

Frye, Northrop. *Fearful Symmetry: A Study of William Blake* (1947). Princeton, N.J.: Princeton University Press, 1969.

Giffin, Michael. *Arthur's Dream: The Religious Imagination in the Fiction of Patrick White*. Paddington, N.S.W., Australia: Spaniel Books, 1996.

Hick, John. *Evil and the God of Love*. London: Macmillan & Co., 1966.

Prickett, Stephen, ed. *Reading the Text: Biblical Criticism and Literary Theory*. Cambridge, Mass.: Basil Blackwell Publisher, 1991.

Spark, Muriel. *The Only Problem*. London: Bodley Head, 1984.

Stern, David. *Parables in Midrash: Narrative and Exegesis in Rabbinic Literature*. Cambridge, Mass.: Harvard University Press, 1991.

6

Religious Dimensions
of Literary Text Genres

This chapter addresses the central question of how literature reflects and generates religious significance, concentrating on motifs and images from the Bible as they are rediscovered in secular forms. In different ways we look at the biblical tradition explored in new "realities," producing different kinds of revelation. These passages show how metaphoric revealing operates in the context of narrative via delayed recognition to produce what Aristotle called *anagnorisis*, or recognition, and James Joyce called "epiphany."

In this chapter we work from the immediate discussion of literary texts rather than by abstraction or theory. In each case we look back to the Bible or to Christian origins to trace a continuing tradition of thought and reflection continually revisited in new and ever-expanding contexts and in different literary forms, keeping alive the constant yet changing assumptions of community beliefs.

The first text, from the modern French philosopher and "pilgrim of the absolute" Simone Weil, traces comparisons between Christian themes and the ancient Greek mysteries. Beginning with the Chorus of Aeschylus's tragedy the *Agamemnon*, she considers questions of the nature of suffering, the "dark night of the soul" (linked with the experience of the sixteenth-century Spanish mystic John of the Cross), and the thematic links between Prometheus and Zeus, Christ and God, concluding with a comparison between Greek tragedy and the book of Job.

From there we look at one of the most familiar passages in English literature, the last lines of John Milton's epic poem *Paradise Lost* (1667), which rehearses the drama of the myth of the Fall and the expulsion of Adam and Eve from paradise—Genesis 2 and 3. The propriety of a poet rewriting a narrative of sacred scripture was questioned by Milton's contemporary, poet Andrew Marvell, who in his poem "On Mr. Milton's *Paradise Lost*" wrote:

> The Argument
> Held me a while misdoubting his Intent,
> That he would ruin (for I saw him strong)
> The sacred Truths to Fable and old Song.

The fear that the poet may have overreached himself in the "ruin of sacred truth" appears in later commentary on *Paradise Lost* in Dr. Samuel Johnson's

Life of Milton (*Lives of the Poets*, 1779–81) and lies behind the irony of William Blake's notorious Note in *The Marriage of Heaven and Hell* (circa 1790–93): "The reason Milton wrote in fetters when he wrote of Angels & God, and at liberty when of Devils & Hell, is because he was a true Poet and of the Devil's party without knowing it."

In these final lines of the poem, Adam and Eve have come to terms with their punishment of expulsion from the Garden of Eden. The image of the paradise garden is replaced by imagery of the laborer in the fields of the earth who earns his living by honest toil. In the much-quoted last four lines the couple become representatives of a Renaissance humanism that is mature and adult in a now-uncertain world. This Miltonic image of a fallen world is revisited in Thomas Gray's great poem "Elegy Written in a Country Churchyard" (1751) and is used to great effect by Thomas Hardy at the end of his novel *Tess of the d'Urbervilles* (1891) as Tess's husband, Angel Clare, and her sister 'Liza-Lu walk away from Tess's execution in Wintoncester.

The dialogue between Faust and Margareta in Goethe's *Faust Part One* (1808) takes place in a garden and also explores themes of innocence and experience, and the first dawning of awareness of sin or possible guilt. Margareta admits to Faust her sense of shock when she was insulted by him outside the church: " . . . you see, it has never / Happened before. No one ever says bad / Things of me." A few years before Goethe's great poem was published, Blake had written his brief poem "The Garden of Love," in *Songs of Innocence and Experience* (1795), again with the image of the church and memories of the paradise garden, the Garden of Love. Here Blake seems to equate the consequences of the fall from innocence with the repressive authority of the church and its institutions, in particular the sinister "Priests in black gowns" who strangle human joy with the briars that symbolize the ruin of the perfection of the primal Garden of Eden.

In our final "garden" passage, Augustine of Hippo again draws directly from the Bible. Here is the moment of his conversion—another kind of epiphany or *anagnorisis* that in the New Testament is linked with *metanoia*, or repentance. It is the word used at the heart of Jesus' first preaching of the gospel in Mark: "The time is fulfilled, and the kingdom of God has come near; repent, and believe in the good news" (Mark 1:15). The Greek word *metanoia* literally means a turning of the mind and is enacted precisely by Augustine when he writes of God bringing him face to face with himself. He is also drawing here upon the great parable of the prodigal son (Luke 15:11–32), in which, at the crucial moment among the swine, the boy "comes back into himself" and resolves to return to his father and ask for forgiveness.

We see, then, how literature continually returns to the great moments or epiphanies of the Fall and redemption, experienced in countless ways in human life.

Sylvia Plath's poem "Lady Lazarus" eerily revisits another moment in the Bible, the raising to life by Jesus of the dead Lazarus in John 11. Seeing herself as Lazarus, the poet, with infinite irony, enters into the experience of the miracle—not a resurrection, but a resuscitation of a dead body, drawing upon nightmare images like the Nazi practice of using the skin of their human victims in the concentration camps to make lampshades. Plath explores her sense of her own body, concluding with another image from the death camps—the burning of the bodies, which she combines with the biblical image of the body returning to the dust and ashes from whence it was created (only the gold rings and fillings remaining unburnt in the holocaust), and arising out of the ashes in a ghastly resurrection in which she, a new scarlet woman, will "eat men like air."

Another woman poet, Emily Dickinson, is represented here by her brief and enigmatic poem "Title divine—is mine!" Allusively and indirectly, like Plath, Dickinson absorbs biblical images into herself, this time the great central images of the passion narratives. She is celebrating her whole life from birth through marriage to death ("Born—Bridalled—Shrouded") in her "victory." She concludes with a question—is the triumph of women, perceived as the day when they become a bride, the day of their "passion" (when Christ won his victory), really such a triumph: "Is *this*—the way?" The Christ of the Fourth Gospel, of course, claims to be the way, the truth, and the life (John 14:6).

The next two pieces in this chapter represent the huge literary tradition that draws on the apocalyptic writings of the Bible. The themes of apocalypse (the Greek means "laying bare" or "uncovering"), which we briefly alluded to in the section on Ezekiel, Blake, and Patrick White in the previous chapter, deal with things at the end of time when everything will finally be revealed. The two great apocalypses of the Bible are the book of Daniel and the Revelation to John, although other passages such as Mark 13 also contain material from the great tradition of apocalyptic writing, which flourished in Jewish traditions alongside the canonical writings of scripture from about 200 B.C.E. to 100 C.E. Yeats's poem "The Second Coming" translates apocalyptic themes into the experience of the twentieth century with the "blood-dimm'd tide" of its terrible wars and the sense that everything is falling apart. His powerful images, drawn from the Bible, but also from classicism with the figure of the Sphinx, combine to herald ironically the promised "second coming," the "parousia" that the Christian church has expected from its earliest days, according to the writings of Paul.

The next passage is from the final pages of perhaps the one truly tragic novel in the English language in the twentieth century, Malcolm Lowry's *Under the Volcano* (1947). The death of the English consul, a character modeled to a large extent on Lowry himself, is portrayed in terrifying apocalyptic images, which also owe much to Dante's *Divine Comedy* (a crucial work for Lowry), and the parable of the good Samaritan (Luke 10:29–37), a story that continually reappears in the novel. At last, for the consul, there is no Samaritan to rescue him. Scripture is rendered inert. He falls into the pit of hell, under the volcano, and this final apocalyptic image is made worse by its ultimate insult and trivialization—when the dead dog is flung in after the body of the consul himself. Here, indeed, is the final "fall," without resurrection or hope.

The final two poems of this chapter have a very different mood. Peter Meinke, a contemporary American poet, finds biblical images of redemption in the stuff of everyday life, even in the stationery and equipment that litter our desktops.

Literature has appropriated the Bible and religious images in many ways, drawing on their power and their central position in the Western mind and imagination to explore the nature of human experience both within and outside the belief systems within which these images and symbols gained power.

SIMONE WEIL, INTIMATIONS OF CHRISTIANITY AMONG THE ANCIENT GREEKS

Simone Weil (1909–1943), a mystic, social philosopher, and ethicist, as well as an activist in the French Resistance during World War II, died young, but she has become one of the most widely read of spiritual writers of the twentieth century. Qualified as a teacher of philosophy, she achieved a conception of the absolute good that lifted her outside all institutions and schools of thought, including the religious.

Weil's writings range across philosophy and religion, history, mathematics, and literature, and include poems and a play. Her spiritual works include *Gravity and Grace, Gateway to God, Waiting on God,* and various collections of essays, all published posthumously and widely translated from the French. In Weil's theory of spiritual development, the individual becomes the spontaneous instrument of a timeless goodness. She has been described as a pilgrim of absolute truth. In the excerpt below she links Aeschylean tragedy with her sense of the Bible and Christianity.

From Intimations of Christianity among the Ancient Greeks, *"Zeus and Prometheus"*

Aeschylus, *Agamemnon,* 160–183

> Ζεύς, ὅστις ποτ᾽ ἐστίν, εἰ τόδ᾽ αὐτῷ φίλον κεκλημένῳ
> τοῦτό νιν προσεννέπω. . . .
> Zeus, whoever he may be, if by this name it pleases him
>   to be invoked,
> By this name I call him.
> Nothing is left that I can compare with him, having weighed all things,
> Except Zeus,
> If I am to cast this vain burden of anxiety from me.
> Nor shall he who was great long ago, bursting with a victor's
>   boldness,
> Be said even to have existed,
> Nor shall he who followed, and has disappeared in finding
>   his vanquisher.
> But whoever, with thoughts turned to Zeus, shall cry his glory,
> Shall receive the fullness of wisdom.

> He has opened the way of wisdom to mortals, proclaiming as
> sovereign law:
> By suffering comes understanding.
> So accrues to the heart, drop by drop, during sleep,
> The wage of dolorous memory;
> And even without willing it, wisdom comes.
> From the gods who sit at the celestial helm,
> grace comes violently.

This passage from a chorus of the *Agamemnon* of Aeschylus, which as Greek is difficult and almost untranslatable, is interesting as being one of those which obviously reflects the doctrine taught to the initiates of the Mysteries, notably that of Eleusis. The tragedies of Aeschylus are clearly impregnated by this doctrine. Zeus seems to be regarded therein as the supreme God, that is to say, the only God, and as being above all the God of Moderation, and of the chastisements that punish excess, the excess and the abuse of power under all their forms. To understand is presented as the supreme end, that is, of course, to understand the relationship of man and the universe, of men among themselves, of man with himself. According to this passage, suffering was regarded as the indispensable condition for such knowledge, and precious by this token, but by this token only. Unlike certain morbid valuations of our time, the Greeks never attributed value to suffering for its own sake. The word they chose to designate suffering, $\pi\grave{\alpha}\Theta os$, is one which evoked above all the idea of enduring much more than of suffering. Man must endure that which he does not want. He must find himself in submissio n to necessity. Misfortunes leave wounds which bleed drop by drop even during sleep; and thus, little by little, they break a man by violence and make him fit, in spite of himself, to receive wisdom, that wisdom which expresses itself as moderation. Man must learn to think of himself as a limited and dependent being, suffering alone can teach him this. . . .

By its very colour this passage clearly reveals the origin of its inspiration to be that of the Mysteries. (The two solitary divinities are certainly not, as affirmed in a note by an unfortunate Sorbonne professor, those of Hesiodic or Orphic genealogy, but false gods anterior to a revelation, which for the Greeks is probably that brought in by contact with the Pelasgians, the Phoenicians, and the Egyptians.) These lines contain the sufficient and infallible method of perfection, which is to keep the mind turned in loving contemplation towards the true God, that God who has no name. The "dolorous memory" is Plato's reminiscence, the remembrance of what the soul saw upon the further side of heaven; that dolorous memory which distils in sleep, is the "dark night" of St. John of the Cross.

If one compares lines from the Prometheus, the similarity of the story of Prometheus with that of the Christ appears with blinding evidence. Prometheus is the preceptor of men, who has taught them all things. Here he (the preceptor) is said to be Zeus. That is all the same thing; the two are really one. It is in crucifying Prometheus that Zeus has opened the way of wisdom to men.

Henceforth the law, "by suffering comes understanding," may be brought in line with the thought of St. John of the Cross: that participation in the suffering of the Cross of Christ alone allows penetration into the depths of divine wisdom.

Moreover, if one compares the first lines spoken by Prometheus with the end of the Book of Job, one sees in these two texts the same mysterious linking between extreme physical suffering, accompanied by an extreme distress of soul, and the complete revelation of the beauty of the world.

JOHN MILTON,
PARADISE LOST

Milton's *Paradise Lost* is one the of the greatest poems in the English language, exploring with enormous erudition and tremendous drama the theological problem of theodicy through the narrative of the account of the creation and fall of humankind in the early chapters of the Hebrew Bible.

A Renaissance man in his learning and sense of religious, civil, and domestic liberties, Milton (1608–1674) spent much of his life involved in the politics of the English Republic after the execution of Charles I in 1649. *Paradise Lost* is written in the heroic epic tradition and celebrates a Renaissance humanism that finally draws Milton's defense of the Christian faith into a recognition that God's ways are justified through the ability of his creatures, Adam and Eve, to adapt to a fallen world, admit their responsibilities, and live as husband and wife in a world full of possibilities as well as honest toil, loving one another in spite of all that has happened. The poem is one of the greatest literary meditations on the Bible ever written.

From Paradise Lost,
Book 12, Lines 624–49

> So spake our mother Eve, and Adam heard
> Well pleased, but answered not; for now too nigh
> Th' Archangel stood, and from the other hill
> To their fixed station, all in bright array
> The Cherubim descended; on the ground
> Gliding metéorous, as ev'ning mist
> Ris'n from a river o'er the marish glides,
> And gathers ground fast at the laborer's heel
> Homeward returning. High in front advanced,
> The brandished sword of God before them blazed
> Fierce as a comet; which with torrid heat,
> And vapor as the Libyan air adust,
> Began to parch that temperate clime; whereat
> In either hand the hast'ning Angel caught
> Our ling'ring parents, and to th' eastern gate
> Led them direct, and down the cliff as fast
> To the subjected plain; then disappeared.

They, looking back, all th'eastern side beheld
Of Paradise, so late their happy seat,
Waved over by that flaming brand, the gate
With dreadful faces thronged and fiery arms.
Some natural tears they dropped, but wiped them soon;
The world was all before them, where to choose
Their place of rest, and Providence their guide:
They hand in hand, with wand'ring steps and slow,
Through Eden took their solitary way.

J. W. VON GOETHE,
FAUST

Goethe (1749–1832) is the greatest poet of German Romanticism, and *Faust* is his greatest achievement. A verse tragedy in two parts written over a period of almost thirty years, the work develops the ancient theme of Faust— its prologue beginning in heaven where God, with his three archangels, Raphael, Gabriel, and Michael, admits Mephistopheles and gives him permission to tempt Faust. God affirms confidence in Faust's steadfastness. The scene is in many ways reminiscent of the early verses of the book of Job.

The scene excerpted below from Part 1, returns to the theme of the paradise garden and the threat to the innocence of the beautiful Margareta (Gretchen). Faust here seems close to the character of the serpent in Genesis, though for a while his lust is chastened by Margareta's simplicity and integrity.

From Faust,
Scene 15, "A Garden"

[*MARGARETA walking up and down with FAUST,
MARTHA with MEPHISTOPHELES.*]

MARGARETA. I'm quite ashamed, I feel you're being so kind
And condescending, just to spare
My feelings, sir! A traveller
Must be polite, and take what he can find.
I know quite well that my poor conversation
Can't entertain a man of education.

FAUST. One look, one word from you—that entertains
Me more than any this wise world contains.
   [*He kisses her hand.*]

MARGARETA. Sir, you put yourself out! How can you kiss my hand?
It's so nasty and rough; I have to do
Such a lot of housework with it. If you knew
How fussy Mother is, you'd understand! . . .

MARGARETA. Yes, out of sight out of mind it will be!
And though you talk politely—after all,
You've many friends, and I'm sure they are all
More intellectual than me.

FAUST. My sweet, believe me, what's called intellect
Is often shallowness and vanity.

MARGARETA. How so?

FAUST. Oh, why can simple innocence not know
Itself, or humble lowliness respect
Its own great value, feel the awe that's due
To generous Nature's dearest, greatest boon—

MARGARETA. You'll sometimes think of me, and then forget me soon;
But I'll have time enough to think of you.

FAUST. So you're alone a lot?

MARGARETA. Oh yes, you see, our household's not
Big, but one has to see to it;
And we've no maid. I cook and sweep and knit
And sew, all day I'm on my feet.
And my mother insists everything's got
To be so neat!
Not that she's really poor in any way,
In fact, we're better off than most folk, I should say.
We got some money when my father died,
A little house and garden just outside
The town. But mine's a quiet life now, that's true.
My brother's a soldier, he's not here.
My little sister, she died too.
I had such trouble with her, the poor little dear,
And yet I'd gladly have it all again to do,
I loved her so.

FAUST. A darling, just like you.

MARGARETA. I brought her up: she got so fond of me.
She was born after Father's death, you see,
And Mother was so desperately ill then
We thought she never would be well again,
And she got better slowly, very gradually.
She couldn't possibly, you know,
Give the baby her breast; and so
I had to feed her, all alone,

With milk and water; she became my own,
And in my arms and on my breast
She smiled and wriggled and grew and grew.

FAUST. That must have been great happiness for you.

MARGARETA. But very hard as well, although I did my best.
At night she had her little cradle by
My bed; she'd hardly need to move, and I
Was wide awake.
Then I would have to feed her, or else take
Her into bed with me, or if she went
On crying, I'd get up and jog her to and fro.
And then, the washing started at cockcrow;
Then I would shop and cook. That's how I spent
The whole of every blessed day.
So you see, sir, it's not all play!
But you eat well, and you sleep well that way. . . .

FAUST. You knew me again, sweetheart, immediately,
Here in the garden? Is it really true?

MARGARETA. You saw me cast my eyes down, didn't you.

FAUST. And you've forgiven the liberty
I took outside the church, the insulting way
I spoke to you the other day?

MARGARETA. It was a shock—you see, it never had
Happened before. No one ever says bad
Things of me, and I thought: did I somehow
Seem lacking in modesty to him just now?
He suddenly just thinks, quite without shame:
"I'll pick this girl up"; maybe I'm to blame?—
I must confess that something in my heart,
I don't know what, began quite soon to take your part;
In fact I got quite cross with myself, too,
For not being quite cross enough with you.

FAUST. Oh my sweet!

MARGARETA. Wait!
    [*She picks a daisy and begins pulling off the petals one by one.*]

FAUST. What's this for? A bouquet?

MARGARETA. No!

114

FAUST. What?

MARGARETA. You'll laugh at me; it's just a game we play.
   [*She murmurs as she picks off the petals.*]

FAUST. What's this you're murmuring?

MARGARETA [*half aloud*]. He loves me—loves me not—

FAUST. You dear beloved little thing!

MARGARETA [*continuing*]. Loves me—not—loves me—not—
   [*pulling off the last petal and exclaiming with joy*].
   He loves me!

FAUST. Yes my love! The flower speaks,
And let it be your oracle! He loves you:
Do you know what that means? He loves you!
   [*He clasps both her hands in his.*]

MARGARETA. I'm trembling all over!

FAUST. Don't be afraid! Oh let my eyes,
My hands on your hands tell you what
No words can say:
To give oneself entirely and to feel
Ecstasy that must last for ever!
For ever!—For its end would be despair.
No, never-ending! Never ending!
   [*MARGARETA presses his hands, frees herself and runs away. He stands
   lost in thought for a moment, then follows her.*]

WILLIAM BLAKE,
"THE GARDEN OF LOVE"

William Blake (see also pp. 90–91), published his *Songs of Experience* in
1794, five years after the *Songs of Innocence.* These lyrics of great tenderness and disarming simplicity were accompanied by Blake's own illustrations, and in a sense cannot be fully appreciated without the pictures
that frame them.

In this poem from the *Songs of Experience,* Blake takes us to the garden,
the natural place of one of his favorite images, flowers, which for him are
symbols of love. But the garden is corrupted by the presence of the chapel,
surrounded by the graves of the instincts that organized religion and its
priests have repressed and negated. In Blake's illustration, a kneeling priest
instructs two children in the doctrines of his deathly religion. Their heads

115

are bowed, and at the bottom of the page the graves of his "joys and desires" are seen bound with briars.

Blake was typical of many Romantics in his loathing of the churches. His fellow poet Samuel Taylor Coleridge, in a letter of 1800, celebrates the natural innocence of his son Hartley, who is the "darling of the Sun and of the Breeze," and asks, "Shall I suffer the Toad of Priesthood to spurt out his foul juice in this Babe's face?"

The Garden of Love

I went to the Garden of Love,
And saw what I never had seen:
A Chapel was built in the midst,
Where I used to play on the green.

And the gates of this Chapel were shut,
And Thou shalt not, writ over the door;
So I turn'd to the Garden of Love,
That so many sweet flowers bore.

And saw it was filled with graves,
And tomb-stones where flowers should be:
And Priests in black gowns, were walking their rounds,
And binding with briars, my joys & desires.

AUGUSTINE OF HIPPO, CONFESSIONS

Augustine, Bishop of Hippo (see above, chapter 3), received a Christian education, but abandoned his religion until, much later in life, he was drawn back into a Christian profession in a conversion dramatically described in his *Confessions*. Augustine, like Paul before him, experiences a moment of "recognition" in the garden near Milan, a further example of the themes explored in this chapter, but now an experience of restoration rather than exile and decay.

Confessions is a dramatic acknowledgment of the writer's sin and error, a recognition of God's goodness and truth, and finally a confession of God's glory. They have been hugely influential on Western literature, and were first translated into English in 1620.

From Confessions,
Book 8, Chapter 7

This was what Ponticianus told us. But while he was speaking, O Lord, you were turning me around to look at myself. For I had placed myself behind my own back, refusing to see myself. You were setting me before my own eyes so that I could see how sordid I was, how deformed and squalid, how tainted with ulcers and sores. I saw it all and stood aghast, but there was no place where I could escape from myself. If I tried to turn my eyes away they fell on Ponticianus, still telling his tale, and in this way you brought me face to face with myself once more, forcing me upon my own sight so that I should see my wickedness and loathe it. I had known it all along, but I had always pretended that it was something different. I had turned a blind eye and forgotten it.

But now, the more my heart warmed to those two men as I heard how they had made the choice that was to save them by giving themselves up entirely to your care, the more bitterly I hated myself in comparison with them. Many years of my life had passed—twelve, unless I am wrong—since I had read Cicero's *Hortensius* at the age of nineteen and it had inspired me to study philosophy. But I still postponed my renunciation of this world's joys, which would have left me free to look for that other happiness, the very search for which, let alone its discovery, I ought to have prized above the discovery of all human treasures and kingdoms or the ability to enjoy all the pleasures of the body at a mere nod of the head. As a youth I had been woefully at fault, particularly in early adolescence. I had prayed to you for chastity and said "Give me chastity and continence, but not yet." For I was afraid that you would answer my prayer at once and cure me too soon of the disease of lust, which I wanted satisfied, not quelled. I had wandered on along the road of vice in the sacrilegious superstition of the Manichees, not because I thought that it was right, but because I preferred it to the Christian belief, which I did not explore as I ought but opposed out of malice.

I had pretended to myself that the reason why, day after day, I staved off the decision to renounce worldly ambition and follow you alone was that I could see no certain goal towards which I might steer my course. But the time had now come when I stood naked before my own eyes, while my conscience upbraided me. "Am I to be silent? Did you not always say that you would not discard your load of vanity for the sake of a truth that was not proved? Now you know that the truth is proved, but the load is still on your shoulders. Yet here are others who have exchanged their load for wings, although they did not wear themselves out in the search for truth or spend ten years or more in making up their minds."

All the time that Ponticianus was speaking my conscience gnawed away at me like this. I was overcome by burning shame, and when he had finished his tale and completed the business for which he had come, he went away and I was left to my own thoughts. I made all sorts of accusations against myself. I cudgelled my soul and belaboured it with reasons why it should follow me now that I was trying so hard to follow you. But it fought back. It would not obey and yet could offer no excuse. All its old arguments were exhausted and had been shown to be false. It remained silent and afraid, for as much as the loss of life itself it feared the stanching of the flow of habit, by which it was wasting away to death.

SYLVIA PLATH,
"LADY LAZARUS"

Sylvia Plath (1932–1963) was born in Boston, Massachusetts, and spent her short life traveling between the United States and England. She was profoundly affected by the early death of her father, and throughout her life suffered from nervous depressions. In 1953 she suffered a breakdown, and eventually she committed suicide.

The poem excerpted here, from her collection *Ariel* (1965), was published after her death. It clearly draws on two suicide attempts and disturbingly relates biblical and twentieth-century images and themes without any of the sense of revelation or forgiveness experienced by Augustine. It takes the theme of the raising of Lazarus and turns it into a nightmare of death and despair.

"Lady Lazarus"

I have done it again.
One year in every ten
I manage it—

A sort of walking miracle, my skin
Bright as a Nazi lampshade,
My right foot

A paperweight,
My face a featureless, fine
Jew linen.

Peel off the napkin
O my enemy.
Do I terrify?—

The nose, the eye pits, the full set of teeth?
The sour breath
Will vanish in a day.

Soon, soon the flesh
The grave cave ate will be
At home on me

And I a smiling woman.
I am only thirty.
And like the cat I have nine times to die.

This is Number Three.
What a trash
To annihilate each decade.

What a million filaments.
The peanut-crunching crowd
Shoves in to see

Them unwrap me hand and foot—
The big strip tease.
Gentlemen, ladies

These are my hands
My knees.
I may be skin and bone,

Nevertheless, I am the same, identical woman.
The first time it happened I was ten.
It was an accident.

The second time I meant
To last it out and not come back at all.
I rocked shut

As a seashell.
They had to call and call
And pick the worms off me like sticky pearls.

Dying
Is an art, like everything else.
I do it exceptionally well.

I do it so it feels like hell.
I do it so it feels real.
I guess you could say I've a call.

It's easy enough to do it in a cell.
It's easy enough to do it and stay put.
It's the theatrical

Comeback in broad day
To the same place, the same face, the same brute
Amused shout:

"A miracle!"
That knocks me out.
There is a charge

For the evening, of my scars, there is a charge
For the hearing of my heart—
It really goes.

And there is a charge, a very large charge
For a word or a touch
Or a bit of blood

Or a piece of my hair or my clothes.
So, so Herr Doktor.
So, Herr Enemy.

I am your opus,
I am your valuable,
The pure gold baby

That melts to a shriek.
I turn and burn.
Do not think I underestimate your great concern.

Ash, ash—
You poke and stir.
Flesh, bone, there is nothing there—

A cake of soap,
A wedding ring,
A gold filling.

Herr God, Herr Lucifer
Beware
Beware.

Out of the ash
I rise with my red hair

And I eat men like air.

EMILY DICKINSON, "TITLE DIVINE—IS MINE!"

Emily Dickinson (1830–1886) was born in Amherst, Massachusetts, into a comfortable, middle-class family. Well educated and, in her early years, sociable and lively, she gradually withdrew from society and lived most of her life as a recluse.

Little of Dickinson's poetry was published in her lifetime, although she wrote a great deal. Her style is idiosyncratic, owes much to the tradition of hymnody, and is saturated in powerful religious and biblical themes and images. This eccentric and violently dramatic verse reveals an intense inner life lived behind the curtains of her secluded domesticity. In the poem given here she gives herself the title "Empress of Calvary," using the traditional Christian image of the Bride of Christ to comment wryly on her own unmarried condition. Other women may speak romantically or possessively of "my husband"; Dickinson almost cynically underlines this in the suggestively erotic image of the penultimate line. The final line returns to the allusions to the gospel—linking the claims of the married women for their husbands to Jesus' claims to the way, the truth, and the life.

We see here how literature can daringly expose religious themes to other contexts in troubling and revisioning ways.

"Title divine—is mine!"

Title divine—is mine!
The Wife—without the Sign!
Acute Degree—conferred on me—
Empress of Calvary!
Royal—all but the Crown!
Betrothed—without the swoon
God sends us Women—
When you—hold—Garnet to Garnet—
Gold—to Gold—
Born—Bridalled—Shrouded—
In a Day—
Tri Victory
"My Husband"—women say—
Stroking the Melody—
Is *this*—the way?

WILLIAM BUTLER YEATS, "THE SECOND COMING"

William Butler Yeats (1865–1939) is the leading poet of the Irish literary renaissance, which gave a voice to Irish nationalism in the early years of the twentieth century. Although better known in his life as a playwright, Yeats became perhaps the most influential poet writing in English of his age. Dylan Thomas thought that of all poets of this century "Yeats was the greatest by miles."

"The Second Coming" was published in 1921 in the collection entitled *Michael Robartes and the Dancer*. Written in the wake of the Great War of 1914–18 and the bloody struggle for Irish independence, this poem is also startlingly prophetic of our century with its genocides and anarchy. It laments the loss of innocence and looks forward to a terrible parousia—that is, the second coming looked for by Christians, when Jesus Christ will return at the end of time. But, returning to the nativity scene of Christ's first coming to Bethlehem, Yeats turns this religious hope into a terrible nightmare—linking this with the sphinx that menaces Oedipus. As things fall apart, we could be said to be moving here into the world of postmodernity, with its abandonment of "the center," and its acknowledgments of chaos.

From "The Second Coming"

. . . Surely some revelation is at hand;
Surely the Second Coming is at hand.
The Second Coming! Hardly are those words out
When a vast image out of *Spiritus Mundi*

121

Troubles my sight: somewhere in sands of the desert
A shape with lion body and the head of a man,
A gaze blank and pitiless as the sun,
Is moving its slow thighs, while all about it
Reel shadows of the indignant desert birds.
The darkness drops again; but now I know
That twenty centuries of stony sleep
Were vexed to nightmare by a rocking cradle,
And what rough beast, its hour come round at last,
Slouches towards Bethlehem to be born?

MALCOLM LOWRY,
UNDER THE VOLCANO

Malcolm Lowry (1909–1957) has only gradually been revealed as one of the greatest of twentieth-century novelists. A chronic alcoholic, he died when only forty-eight by "misadventure," leaving a mass of incomplete manuscripts that have slowly been edited and published.

His principal novel, completed and published in his lifetime, is *Under the Volcano,* in which he draws on his experiences as a traveler, a sailor, and an alcoholic. Like all his work, it is permeated with Dantean themes from *The Divine Comedy,* but it is also a kind of extended meditation on the parable of the good Samaritan from the Gospel of Luke (10:30–37). This is brought out in the underrated film of the book by John Huston. The parable is repeatedly returned to with different twists—what if the man had died before he could be rescued? What if he refuses to be rescued?

The last paragraphs of the book, which are excerpted here, recount the death of the principal character, the consul, Geoffrey Firmin, and his descent into the "Hell" of the ravine.

From Under the Volcano

At first the Consul felt a queer relief. Now he realized he had been shot. He fell on one knee, then, with a groan, flat on his face in the grass. "Christ," he remarked, puzzled, "this is a dingy way to die."

A bell spoke out:

Dolente . . . dolore!

It was raining softly. Shapes hovered by him, holding his hand, perhaps still trying to pick his pockets, or to help, or merely curious. He could feel life slivering out of him like liver, ebbing into the tenderness of the grass. He was alone. Where was everybody ? Or had there been no one? Then a face shone out of the gloom, a mask of compassion. It was the old fiddler, stooping over him. "*Compañero*—" he began. Then he had vanished.

Presently the word *pelado* began to fill his whole consciousness. That had been Hugh's word for the thief: now someone had flung the insult at him. And it was as if, for a moment, he had become the *pelado,* the thief—yes, the pilferer of meaningless muddled ideas out of which his rejection of life had grown, who had worn his two or three little bowler hats, his disguises, over these abstractions: now the realest of them all was close. But someone had called him *compañero* too, which was better, much better. It made him happy. These thoughts drifting through his mind were accompanied by music he could hear only when he listened carefully. Mozart was it? The Siciliana. Finale of the D minor quartet by Moses. No, it was something funereal, of Gluck's perhaps, from Alcestis. Yet there was a Bach-like quality to it. Bach? A clavichord, heard from far away, in England in the seventeenth century. England. The chords of a guitar too, half lost, mingled with the distant clamour of a waterfall and what sounded like the cries of love.

He was in Kashmir, he knew, lying in the meadows near running water among violets and trefoil, the Himalayas beyond, which made it all the more remarkable he should suddenly be setting out with Hugh and Yvonne to climb Popocatepetl. Already they had drawn ahead. "Can you pick bougainvillea?" he heard Hugh say, and, "Be careful," Yvonne replied, "it's got spikes on it and you have to look at everything to be sure there're no spiders." "We shoota de espiders in Mexico," another voice muttered. And with this Hugh and Yvonne had gone. He suspected they had not only climbed Popocatepetl but were by now far beyond it. Painfully he trudged the slope of the foothills toward Amecameca alone. With ventilated snow goggles, with alpenstock, with mittens and a wool cap pulled over his ears, with pockets full of dried prunes and raisins and nuts, with a jar of rice protruding from one coat pocket, and the Hotel Fausto's information from the other, he was utterly weighed down. He could go no farther. Exhausted, helpless, he sank to the ground. No one would help him even if they could. Now he was the one dying by the wayside where no good Samaritan would halt. Though it was perplexing there should be this sound of laughter in his ears, of voices: ah, he was being rescued at last. He was in an ambulance shrieking through the jungle itself, racing uphill past the timberline toward the peak—and this was certainly one way to get there!—while those were friendly voices around him, Jacques's and Vigil's, they would make allowances, would set Hugh and Yvonne's minds at rest about him. "*No se puede vivir sin amar,*" they would say, which would explain everything, and he repeated this aloud. How could he have thought so evil of the world when succour was at hand all the time? And now he had reached the summit. Ah, Yvonne, sweetheart, forgive me! Strong hands lifted him. Opening his eyes, he looked down, expecting to see, below him, the magnificent jungle, the heights, Pico de Orizabe, Malinche, Cofre de Perote, like those peaks of his life conquered one after another before this greatest ascent of all had been successfully, if unconventionally, completed. But there was nothing there: no peaks, no life, no climb. Nor was this summit a summit exactly: it had no substance, no firm base. It was crumbling too, whatever it was, collapsing, while he was falling, falling into the volcano, he must have climbed it after all, though now there was this noise of foisting lava in his ears, horribly, it was in eruption, yet no, it wasn't the volcano, the world itself was bursting, bursting into black spouts of villages catapulted into space, with himself falling through it all, through the inconceivable pandemonium of a million tanks, through the blazing of ten million burning bodies, falling, into a forest, falling—

Suddenly he screamed, and it was as though this scream were being tossed from one tree to another, as its echoes returned, then, as though the trees themselves were crowding nearer, huddled together, closing over him, pitying . . .

Somebody threw a dead dog after him down the ravine.

PETER MEINKE,
"LIQUID PAPER," "M3"

Peter Meinke was born in Brooklyn but has lived in St. Petersburg, Florida, since 1966. He has written ten collections of poetry and a collection of stories, *The Piano Tuner*, which won the Flannery O'Connor Award for 1986.

In "Liquid Paper" Meinke reflects on the themes of sin and redemption, using the image of the little bottles of liquid paper that are black with a white cap, and look like ministers in their clerical collars. The seven years refers to the custom of temporary enslavement in Israel under which, according to law, slaves should be set free in the seventh year after six years of service (Ex. 21:2–6; Deut. 15:12–17). In the final lines of the poem, the poet ponders the possibility of returning to the innocence of childhood, before the "fall" of our guilty lives.

In "M3," Meinke links his stay at the University of North Carolina at Greensboro, where he has served as writer-in-residence, with the themes that have permeated this chapter: "recognition," innocence and guilt, and the biblical image of the Promised Land as flowing with milk and honey. He also looks back to his fellow poet William Blake.

"Liquid Paper"

Smooth as a snail, this little parson
pardons our sins. Touch the brush tip
lightly and—*abracadabra!*—a clean slate.

We know those who blot their brains
by sniffing it, which shows
it erases more than ink
and with imagination anything
can be misapplied. . . . In the army,
our topsergeant drank aftershave, squeezing
my Old Spice to the last slow drop.

It worked like Liquid Paper in his head

until he'd glide across the streets of Heidelberg
hunting for the house in Boise, Idaho,
where he was born. . . . If I were God
I'd authorize Celestial Liquid Paper
every seven years to whiten our mistakes:
we should be sorry and live with what we've done
but seven years is long enough and all of us
deserve a visit now and then
to the house where we were born
before everything got written so far wrong.

"M3"

Meaning (call it "M3") is the increasingly invisible
odorless tasteless element in our universe long ago
slipped by Someone's god into our water which if only we had
the proper instruments we'd recognize as I I2OM3
But we who specialize in seeing trees instead of forests can
find in its place only particles of emptiness vibrating
randomly like the snowflakes in Greensboro during this Blizzard
of '96 for which we are as unprepared as Sodom or
Gomorra were for flames

Of course we're as innocent and guilty as either of those doomed
cities without having had as much fun: our exercise and food
increasingly designed to extend our lives and make them not worth
living   Winters are getting colder and soon by geologic
time the curled wave will freeze the stars wink shut the last love letter
    sent
All this is good as the storm has shown us over and over: wheels
without friction spin uselessly digging existential ditches
heading nowhere at high speed   Clearly we should stay at home
    stock some
staples renew our vows

Without contraries there is no progression Blake proclaimed   That's
    why
I'm counting syllables here as a ground to grip: the miracle
of ordinary happiness demands connection lip to lip
hand on hand a boot biting into snow   It's the *recognition*
of connection (call *it* M3 as well) that's become so hard: here
in Greensboro too far from you I know you've sent with deepest faith
your guardian spirit in whom I'm striving to believe and who
indeed seems to have brought me through to this snowed-in sunlit
    land of
dwindling milk and honey

FURTHER READING

Aichele, George, Jr. *The Limits of Story.* Chico, Calif.: Scholars Press; Philadelphia: Fortress Press, 1985.

Bennett, J. A. W. *Poetry of the Passsion: Studies in Twelve Centuries of English Verse.* Oxford: Clarendon Press; New York: Oxford University Press, 1982.

Daiches, David. *God and the Poets.* Oxford: Clarendon Press, and New York: Oxford University Press, 1984.

Frye, Northrop. *The Secular Scripture: A Study of the Structure of Romance.* Cambridge, Mass.: Harvard University Press, 1976.

Graham, William C. *Half-Finished Heaven: The Social Gospel in American Literature.* Lanham, Md.: University Press of America, 1995.

Gunn, Giles B. *The Interpretation of Otherness: Literature, Religion and the American Imagination.* New York: Oxford University Press, 1979.

Hartman, Geoffrey H., and Sanford Budick, eds. *Midrash and Literature.* New Haven, Conn., and London: Yale University Press, 1986.

Kort, Wesley A. *Narrative Elements and Religious Meaning.* Philadelphia: Fortress Press, 1975.

Ledbetter, Mark. *Virtuous Intentions: The Religious Dimension of Narrative.* Atlanta: Scholars Press, 1989.

Liptzin, Sol. *Biblical Themes in World Literature.* Hoboken, N.J.: KTAV Publishing House, 1985.

Lynch, William F. *Christ and Apollo: The Dimensions of the Literary Imagination.* New York: New American Library, 1963; Notre Dame, 1975.

The Great Themes
of Literature and Religion

Much of the impetus toward the founding of the formal study of literature and religion as a field came from the desire of teachers and critics to treat prominent themes of the Judeo-Christian religious tradition as rendered in imaginative literature. In this chapter we identify four such thematic areas, though many others have equal claim for inclusion, and each area opens up a wide series of questions and issues.

Death, the first theme, might suggest also immortality, resurrection, and the traditional "last four things" of Christian eschatology—heaven, hell, death, and judgment. The dynamics of religious conversion, the second theme, is a vast subject varying enormously in different traditions of religious practice. The third theme, or rather themes, of love and evil might seem an odd pair, though they both find their origin, in a sense, in the Genesis story of the Fall in Eden. We do not pursue the question of the relationship between erotic and spiritual love, or more broadly between what C. S. Lewis designated as the four loves—affection, friendship, eros, and charity—or some of the theological problems which inevitably arise out of the experience of evil and suffering, though these are touched upon. Finally, the traditions of apocalyptic literature—the visions of the end in both the Jewish and Christian faiths—are many and complex, and can only be suggested here in our excerpts and proposed further reading.

Other themes, not included except tangentially, might be those of religious persecution and martyrdom; justice, law, and grace; community; revelation and prophecy; sacred space and time; sin, redemption, and the "savior" figure; transcendence; virtue and sainthood. The list is almost endless, and many of these are implicitly discussed elsewhere in this anthology. We leave the attentive reader to continue from where we have left off.

As in other chapters the starting point is biblical literature, and while acknowledging the art of the works discussed, in this chapter we emphasize what the narratives, plays, and poems "say" about these great themes and about the writers and cultures that have produced them. Elsewhere we have been more concerned with the "how" of literature—its devices and techniques, but here we concentrate upon the "what," both theologically and within cultures. Thus, by including a passage from Elie Wiesel's autobiographical novel *Night*, we wish to stress the author's personal as well as poetic role as a witness to World War II holocaust atrocities and explore the theme

127

of theodicy (see "Love and Evil" section, below) in the context of Wiesel's witness. This is not to deny that the harrowing passage here reproduced is not literature of the highest order; indeed, it is included for that very reason.

DEATH

It might seem somewhat strange to begin with the theme of death, though in many ways this lies at the heart of almost all great religious traditions, and Christianity in particular focuses upon the "defeat" of death. As Paul states in 1 Corinthians 15:54, in Christ is fulfilled the prophecy of Isaiah 25:8, and "Death has been swallowed up in victory." First we return to Ovid's *Metamorphoses* and the account there of the death of Orpheus, torn to shreds by the Thracian Maenads, the Ciconian women. Orpheus's head continues to sing even after it is severed from his body, and in death he is reunited with his beloved Eurydice, whom he had followed even into the Underworld, or Hades. This story of pursuit of the beloved into hell or Hades is found in the folklore of widely distant countries, and finds an echo in the Christian theme of Christ's descent into hell after his Passion to recover the souls of the lost. Milton draws upon the myth of Orpheus in *Paradise Lost* (Book 8, lines 30ff.).

Emily Dickinson's poem is elegant and gothic, linking Christian imagery with the theme of a carriage drive on a journey "toward Eternity." With typical terseness she portrays Death as a kindly and civil driver, carrying the poet through scenes of her earthly life as she is divested of the concerns and anxieties of mortal life, ending at the grave, which is described in the penultimate verse. Time is swallowed up in eternity, and the experience of death is gentle and described almost as the encounter with the lover who takes his beloved on a country drive in a carriage made just for the two of them.

T. S. Eliot, on the other hand, deals with the theme of the murder of the Christian martyr Thomas Becket, the archbishop of Canterbury who defied his king, Henry II of England, in 1170. Thomas represents the defiance of the state by the church, of temporal by spiritual power, and he follows his true master, that is, Christ, in his own shedding of blood; "My blood given to pay for His death." In Eliot's play, written to be acted in Canterbury Cathedral itself, Thomas dies commending his soul to God and the saints of his church, beginning with the blessed Virgin Mary and including the earlier martyr and bishop, Denys of Paris, popularly regarded as the patron saint of France, who was reputed to have been put to death about 258 C.E. while serving as a missionary in Gaul.

CONVERSION AND ECSTASY

The theme of religious conversion is widespread in literature and often linked with ecstatic experiences—that is, literally, experiences outside the body, from the Greek *ek-stasis*, a standing outside of the self. The conversion of Saul, a persecutor of the first Christians and above all of the first martyr

Stephen (Acts 7) is recounted in the Acts of the Apostles, the book that describes the earliest history of the Christian church. Saul, a rabbinic Jew, became Paul, the church's first theologian, in a sudden conversion that is characterized by a direct experience of God and physical trauma. Augustine's experience of the "voice" of God is through the word of scripture from which his conversion is equally instantaneous, though in each case this is clearly the culmination of a long period of struggle. The third excerpt, from James Baldwin's autobiographical novel *Go Tell It on the Mountain*, stresses the physical nature of religious experience as the Power strikes and possesses the worshipers. From Paul to Baldwin, and through Augustine, the strong sense of sin precedes conversion, and the language of the Bible is sustained as the word of God.

LOVE AND EVIL

The linking of these two themes begins with the story of Adam and Eve in Genesis 2–3, a narrative that recounts the beginning of human love, and also the origin of Adam's "curse," from which there is no fine thing "but needs much labouring." Both Yeats and Milton return to these chapters at the beginning of the Bible, and in his epic of the fall from innocence, Milton creates one of the great and most disturbing figures in Western literature, the Archenemy and fallen archangel Satan. We have taken here Satan's first speech in *Paradise Lost*, which wonderfully captures his evil power and his seductive rhetoric.

Milton's epic poem, with its declared intention to "justify the ways of God to men," is perhaps the greatest of all poetic attempts to address one of the most troubling of all theological problems, and one to which we return again and again, known as theodicy: to justify the Christian belief in a good and loving, all-powerful creator God in a world full of evil and unmerited suffering. Why, under such a God, should the innocent suffer as they do?

This question is asked again with unbearable poignancy in the passage from Elie Wiesel's *Night*, in which Wiesel describes the hanging of a small boy by the SS in a Nazi concentration camp. Wiesel deliberately uses religious images to underline the horror of the event—the boy has "the face of a sad angel," and finally the execution is linked to Calvary itself as the ultimate paradox is articulated, that to witness such an atrocity is to witness the very death of God. The resonances are all the more terrible as we recall that the author is not a Christian but a Jew, himself a prisoner in the death camp. What in the Christian tradition is the greatest of all acts of God's love for God's people is here an act of inhumanity so extreme as to banish the sense of the presence of God entirely.

VISIONS OF THE END

The final section begins with Daniel's dream (Daniel 7), one of the greatest of all "apocalyptic" writings—a genre that is found in both Judaism and

129

Christianity. The word is taken from a Greek verb meaning "to reveal or disclose," and these writings are often strange visions of the end of all things. The last book of the Christian Bible, Revelation, is one of the first and most elusive of Christian apocalypses, marking subsequent literature perhaps more deeply than any other single book of the Bible.

Omitting poetry as strange and profound as that of Dante and William Blake, we move straight from the Bible to a modern apocalypse, J. G. Ballard's deeply disturbing (and biblical) novel *The Atrocity Exhibition*, which begins with the word "Apocalypse." The exhibition is of pictures by patients in a mental institution, true to the apocalyptic insight that often it is the insane whose bizarre visions give us something profoundly important that is easy to miss in the ordered "sanity" of our lives. As Ballard notes in his recent annotations to his own work (which we have included here), " 'To the insane.' I owe them everything." The novel, which defies organized narrative or even identity to its characters, focuses on such "apocalyptic" events in American experience as the assassination of President Kennedy, the Vietnam War, and the obsession with the tragic beauty of Marilyn Monroe.

We step back nearly two hundred years in literary history to Samuel Taylor Coleridge's remarkable fragment "Kubla Khan," a "vision in a dream," like that of Daniel, which concludes with the figure of the terrible poet/prophet who has not only seen but actually experienced the beauties of paradise itself, before the Fall.

Thus we see how our themes are inextricably interwoven, and so, at the end of the chapter we return to where we began, with the experience of death—here the death of Flannery O'Connor's Hazel Motes, the central character of her novella *Wise Blood*. Again, the Bible and its imagery saturate this work, even to the name of Motes himself, looking back to the words from the Sermon on the Mount in Matthew 7:4 (in the King James Version): "Or how wilt thou say to thy brother, Let me pull out the mote out of thine eye; and, behold, a beam is in thine own eye?" Motes dies unnoticed in the squad car with his final words, "I want to go on where I'm going," in the end disappearing into the darkness as a mere point of light in another rehearsal of the great cosmic battle between light and dark which underlies so much of the imagery of the Gospels themselves.

Death

OVID,
METAMORPHOSES

The death of Orpheus in Ovid's *Metamorphoses* may be connected with the ritual of Dionysus and the death of Pentheus as found in Euripides' tragedy *The Bacchae*. But in this dramatic narrative there are also overtones of the Christian Passion. The ritual dismemberment of the body, sometimes described by the Greek word *sparagmos*—a tearing or mangling—probably has its origins in ancient times in a fertility ritual that had as its myth a cosmogony wherein the world is created by the dismemberment of a god whose body portions are then used to form the various parts of the earth. Other examples may be found as far apart in time and place as the *Enuma Elish*, the Mesopotamian creation myth, and the *Rig Veda* of India. The motif continues to haunt modern fiction, from Russell Hoban's *Riddley Walker* to D. M. Thomas's *The White Hotel*.

In Ovid's beautiful rendering of the myth, nature itself joins in the grief initiated by the terrible death of the poet whom Apollo loved. But his death is not an end, and Orpheus is finally reunited in paradisal bliss with his beloved Eurydice.

Milton refers to the story in *Paradise Lost* (Book 7, lines 30–39).

From Metamorphoses,
Book 11, "The Death of Orpheus"

By such songs as these the Thracian poet was drawing the woods and rocks to follow him, charming the creatures of the wild, when suddenly the Ciconian women caught sight of him. Looking down from the crest of a hill, these maddened creatures, with animal skins slung across their breasts, saw Orpheus as he was singing and accompanying himself on the Lyre. One of them, tossing her hair till it streamed in the light breeze, cried out: "See! Look here! Here is the man who scorns us!" and flung her spear at the poet Apollo loved, at the lips which produced such melodies. Her weapon, tipped with leaves, left its mark, but did not wound him. Another picked up a stone, and hurled it at Orpheus: but even as it flew through the air it was charmed by the blending harmonies of voice and lyre, and fell at his feet, as if to ask pardon for so daring an assault. None the less, the women's rash attack increased in violence, till all restraint was lost, and maniac fury had them under its sway. All their weapons would have been rendered harmless by the charm of Orpheus' songs, but clamorous shouting, Phrygian flutes with curving horns, tambourines, the beating of breasts, and Bacchic howlings, drowned the music of the lyre. Then at last the stones grew crimson with the blood of the poet, whose voice they did not hear.

The first victims were the countless birds, still spell-bound by the voice of the singer, the snakes and the throng of wild animals, the audience which had brought Orpheus such renown. The frenzied women began by seizing upon these; then, with bloodstained hands, they turned on Orpheus himself, flocking together just as birds do, if they see the bird of night abroad by day. It was like the scene in an amphitheater when, for a morning's entertainment in the arena, a doomed stag is hunted down by dogs. Hurling their leaf-decked thyrsi, made for a far different purpose, the women launched the attack on the poet. Some threw sods of earth, others tore branches from the trees, others again flung stones. To provide real weapons for their mad intent, it happened that there were oxen ploughing in the fields, and not far off sturdy farmers were digging the hard ground, toiling and sweating to secure their harvest.

When the farmers saw the horde of women, they fled, leaving their imple-
ments behind, so that hoes and heavy rakes and long mattocks lay scattered
about the deserted fields. Savagely the women seized hold of these, tore apart
the oxen which threatened them with their horns, and rushed once more to
the destruction of the poet. He stretched out his hands towards his assailants,
but now, for the first time, his words had no effect, and he failed to move them
in any way by his voice. Dead to all reverence, they tore him apart and,
through those lips to which rocks had listened, which wild beasts had understood, his last breath slipped away and vanished in the wind.

The grief-stricken birds, the host of wild creatures, the flinty rocks and
the woods that had so often followed his songs, all wept for Orpheus. The
trees shed their leaves and, with bared heads, mourned his loss. Men say
that the rivers too were swollen with their own tears, and naiads and dryads
tore their hair, and pulled on black garments, over their fine robes. The
poet's limbs were scattered in different places, but the waters of the Hebrus
received his head and Lyre. Wonderful to relate, as they floated down in
midstream, the Lyre uttered a plaintive melody and the lifeless tongue made
a piteous murmur, while the river banks lamented in reply. Carried down
to the sea, they left their native river, and were washed up on the shore of
Lesbos, near Methymna. Here, as the head lay exposed on that foreign
shore, its hair dripping with beads of foam, it was attacked by a savage
snake: but Phoebus at last appeared, and checked the snake in the very act
of biting, turning its open mouth to stone, and petrifying its gaping jaws.
The ghost of Orpheus passed beneath the earth; he recognized all the
places he had seen before and, searching through the fields of the blessed,
found his Eurydice, and clasped her in eager arms. There they stroll
together, side by side: or sometimes Orpheus follows, while his wife goes
before, sometimes he leads the way and looks back, as he can do safely
now, at his Eurydice.

EMILY DICKINSON,
"BECAUSE I COULD NOT STOP FOR DEATH"

This is one of Emily Dickinson's most perfect pieces, presenting in a
series of remarkable images, and without explanation, the confrontation of
human life with immortality. We "see" without being told what to think. In
1924, the poet Conrad Aiken wrote of Dickinson and this poem: "She has
presented a typical Christian theme in its final irresolution, without making any final statements about it."

Death is mysteriously portrayed as a gentleman taking a lady out for a
drive. In its reserved way, the poem is highly erotic, making the Romantic
connection between love and death. What is particularly striking is the precision of the imagery, the drawing together of the changing scenes of the
journey (especially in stanza 3), and the gentle but menacing irony linking
these domestic pictures with what Aiken calls "the pattern of suspended
rhythm back of the poem."

As with so many of Dickinson's poems, final definition is elusive. With the poet we are invited to see, and then left to think and draw our own conclusions.

Because I could not stop for Death

> Because I could not stop for Death—
> He kindly stopped for me—
> The Carriage held but just Ourselves—
> And Immortality.
>
> We slowly drove—He knew no haste
> And I had put away
> My labor and my leisure too,
> For His Civility—
>
> We passed the School, where Children strove
> At Recess—in the Ring—
> We passed the Fields of Gazing Grain—
> We passed the Setting Sun—
>
> Or rather—He passed Us—
> The Dews drew quivering and chill—
> For only Gossamer, my Gown—
> My Tippet—only Tulle—
>
> We paused before a House that seemed
> A Swelling of the Ground—
> The Roof was scarcely visible—
> The Cornice—in the Ground—
>
> Since then—'tis Centuries—and yet
> Feels shorter than the Day
> I first surmised the Horses' Heads
> Were toward Eternity—

T. S. ELIOT,
MURDER IN THE CATHEDRAL

T. S. Eliot (1888–1965) wrote *Murder in the Cathedral* (1935) to be performed in Canterbury Cathedral, the scene of the actual murder of Archbishop Thomas Becket on December 29, 1170. To a large extent this accounts for the solemn ritualistic language and rhythms of the play, which also draw immediately on Greek tragedy (note the extended use of the Chorus) and the Vedic tradition of the *Upanishads*, with which Eliot was fascinated.

Murder in the Cathedral is self-consciously tragic theater, exploring the conflict between the values of the world—as represented by the murderous knights and King Henry II—and the values of the spirit. Becket, former royal favorite and chancellor, having become archbishop of Canterbury in a political move by the king, has now embraced the Christian faith and its spiritual values and is ready to follow Christ into martyrdom, to "suffer with his blood." He is compared by the four knights with the biblical figure of Daniel (see Daniel 6), who, having been a great favorite of King Darius, refuses to obey the king's edict that he should forgo the worship of God. Darius, like Henry II, is trapped by his own law into punishing his favorite. It is ironic, therefore, that the knights should taunt Thomas with the story of Daniel in the lions' den—a story that Thomas turns against them as he describes himself as "like a bold lion"—the victim become the victor in Christian death.

From Murder in the Cathedral

[*The door is opened. The KNIGHTS enter, slightly tipsy.*]
PRIESTS. This way, my Lord! Quick. Up the stair. To the roof.
   To the crypt. Quick. Come. Force him.
KNIGHTS. Where is Becket, the traitor to the King?
   Where is Becket, the meddling priest?
   Come down Daniel to the lions' den,
   Come down Daniel for the mark of the beast.

Are you washed in the blood of the Lamb?
   Are you marked with the mark of the beast?
   Come down Daniel to the lions' den,
   Come down Daniel and join in the feast.

Where is Becket the Cheapside brat?
   Where is Becket the faithless priest?
   Come down Daniel to the lions' den,
   Come down Daniel and join in the feast.
THOMAS. It is the just man who
   Like a bold lion, should be without fear.
   I am here.
   No traitor to the King. I am a priest,
   A Christian, saved by the blood of Christ,
   Ready to suffer with my blood.
   This is the sign of the Church always,
   The sign of blood. Blood for blood.
   His blood given to buy my life,
   My blood given to pay for His death,
   My death for His death.
FIRST KNIGHT. Absolve all those you have excommunicated.
SECOND KNIGHT. Resign the powers you have arrogated.
THIRD KNIGHT. Restore to the King the money you appropriated.
FIRST KNIGHT. Renew the obedience you have violated.

THOMAS. For my Lord I am now ready to die,
> That his Church may have peace and liberty.
> Do with me as you will, to your hurt and shame;
> But none of my people, in God's name,
> Whether layman or clerk, shall you touch.
> This I forbid.

KNIGHTS. Traitor! traitor! traitor!

THOMAS. You, Reginald, three times traitor you:
> Traitor to me as my temporal vassal,
> Traitor to me as your spiritual lord,
> Traitor to God in desecrating His Church.

FIRST KNIGHT. No faith do I owe to a renegade,
> And what I owe shall now be paid.

THOMAS. Now to Almighty God, to the Blessed Mary ever Virgin, to the blessed John the Baptist, the holy apostles Peter and Paul, to the blessed martyr Denys, and to all the Saints, I commend my cause and that of the Church.

While the KNIGHTS kill him, we hear the

CHORUS. Clear the air! clean the sky ! wash the wind! take stone from stone and wash them.
> The land is foul, the water is foul, our beasts and ourselves defiled with blood.
> A rain of blood has blinded my eyes. Where is England? where is Kent? where is Canterbury?
> O far far far far in the past; and I wander in a land of barren boughs: if I break them, they bleed; I wander in a land of dry stones: if I touch them they bleed.
> How how can I ever return, to the soft quiet seasons?
> Night stay with us, stop sun, hold season, let the day not come, let the spring not come.
> Can I look again at the day and its common things, and see them all smeared with blood, through a curtain of falling blood?
> We did not wish anything to happen.
> We understood the private catastrophe,
> The personal loss, the general misery,
> Living and partly living;
> The terror by night that ends in daily action,
> The terror by day that ends sleep;
> But the talk in the market-place, the hand on the broom,
> The night-time heaping of the ashes,
> The fuel laid on the fire at daybreak,
> These acts marked a limit to our suffering.
> Every horror had its definition,
> Every sorrow had a kind of end:
> In life there is not time to grieve long.
> But this, this is out of life, this is out of time,
> An instant eternity of evil and wrong.

We are soiled by a filth that we cannot clean, united to supernatural
   vermin,
It is not we alone, it is not the house, it is not the city that is defiled,
But the world that is wholly foul.
Clear the air! clean the sky! wash the wind! take the stone from the
   stone, take the skin from the arm, take the muscle from the bone, and
   wash them. Wash the stone, wash the bone, wash the brain, wash the
   soul, wash them wash them!

Conversion and Ecstasy

THE ACTS OF THE APOSTLES

The story of the conversion of Saul to Christianity is recounted three
times in the New Testament book, the Acts of the Apostles (9:1–31; 22:4–16;
26:12–18), and this, 9:1–31, is the longest and most dramatic of the accounts.

It has many of the classic elements of conversion stories, above all the call
to repentance after a previously ill-spent life. Saul, the Jewish persecutor of
the young Christian church, would now make a dramatic turnabout and
become the greatest of its apostles and teachers. Here the story is told with
panache and dramatic verve. After his extraordinary encounter on the road
to Damascus—the "Damascus road" has become proverbial in conversion
experiences—Saul (later renamed Paul) fasts and lives in blindness for three
days, reminiscent of the three days between the crucifixion and the resurrection, and perhaps also symbolic of Christian baptism as it follows the
death, burial, and resurrection of Jesus.

This rich and heavily symbolic narrative sets a pattern for the vast literature of conversion within the Christian tradition.

"The Conversion of Saul," Acts 9:1–31

9:1 Meanwhile Saul, still breathing threats and murder against the disciples
of the Lord, went to the high priest [2]and asked him for letters to the synagogues
at Damascus, so that if he found any who belonged to the Way, men or
women, he might bring them bound to Jerusalem. [3]Now as he was going
along and approaching Damascus, suddenly a light from heaven flashed
around him. [4]He fell to the ground and heard a voice saying to him, "Saul,
Saul, why do you persecute me?" [5]He asked, "Who are you, Lord?" The reply
came, "I am Jesus, whom you are persecuting. [6]But get up and enter the city,
and you will be told what you are to do." [7]The men who were traveling with
him stood speechless because they heard the voice but saw no one. [8]Saul got
up from the ground, and though his eyes were open, he could see nothing; so
they led him by the hand and brought him into Damascus. [9]For three days he
was without sight, and neither ate nor drank.

10 Now there was a disciple in Damascus named Ananias. The Lord said to him in a vision, "Ananias." He answered, "Here I am, Lord." [11]The Lord said to him, "Get up and go to the street called Straight, and at the house of Judas look for a man of Tarsus named Saul. At this moment he is praying, [12]and he has seen in a vision a man named Ananias come in and lay his hands on him so that he might regain his sight." [13]But Ananias answered, "Lord, I have heard from many about this man, how much evil he has done to your saints in Jerusalem; [14]and here he has authority from the chief priests to bind all who invoke your name." [15]But the Lord said to him, "Go, for he is an instrument whom I have chosen to bring my name before Gentiles and kings and before the people of Israel; [16]I myself will show him how much he must suffer for the sake of my name." [17]So Ananias went and entered the house. He laid his hands on Saul and said, "Brother Saul, the Lord Jesus, who appeared to you on your way here, has sent me so that you may regain your sight and be filled with the Holy Spirit." [18]And immediately something like scales fell from his eyes, and his sight was restored. Then he got up and was baptized, [19]and after taking some food, he regained his strength.

For several days he was with the disciples in Damascus, [20]and immediately he began to proclaim Jesus in the synagogues, saying, "He is the Son of God." [21]And all who heard him were amazed and said, "Is not this the man who made havoc in Jerusalem among those who invoked this name? And has he not come here for the purpose of bringing them bound before the chief priests?" [22]Saul became increasingly more powerful and confounded the Jews who lived in Damascus by proving that Jesus was the Messiah.

23 After some time had passed, the Jews plotted to kill him, [24]but their plot became known to Saul. They were watching the gates day and night so that they might kill him; [25]but his disciples took him by night and let him down through an opening in the wall, lowering him in a basket.

26 When he had come to Jerusalem, he attempted to join the disciples; and they were all afraid of him, for they did not believe that he was a disciple. [27]But Barnabas took him, brought him to the apostles, and described for them how on the road he had seen the Lord, who had spoken to him, and how in Damascus he had spoken boldly in the name of Jesus. [28]So he went in and out among them in Jerusalem, speaking boldly in the name of the Lord. [29]He spoke and argued with the Hellenists; but they were attempting to kill him. [30]When the believers learned of it, they brought him down to Caesarea and sent him off to Tarsus.

31 Meanwhile the church throughout Judea, Galilee, and Samaria had peace and was built up. Living in the fear of the Lord and in the comfort of the Holy Spirit, it increased in numbers.

AUGUSTINE OF HIPPO, *CONFESSIONS*

Augustine wrote his *Confessions* in the last years of the fourth century when he was about forty-three and already bishop of Hippo in North

Africa. It covers the first thirty-three years of his life and is an intense, intellectual reflection on Augustine's inner life, his "heart," or *affectus*.

Confessio meant for Augustine "accusation of oneself; praise of God." In this one word he attempted to sum up his thoughts about the human condition and the riddle of evil which lay at its heart. He describes the process of his conversion to Christianity as a conversation or wrestling with the Lord, analyzing his feelings with relentless honesty. At every point, the Bible is crucial (as it was later for Martin Luther), and the words with which he addresses God ("Lord, will you never be content?") are taken directly from the Psalms (Ps. 6:3, etc.).

From turmoil, Augustine finds a new calm in his conversion, and he turns immediately to the person who dominates his inner life throughout the *Confessions*—his mother, Monica. This fact, and the further fact that Augustine had left his mistress to whom he had been faithful for some fifteen years, give pause for thought in our post-Freudian age.

From Confessions, Book 8, Chapter 12

I probed the hidden depths of my soul and wrung its pitiful secrets from it, and when I mustered them all before the eyes of my heart, a great storm broke within me, bringing with it a great deluge of tears. I stood up and left Alypius so that I might weep and cry to my heart's content, for it occurred to me that tears were best shed in solitude. I moved away far enough to avoid being embarrassed even by his presence. He must have realized what my feelings were, for I suppose I had said something and he had known from the sound of my voice that I was ready to burst into tears. So I stood up and left him where we had been sitting, utterly bewildered. Somehow I flung myself down beneath a fig tree and gave way to the tears which now streamed from my eyes, the sacrifice that is acceptable to you. I had much to say to you, my God, not in these very words but in this strain: *Lord, will you never be content? Must we always taste your vengeance? Forget the long record of our sins.* For I felt that I was still the captive of my sins, and in my misery I kept crying "How long shall I go on saying 'tomorrow, tomorrow'? Why not now? Why not make an end of my ugly sins at this moment?"

I was asking myself these questions, weeping all the while with the most bitter sorrow in my heart, when all at once I heard the singsong voice of a child in a nearby house. Whether it was the voice of a boy or a girl I cannot say, but again and again it repeated the refrain "Take it and read, take it and read." At this I looked up, thinking hard whether there was any kind of game in which children used to chant words like these, but I could not remember ever hearing them before. I stemmed my flood of tears and stood up, telling myself that this could only be a divine command to open my book of Scripture and read the first passage on which my eyes should fall. For I had heard the story of Antony, and I remembered how he had happened to go into a church while the Gospel was being read and had taken it as a counsel addressed to himself when he heard the words *Go home and sell all that belongs to you. Give it to the poor, and so the treasure you have shall be in heaven; then come back and follow me.* By this divine pronouncement he had at once been converted to you.

So I hurried back to the place where Alypius was sitting, for when I stood up to move away I had put down the book containing Paul's Epistles. I seized it and opened it, and in silence I read the first passage on which my eyes fell: *Not in revelling and drunkenness, not in lust and wantonness, not in quarrels and rivalries. Rather, arm yourselves with the Lord Jesus Christ; spend no more thought on nature and nature's appetites.* I had no wish to read more and no need to do so. For in an instant, as I came to the end of the sentence, it was as though the light of confidence flooded into my heart and all the darkness of doubt was dispelled.

I marked the place with my finger or by some other sign and closed the book. My looks now were quite calm as I told Alypius what had happened to me. He too told me what he had been feeling, which of course I did not know. He asked to see what I had read. I showed it to him and he read on beyond the text which I had read. I did not know what followed, but it was this: *Find room among you for a man of over-delicate conscience.* Alypius applied this to himself and told me so. This admonition was enough to give him strength, and without suffering the distress of hesitation he made his resolution and took this good purpose to himself. And it very well suited his moral character, which had long been far, far better than my own.

Then we went in and told my mother, who was overjoyed. And when we went on to describe how it had all happened, she was jubilant with triumph and glorified you, *who are powerful enough, and more than powerful enough, to carry out your purpose beyond our hopes and dreams.* For she saw that you had granted her far more than she used to ask in her tearful prayers and plaintive lamentations. You converted me to yourself, so that I no longer desired a wife or placed any hope in this world but stood firmly upon the rule of faith, where you had shown me to her in a dream so many years before. And you *turned her sadness into rejoicing,* into joy far fuller than her dearest wish, far sweeter and more chaste than any she had hoped to find in children begotten of my flesh.

JAMES BALDWIN,
GO TELL IT ON THE MOUNTAIN

James Baldwin (1924–1987) was born in Harlem, and for a while in his youth was, like his father, a preacher. "The rhetoric of the store-front church" imprinted itself on his prose style long after he left the church. In his essay "Down at the Cross," Baldwin writes of how he experienced a "prolonged religious crisis" when he was fourteen, though as he describes his "conversion" he admits that he became for the first time in his life "afraid of the evil within me and afraid of the evil without." The themes of conversion remain constant from Paul to Augustine to Baldwin.

In his first novel, *Go Tell It on the Mountain* (1953), Baldwin looks back on his experiences as a boy, and re-creates them in his fictional character John

Grimes. The excerpt below is taken from early in the book and describes the Sunday morning service in the Temple of the Fire Baptized in Harlem. The prose, with its echoes of the Bible, reflects the sense of physical ecstasy in music and dance, and the fearfulness of the boy who stands apart yet feels the tangible "real presence."

In the final paragraph, which deals with the uncovering of sin, there is a sense of menace, particularly in the last sentences, looking back to Jesus' words in Mark 10:29 about the leaving of brothers, sisters, and mothers for the sake of the gospel, and the affirmation of the exclusion of the coward heart in biblical tones by the whole church.

From Go Tell It on the Mountain

The song might be: *Down at the cross where my Saviour died!*
Or: *Jesus, I'll never forget how you set me free!*
Or: *Lord, hold my hand while I run this race!* . . .

On Sunday mornings the women all seemed patient, all the men seemed mighty. While John watched, the Power struck someone, a man or woman; they cried out, a long, wordless crying, and, arms outstretched like wings, they began the Shout. Someone moved a chair a little to give them room, the rhythm paused, the singing stopped, only the pounding feet and the clapping hands were heard; then another cry, another dancer; then the tambourines began again, and the voices rose again, and the music swept on again, like fire, or flood, or judgment. Then the church seemed to swell with the Power it held, and, like a planet rocking in space, the temple rocked with the Power of God. John watched, watched the faces, and the weightless bodies, and listened to the timeless cries. One day, so everyone said, this Power would possess him; he would sing and cry as they did now, and dance before his King. He watched young Ella Mae Washington, the seventeen-year-old granddaughter of Praying Mother Washington, as she began to dance. And then Elisha danced.

At one moment, head thrown back, eyes closed, sweat standing on his brow, he sat at the piano, singing and playing; and then, like a great black cat in trouble in the jungle, he stiffened and trembled, and cried out. *Jesus, Jesus, oh Lord Jesus!* He struck on the piano one last, wild note, and threw up his hands, palms upward, stretched wide apart. The tambourines raced to fill the vacuum left by his silent piano, and his cry drew answering cries. Then he was on his feet, turning, blind, his face congested, contorted with this rage, and the muscles leaping and swelling in his long, dark neck. It seemed that he could not breathe, that his body could not contain this passion, that he would be, before their eyes, dispersed into the waiting air. His hands, rigid to the very fingertips, moved outward and back against his hips, his sightless eyes looked upward, and he began to dance. Then his hands closed into fists, and his head snapped downward, his sweat loosening the grease that slicked down his hair; and the rhythm of all the others quickened to match Elisha's rhythm; his thighs moved terribly against the cloth of his suit, his heels beat on the floor, and his fists moved beside his body as though he were beating his own drum. And so, for a while, in the centre of the dancers, head down, fists beating, on, on, unbearably, until it seemed the walls of the church would fall for very sound; and then, in a moment, with a cry, head up, arms high in the air, sweat pouring from his forehead, and all his body dancing as though it would never stop. Sometimes he did not stop until he fell—until he dropped like some animal felled by a hammer—moaning, on his face. And then a great moaning filled the church.

There was sin among them. One Sunday, when regular service was over, Father James had uncovered sin in the congregation of the righteous. He had uncovered Elisha and Ella Mae. They had been "walking disorderly"; they were in danger of straying from the truth. And as Father James spoke of the sin that he knew they had not committed yet, of the unripe fig plucked too early from the tree—to set the children's teeth on edge—John felt himself grow dizzy in his seat and could not look at Elisha where he stood, beside Ella Mae, before the altar. It was not an easy thing, said Father James, to be the pastor of a flock. It might look easy to just sit up there in the pulpit night after night, year in, year out, but let them remember the awful responsibility placed on his shoulders by almighty God—let them remember that God would ask an accounting of him one day for every soul in his flock. Let them remember this when they thought he was hard, let them remember that the Word was hard, that the way of holiness was a hard way. There was no room in God's army for the coward heart, no crown awaiting him who put mother, or father, sister, or brother, sweetheart, or friend above God's will. Let the church cry amen to this! And they cried. "Amen! Amen!"

Love and Evil

WILLIAM BUTLER YEATS, "ADAM'S CURSE"

After Adam and Eve have eaten the forbidden fruit in the Garden of Eden, the Lord God pronounces punishments on them for their disobedience (Gen. 3:16–19). To Adam he says that his lot shall be one of toil on the earth so that he might eat from what the ground produces, though "thorns and thistles" will also grow among the good food.

Yeats's early poem reflects on this curse. It is set, significantly, at "summer's end"—reminding one of the expulsion from paradise. It is a poem of love that has grown old and lost its initial innocence and happiness. It is also a reflection on the vocation of the poet—Adam, we should recall, was sent by God to establish language by the naming of the animals (Gen. 2:19–20), reminding us that the labor of the poet after the Fall in creating beauty is harder than that of the "noisy set" of those who think themselves busy. Now even to be beautiful is a labor—such is the curse of Adam.

A poem that bears comparison with this one is Thomas Hardy's "Neutral Tones" (1867).

From Adam's Curse

We sat together at one summer's end,
That beautiful mild woman, your close friend,
And you and I, and talked of poetry.
I said, "A line will take us hours maybe;
Yet if it does not seem a moment's thought,
Our stitching and unstitching has been naught." . . .

I said, "It's certain there is no fine thing
Since Adam's fall but needs much labouring.
There have been lovers who thought love should be
So much compounded of high courtesy
That they would sigh and quote with learned looks
Precedents out of beautiful old books;
Yet now it seems an idle trade enough."

We sat grown quiet at the name of love;
We saw the last embers of daylight die,
And in the trembling blue-green of the sky
A moon, worn as if it had been a shell
Washed by time's waters as they rose and fell
About the stars and broke in days and years.

JOHN MILTON,
PARADISE LOST

In the opening lines of Milton's *Paradise Lost* (1667), Satan is presented as the archangel who has been hurled from heaven because of his presumption in opposing and claiming to "equal" God. For his sin of pride he is cast into perdition, and with Beelzebub and other rebellious angels he builds his palace of Pandemonium (a word coined by Milton, meaning "all demons").

In his first speech—excerpted in full here—Satan summons his legions to revenge and eternal war against God. Later in the epic, this war will take the form of Satan's beguiling of God's innocent creation in the form of Eve. Satan—a perverted form of the heroes of classical literature—is one of the great figures of world literature. His nature is wholly committed to evil, but Milton introduces a tragic dimension into his character by revealing in him a conscience that his fellow rebels lack. Throughout the poem he is a seductive, powerful, and terrifying figure, all the more frightening in his evil as he is still capable of evoking sympathy in the reader, even though we know him to be utterly depraved.

From Paradise Lost,
Book 1, Lines 81–127

    To whom th' Arch-Enemy,
And thence in heav'n called Satan, with bold words
Breaking the horrid silence thus began:

    "If thou beest he—but O how fall'n! how changed
From him who in the happy realms of light
Clothed with transcendent brightness didst outshine
Myriads though bright—if he whom mutual league
United thoughts and counsels, equal hope
And hazard in the glorious enterprise,
Joined with me once now misery hath joined
In equal ruin: into what pit thou seest
From what highth fall'n, so much the stronger proved
He with his thunder, and till then who knew
The force of those dire arms? Yet not for those,
Nor what the potent Victor in his rage
Can else inflict, do I repent or change,
Though changed in outward luster, that fixed mind
And high disdain, from sense of injured merit,
That with the mightiest raised me to contend,
And to the fierce contention brought along
Innumerable force of Spirits armed
That durst dislike his reign, and me preferring,
His utmost power with adverse power opposed
In dubious battle: on the plains of heav'n,
And shook his throne. What though the field be lost?
All is not lost; the unconquerable will,
And study of revenge, immortal hate,
And courage never to submit or yield:
And what is else not to be overcome?
That glory never shall his wrath or might
Extort from me. To bow and sue for grace
With suppliant knee, and deify his power
Who from the terror of this arm so late
Doubted his empire, that were low indeed,
That were an ignominy and shame beneath
This downfall; since by fate the strength of gods
And this empyreal substance cannot fail,
Since through experience of this great event,
In arms not worse, in foresight much advanced,
We may with more successful hope resolve
To wage by force or guile eternal war
Irreconcilable to our grand Foe,
Who now triumphs, and in th' excess of joy
Sole reigning holds the tyranny of heav'n."

So spake th' apostate Angel, though in pain,
Vaunting aloud, but racked with deep despair . . .

ELIE WIESEL,
NIGHT

Elie Wiesel was born in Romania in 1928. Brought up in a pious Jewish household, he was deported with his family to Auschwitz and then to Buchenwald, where his parents and sister were killed. After the war, in Paris, he wrote the autobiographical *Night*, describing his experiences as a boy in the death camps. Wiesel won the Nobel Peace Prize in 1986.

In an essay introducing this work the French Catholic novelist François Mauriac wrote, "Have we ever thought about the consequence of a horror that, though less apparent, less striking than the other outrages, is yet the worst of all to those of us who have faith: the death of God in the soul of a child who suddenly discovers absolute evil?"

In the passage below, the boy Wiesel is forced to look into the face of another child who has been hanged in the camp. It is, for him, an experience of the death of God, and at the same time God becomes the accused. The overtones of the crucifixion story are clear, but there is nothing here to place a limit on the presence of evil and death. Theology is silent and the narrative stretches the imagination beyond the imaginable. Mauriac, the Christian commentator, is lost for words and concludes, "I could only embrace him, weeping."

From Night

I witnessed other hangings. I never saw a single one of the victims weep. For a long time those dried-up bodies had forgotten the bitter taste of tears.

Except once. The Oberkapo of the fifty-second cable unit was a Dutchman, a giant, well over six feet. Seven hundred prisoners worked under his orders, and they all loved him like a brother. No one had ever received a blow at his hands, nor an insult from his lips.

He had a young boy under him, a *pipel,* as they were called—a child with a refined and beautiful face, unheard of in this camp.

(At Buna, the *pipel* were loathed; they were often crueler than adults. I once saw one of thirteen beating his father because the latter had not made his bed properly. The old man was crying softly while the boy shouted: "If you don't stop crying at once I shan't bring you any more bread. Do you understand?" But the Dutchman's little servant was loved by all. He had the face of a sad angel.)

One day, the electric power station at Buna was blown up. The Gestapo, summoned to the spot, suspected sabotage. They found a trail. It eventually led to the Dutch Oberkapo. And there, after a search, they found an important stock of arms.

The Oberkapo was arrested immediately. He was tortured for a period of weeks, but in vain. He would not give a single name. He was transferred to Auschwitz. We never heard of him again.

But his little servant had been left behind in the camp in prison. Also put to torture, he too would not speak. Then the SS sentenced him to death, with two other prisoners who had been discovered with arms.

One day when we came back from work, we saw three gallows rearing up in the assembly place, three black crows. Roll call. SS all round us, machine guns trained: the traditional ceremony. Three victims in chains—and one of them, the little servant, the sad-eyed angel.

The SS seemed more preoccupied, more disturbed than usual. To hang a young boy in front of thousands of spectators was no light matter. The head of the camp read the verdict. All eyes were on the child. He was lividly pale, almost calm, biting his lips. The gallows threw its shadow over him.

This time the Lagerkapo refused to act as executioner. Three SS replaced him.

The three victims mounted together on to the chairs.

The three necks were placed at the same moment within the nooses.

"Long live liberty!" cried the two adults.

But the child was silent.

"Where is God? Where is He?" someone behind me asked.

At a sign from the head of the camp, the three chairs tipped over.

Total silence throughout the camp. On the horizon, the sun was setting.

"Bare your heads!" yelled the head of the camp. His voice was raucous. We were weeping.

"Cover your heads!"

Then the march past began. The two adults were no longer alive. Their tongues hung swollen, blue-tinged.

But the third rope was still moving, being so light, the child was still alive. . . .

For more than half an hour he stayed there, struggling between life and death, dying in slow agony under our eyes. And we had to look him full in the face. He was still alive when I passed in front of him. His tongue was still red, his eyes were not yet glazed.

Behind me, I heard the same man asking:

"Where is God now?"

And I heard a voice within me answer him:

"Where is He? Here He is—He is hanging here on this gallows. . . . "

That night the soup tasted of corpses.

Visions of the End

THE BOOK OF DANIEL

The book of Daniel was written about 170 B.C.E. and was occasioned by the persecution of the Jews by the Seleucid king Antiochus Epiphanes, who reigned from 175 to 163 B.C.E. The writer uses the persona of Daniel, a Jewish sage living in the time of the exile in Babylon, about 586–538 B.C.E. His book contains some of the most familiar stories in the Jewish Bible, including Shadrach, Meshach, and Abednego in the fiery furnace, and Daniel in the den of lions (see above, T. S. Eliot's *Murder in the Cathedral*).

Daniel 7 is one of the most important passages in the Bible. Its powerful and extraordinary imagery has found its way into both Jewish and Christian apocalyptic literature, of which perhaps the best-known example is the book of Revelation. The "one like a son of man" in verse 13 (RSV) is the origin of the words used by Jesus to the High Priest at his trial in Mark 14:62, while the figure of the ancient of days is familiar in the art and poetry of William Blake.

The message of the chapter is essentially simple. Despite persecution, God has not abandoned his people, and those who remain faithful will share the final victory of God's purpose in an end that is near. The writer draws immediately on the psalms of lament, especially 74 and 89, and behind them on the stories of the ancient Babylonian myths of creation. These fantastic pictures are an exercise in intertextuality that stretches back to the very beginnings of literature and continues energetically to the present day as we find apocalyptic images in contemporary film and literature exploring visions of the end of all things. There is, for example, a direct link between Daniel's terrible beasts and the machine horrors of the two Terminator films.

Daniel 7

1 In the first year of King Belshazzar of Babylon, Daniel had a dream and visions of his head as he lay in bed. Then he wrote down the dream: 2I, Daniel, saw in my vision by night the four winds of heaven stirring up the great sea, 3and four great beasts came up out of the sea, different from one another. 4The first was like a lion and had eagles' wings. Then, as I watched, its wings were plucked off, and it was lifted up from the ground and made to stand on two feet like a human being; and a human mind was given to it. 5Another beast appeared, a second one, that looked like a bear. It was raised up on one side, had three tusks in its mouth among its teeth and was told, "Arise, devour many bodies!" 6After this, as I watched, another appeared, like a leopard. The beast had four wings of a bird on its back and four heads; and dominion was given to it. 7After this I saw in the visions by night a fourth beast, terrifying and dreadful and exceedingly strong. It had great iron teeth and was devouring, breaking in pieces, and stamping what was left with its feet. It was different from all the beasts that had preceded it, and it had ten horns. 8I was considering the horns, when another horn appeared, a little one coming up among them; to make room for it, three of the earlier horns were plucked up by the roots. There were eyes like human eyes in this horn, and a mouth speaking arrogantly.
9   As I watched,
        thrones were set in place,
            and an Ancient One took his throne,
        his clothing was white as snow,
            and the hair of his head like pure wool;

his throne was fiery flames,
    and its wheels were burning fire.
10 A stream of fire issued
    and flowed out from his presence.
A thousand thousands served him,
    and ten thousand times ten thousand stood attending him.
The court sat in judgment,
    and the books were opened.
¹¹I watched then because of the noise of the arrogant words that the horn was speaking. And as I watched, the beast was put to death, and its body destroyed and given over to be burned with fire. ¹²As for the rest of the beasts, their dominion was taken away, but their lives were prolonged for a season and a time. ¹³As I watched in the night visions,
    I saw one like a human being
        coming with the clouds of heaven.
    And he came to the Ancient One
        and was presented before him.
¹⁴To him was given dominion
    and glory and kingship,
    that all peoples, nations, and languages
        should serve him.
His dominion is an everlasting dominion
    that shall not pass away,
    and his kingship is one
        that shall never be destroyed.

15 As for me, Daniel, my spirit was troubled within me, and the visions of my head terrified me. ¹⁶I approached one of the attendants to ask him the truth concerning all this. So he said that he would disclose to me the interpretation of the matter: ¹⁷"As for these four great beasts, four kings shall arise out of the earth. ¹⁸But the holy ones of the Most High shall receive the kingdom and possess the kingdom forever—forever and ever."

19 Then I desired to know the truth concerning the fourth beast, which was different from all the rest, exceedingly terrifying, with its teeth of iron and claws of bronze, and which devoured and broke in pieces, and stamped what was left with its feet; ²⁰and concerning the ten horns that were on its head, and concerning the other horn, which came up and to make room for which three of them fell out—the horn that had eyes and a mouth that spoke arrogantly, and that seemed greater than the others. ²¹As I looked, this horn made war with the holy ones and was prevailing over them, ²²until the Ancient One came; then judgment was given for the holy ones of the Most High, and the time arrived when the holy ones gained possession of the kingdom.

23 This is what he said: "As for the fourth beast,
    there shall be a fourth kingdom on earth
        that shall be different from all the other kingdoms;
    it shall devour the whole earth,
        and trample it down, and break it to pieces.

^{24} As for the ten horns,
   out of this kingdom ten kings shall arise,
      and another shall arise after them.
   This one shall be different from the former ones,
      and shall put down three kings.
^{25} He shall speak words against the Most High,
      shall wear out the holy ones of the Most High,
      and shall attempt to change the sacred seasons and the law;
   and they shall be given into his power
      for a time, two times, and half a time.
^{26} Then the court shall sit in judgment,
      and his dominion shall be taken away,
      to be consumed and totally destroyed.
^{27} The kingship and dominion
      and the greatness of the kingdoms under the whole heaven
      shall be given to the people of the holy ones of the Most High;
   their kingdom shall be an everlasting kingdom,
      and all dominions shall serve and obey them."
28 Here the account ends. As for me, Daniel, my thoughts greatly terrified
me, and my face turned pale; but I kept the matter in my mind.

J. G. BALLARD,
THE ATROCITY EXHIBITION

J. G. Ballard was born in Shanghai in 1930. His childhood experience as
a prisoner of the Japanese occupying forces is recounted in *Empire of the Sun*
(1984), which was filmed by Steven Spielberg. Ballard's 1960s science fiction
trilogy (*The Drowned World, The Drought, The Crystal World*) describes the
occurrence of an actual world apocalypse. But in *The Atrocity Exhibition*
(1970) he adopts an apocalyptic mode of writing which is at times unnerv-
ingly biblical in spite of its contemporary images.

The setting is a mental institution. The patients present an annual exhibition of art in which is displayed a "marked preoccupation of the paintings
with the theme of world cataclysm." The division between inner and outer
worlds breaks down, and as in earlier apocalypse, powerful images clash and
narratives disintegrate in a shocking fragmentary vision of chaos and collapse.

The selection below is from the opening pages of the book, specifically
from the author's annotated edition of 1993. Ballard's own marginal
"notes" form part of the actual text, texts feeding on texts as they have
always done in the tradition of apocalyptic writing. *The Atrocity Exhibition*
is still an uncomfortable book to read, nearly thirty years after its writing;
the visual images are so powerful that they almost block thought and defy
interpretation. Like Daniel and Revelation, it is a book that both invites and
deconstructs attempts to interpret and understand it. It simply numbs us
with its sense of utter chaos.

From The Atrocity Exhibition

Apocalypse. A disquieting feature of this annual exhibition—to which the patients themselves were not invited—was the marked preoccupation of the paintings with the theme of world cataclysm, as if these long-incarcerated patients had sensed some seismic upheaval within the minds of their doctors and nurses. As Catherine Austin walked around the converted gymnasium these bizarre images, with their fusion of Eniwetok and Luna Park, Freud and Elizabeth Taylor, reminded her of the slides of exposed spinal levels in Travis's office. They hung on the enamelled walls like the codes of insoluble dreams, the keys to a nightmare in which she had begun to play a more willing and calculated role. Primly she buttoned her white coat as Dr Nathan approached, holding his gold-tipped cigarette to one nostril. "Ah, Dr Austin . . . What do you think of them? I see there's War in Hell."

Notes Towards a Mental Breakdown. The noise from the cine-films of induced psychoses rose from the lecture theatre below Travis's office. Keeping his back to the window behind his desk, he assembled the terminal documents he had collected with so much effort during the previous months: (1) Spectro-heliogram of the sun; (2) Front elevation of balcony units, Hilton Hotel, London; (3) Transverse section through a pre-Cambrian trilobite; (4) "Chronograms," by E. J. Marey; (5) Photograph taken at noon, August 7th, 1945, of the sand-sea, Qattara Depression, Egypt; (6) Reproduction of Max Ernst's "Garden Airplane Traps"; (7) Fusing sequences for "Little Boy" and "Fat Boy," Hiroshima and Nagasaki A-Bombs. When he had finished Travis turned to the window. As usual, the white Pontiac had found a place in the crowded parking lot directly below him. The two occupants watched him through the tinted windshield.

"Eniwetok and Luna Park" may seem a strange pairing, the H-bomb test site in the Marshall Islands with the Paris fun-fair loved by the surrealists. But the endless newsreel clips of nuclear explosions that we saw on TV in the 1960s (a powerful incitement to the psychotic imagination, sanctioning *everything*) did have a carnival air, a media phenomenon which Stanley Kubrick caught perfectly at the end of *Dr Strangelove*. I imagine my mental patients conflating Freud and Liz Taylor in their Warhol-like efforts, unerringly homing in on the first signs of their doctor's nervous breakdown. *The Atrocity Exhibition*'s original dedication should have been "To the Insane." I owe them everything.

The many lists in *The Atroicty Exhibition* were produced by free association, which accounts for the repetition but, I hope, makes more sense of them. "Garden Airplane Traps." "Voracious gardens in turn devoured by a vegetation that springs from the debris of trapped airplanes." Max Ernst, *Informal Life*. The nightmare of a grounded pilot. Why a white Pontiac? A British popstar of the 1960s, Dicky Valentine, drove his daughter in a white Pontiac to the same school that my own children attended near the film studios at Shepperton. The car

The Weapons Range. Travis stopped the car at the end of the lane. In the sunlight he could see the remains of the outer perimeter fence, and beyond this a rusting quonset and the iron-stained roofs of the bunkers. He crossed the ditch and walked towards the fence, within five minutes found an opening. A disused runway moved through the grass. Partly concealed by the sunlight, the camouflage patterns across the complex of towers and bunkers four hundred yards away revealed half-familiar contours—the model of a face, a posture, a neural interval. A unique event would take place here. Without thinking, Travis murmured, "Elizabeth Taylor." Abruptly there was a blare of sound above the trees.

Dissociation: Who Laughed at Nagasaki? Travis ran across the broken concrete to the perimeter fence. The helicopter plunged towards him, engine roaring through the trees, its fans churning up a storm of leaves and paper. Twenty yards from the fence Travis stumbled among the coils of barbed wire. The helicopter was banking sharply, the pilot crouched over the controls. As Travis ran forward the shadows of the diving machine flickered around him like cryptic ideograms. Then the craft pulled away and flew off across the bunkers. When Travis reached the car, holding the torn knee of his trousers, he saw the young woman in the white dress walking down the lane. Her disfigured face looked back at him with indulgent eyes. Travis started to call to her, but stopped himself. Exhausted, he vomited across the roof of the car.

had a powerful iconic presence, emerging from all those American movies into the tranquil TV suburbs. Soon after, Valentine died in a car accident. By chance a telescoped Pontiac starred in my 1969 exhibition of crashed cars at the New Arts Laboratory in London. . . .

Weapons ranges have a special magic, all that destructive technology concentrated on the production of nothing, the closest we can get to certain obsessional states of mind. Even more strange are the bunkers of the Nazi Atlantic Wall, most of which are still standing, and are far larger than one expects. Space-age cathedrals, they threaten the surrounding landscape like lines of Teutonic knights, and are examples of cryptic architecture, where form no longer reveals function. They seem to contain the codes of some mysterious mental process. At Utah Beach, the most deserted stretch of the Normandy coast, they stare out over the washed sand, older than the planet. On visits with my agent and his wife, I used to photograph them compulsively.

SAMUEL TAYLOR COLERIDGE, "KUBLA KHAN"

The reputation of Samuel Taylor Coleridge (1772–1834) has grown in the twentieth century, and he is acknowledged to be one of the most remarkable poets, critics, and thinkers in English literature. His fragment "Kubla Khan" lies at the very heart of the Romantic movement, an extraordinary vision of mysterious and exotic images induced, it may be, by his habit of taking opium.

According to Coleridge's own preface to the poem, it derives from a dream that was disturbed by "a person on business from Porlock," a village in the West of England. Be that as it may, the poem offers an image of the poet as a terrifying, holy figure who has seen and tasted of the milk of paradise from which Adam and Eve were expelled—a glimpsed image of human origins which suggests also a dark and threatening end to all things.

"Kubla Khan"

In Xanadu did Kubla Khan
A stately pleasure-dome decree:
Where Alph, the sacred river, ran
Through caverns measureless to man
   Down to a sunless sea.
So twice five miles of fertile ground
With walls and towers were girdled round:
And here were gardens bright with sinuous rills,
Where blossomed many an incense-bearing tree;
And here were forests ancient as the hills,
Enfolding sunny spots of greenery.

But oh! that deep romantic chasm which slanted
Down the green hill athwart a cedarn cover!
A savage place! as holy and enchanted
As e'er beneath a waning moon was haunted
By woman wailing for her demon-lover!
And from this chasm, with ceaseless turmoil seething,
As if this earth in fast thick pants were breathing,
A mighty fountain momently was forced:
Amid whose swift half-intermitted burst
Huge fragments vaulted like rebounding hail,
Or chaffy grain beneath the thresher's flail:
And 'mid these dancing rocks at once and ever
It flung up momently the sacred river.
Five miles meandering with a mazy motion
Through wood and dale the sacred river ran,
Then reached the caverns measureless to man,
And sank in tumult to a lifeless ocean:
And 'mid this tumult Kubla heard from far
Ancestral voices prophesying war!
   The shadow of the dome of pleasure
   Floated midway on the waves;
   Where was heard the mingled measure
   From the fountain and the caves.
It was a miracle of rare device,
A sunny pleasure-dome with caves of ice!

A damsel with a dulcimer
In a vision once I saw:
It was an Abyssinian maid,
And on her dulcimer she played,
Singing of Mount Abora.
Could I revive within me
Her symphony and song,
To such a deep delight 'twould win me,
That with music loud and long,
I would build that dome in air,
That sunny dome! those caves of ice!
And all who heard should see them there,
And all should cry, Beware! Beware!
His flashing eyes, his floating hair!
Weave a circle round him thrice,
And close your eyes with holy dread,
For he on honey-dew hath fed,
And drunk the milk of Paradise.

FLANNERY O'CONNOR,
WISE BLOOD

Flannery O'Connor (1925–1964) was born in Milledgeville, Georgia, into an old Catholic family. Her short stories and two novels, *Wise Blood* (1952) and *The Violent Bear It Away* (1960) reflect the poor whites of the Protestant Bible Belt of Georgia and Tennessee. In the words of V. S. Prichett, her gothic stories "evoke the disordered images" in the minds of the people around her in fiction—minds that are grimly comic and haunted by the violence of their religious vision—and the grace that pursues her characters relentlessly.

In her note to the second edition of *Wise Blood* (1960), O'Connor describes the central character, Hazel Motes, as a "Christian *malgré lui*" whose "integrity lies in his trying with such vigor to get rid of the ragged figure who moves from tree to tree in the back of his mind." For the author, she continues, "Hazel's integrity lies in his not being able to do so."

The characters of the novel are not rounded figures, but bear the characteristics of their names. Motes is a reference to the scriptural image of the mote and the beam (Matt. 7:3 and Luke 6:41). The passage below is the last few paragraphs of the novel. Hazel has finally blinded himself and "sees" the grace that has been pursuing him throughout the novel. In his death he is freed from the world in which he has been haunted by Christ and finally becomes only a "pin point of light." "Freedom cannot be conceived simply," wrote O'Connor. "It is a mystery and one which a novel, even a comic novel, can only be asked to deepen."

From Wise Blood

"You reckon he's daid?" the first one asked.

"Ast him," the other said.

"No, he ain't daid. He's moving."

"Maybe he's just unconscious," the latter one said, taking out his new billy. They watched him for a few seconds. His hand was moving along the edge of the ditch as if it were hunting something to grip. He asked them in a hoarse whisper where he was and if it was day or night.

"It's day," the thinner one said, looking at the sky. "We got to take you back to pay your rent."

"I want to go on where I'm going," the blind man said.

"You got to pay your rent first," the policeman said. "Ever' bit of it!"

The other, perceiving that he was conscious, hit him over the head with his new billy. "We don't want to have no trouble with him," he said. "You take his feet."

He died in the squad car but they didn't notice and took him on to the land-lady's. She had them put him on her bed and when she had pushed them out the door, she locked it behind them and drew up a straight chair and sat down close to his face where she could talk to him. "Well, Mr. Motes," she said, "I see you've come home!"

His face was stern and tranquil. "I knew you'd come back," she said. "And I've been waiting for you. And you needn't to pay any more rent but have it free here, any way you like, upstairs or down. Just however you want it and with me to wait on you, or if you want to go on somewhere, we'll both go."

She had never observed his face more composed and she grabbed his hand and held it to her heart. It was resistless and dry. The outline of a skull was plain under his skin and the deep burned eye sockets seemed to lead into the dark tunnel where he had disappeared. She leaned closer and closer to his face, looking deep into them, trying to see how she had been cheated or what had cheated her, but she couldn't see anything. She shut her eyes and saw the pin point of light but so far away that she could not hold it steady in her mind. She felt as if she were blocked at the entrance of something. She sat staring with her eyes shut, into his eyes, and felt as if she had finally got to the beginning of something she couldn't begin, and she saw him moving farther and farther away, farther and farther into the darkness until he was the pin point of light.

FURTHER READING

Ahearn, Edward J. *Visionary Fictions: Apocalyptic Writing from Blake to the Modern Age.* New Haven, Conn.: Yale University Press, 1996.

Berger, Alan L. *Children of Job: American Second-Generation Witnesses to the Holocaust.* Albany: State University of New York Press, 1997.

Bull, Malcolm, ed. *Apocalypse Theory and the Ends of the World.* Oxford and Cambridge, Mass.: Basil Blackwell Publisher, 1995.

Collins, John J., *The Apocalyptic Imagination: An Introduction to the Jewish Matrix of Christianity.* New York: Crossroad, 1987.

Detweiler, Robert. "Apocalyptic Fiction and the End(s) of Realism." In *European Literature and Theology in the Twentieth Century,* ed. David Jasper and Colin Crowder. London: Macmillan, 1990.

Fried, Lewis, ed. *Handbook of American-Jewish Literature: An Analytical Guide to Topics, Themes, and Sources.* New York: Greenwood Press, 1988.

Haynes, Stephen R. *Reluctant Witnesses: Jews and the Christian Imagination.* London: Macmillan; Louisville, Ky: Westminster John Knox Press, 1995.

Ingebretsen, Ed. *Maps of Heaven, Maps of Hell: Religious Terror as Memory from the Puritans to Stephen King.* Armonk, N.Y.: M. E. Sharpe, 1996.

Macquarrie, John. *Principles of Christian Theology.* New York: Charles Scribner's Sons, 1981; first edition, London, 1966.

Montgomery, Maxine Lavon. *The Apocalypse in African-American Fiction.* Gainesville: University Press of Florida, 1996.

O'Connor, Flannery. *Mystery and Manners: Occasional Prose.* New York: Farrar, Straus & Giroux, 1969.

Paul, Leslie. *Springs of Good and Evil: Biblical Themes in Literature.* London: Bible Reading Fellowship, 1979.

Plank, Karl A. *Mother of the Wire Fence: Inside and Outside the Holocaust.* Louisville, Ky.: Westminster John Knox Press, 1994.

Williams, Raymond. *Modern Tragedy.* Stanford, Calif.: Stanford University Press, 1966.

Wójcik, Daniel. *The End of the World as We Know It: Faith, Fatalism, and Apocalypse in America.* New York: New York University Press, 1997.

8

Interactions: New Challenges to and from Other Fields

Literature and religion, it should be clear by now, is a field of study which is notoriously hard to pin down and define. Much of the material with which we have been concerned looks back to a great tradition at the heart of which lies the Bible. Now we look at some of the ways forward, links that this study might forge with other disciplines and ways in which its concerns might grow and develop. This chapter addresses some recent theories and practices of interpretation important for literary-religious study as well as some key global-political issues crucial to such study. Inevitably, and as in previous chapters, we have had to be highly selective.

We begin with what we have described as the sociopolitics of the body, race, sexuality, and age. The "body" has become a central issue in contemporary literature and criticism, giving rise to all these concerns within the context of a culture that still focuses, often unconsciously, on the themes of biblical theology, is concerned with the historical background of racial problems in the history of slavery, and has only recently begun to face seriously the implications of gender and its difficulty of definition. Above all, perhaps, we have still to come to terms with the sense that we are an age that, almost uniquely in Western cultures, understands itself, sadly or gladly, as living its life after God, in the aftermath of Nietzsche's resounding proclamation of the death of God in *Also Sprach Zarathustra* (1883–92). We begin with Michèle Roberts's *The Wild Girl*, a novel that explores sexuality and women's spirituality in the context of a "fifth Gospel" of Mary Magdalene.

In the second section we turn to the question of science in the post-Einsteinian age and its effect on the paradigms of literature and the slow encroachment of these into theological and religious thought. Italo Calvino's *Cosmicomics* is a highly amusing account of the universe as a great cosmic joke, introducing the themes of randomness and relativity through a fiction that draws upon the traditions of the surreal, the parable and riddle and the subversive nature of storytelling. Far more somber and serious is the reflection of Tamiki Hara, a Hiroshima survivor, and his vision of the future after the deadly splitting of the atom. Shortly after writing this, Hara committed suicide. Finally, Mark C. Taylor's *Nots*, in this section entitled "Science," mixes liturgy with poetry and philosophy to bring the many-sided conversation into a self-consciously postmodern context.

155

Thus, the third section, "Intermediality," signals the profound interdisciplinarity that inevitably ensues from the study of literature and religion. Those who have been long concerned with this study have come to acknowledge that the critical discussion must also address issues in the other arts, such as the musical and the visual, and that once certain barriers and restrictions in discussions have been broken down, others must follow. We can no longer claim to reside comfortably within our academic expertise as the business of religious discourse haunts every aspect of our lives and experience. Thus, we deliberately begin this section with that most difficult and iconoclastic of musicians and poets, John Cage, who was influenced by figures in the twentieth century as diverse as Arnold Schoenberg, Juan Miro, Max Ernst, Marshall McLuhan, and Buckminster Fuller. In his long poem "Overpopulation and Art," from which we have taken an excerpt, Cage demonstrates how his ideas of aesthetics are highly liturgical and communal. Drawing on biblical images, Cage's poem is also a visual experience, requiring us to *see* the writing as well as to understand its verbal "meaning." It is one of the themes of art historian Leo Steinberg's extraordinary study, *The Sexuality of Christ in Renaissance Art*, that images may "start from no preformed programme to become primary texts." In other words, exploring what has been described as the "word-image opposition," Steinberg reminds us that theological and religious reflection does not necessarily arise immediately and only from the word, but may come also from an experience of art which has not been previously enscripted, but which prompts a literary and religious thinking often blurred or hidden by the verbal priorities of our "modern oblivion."

And so we move to our final section, appropriately concerned with the postmodern in fiction and literature. Discussions and definitions of the postmodern now fill whole libraries, and conclusions remain, necessarily and absurdly, elusive. Our two excerpts from the writers Samuel Beckett and Edmond Jabès, embedded deeply in different European traditions, cut across boundaries of sense and limits of propriety. How can we tell, with all our sophistications of theology and critical thought, the difference between the laughter of the angels and the laughter of the devil, for "we have no word to tell one from the other"? Words in postmodernity have become slippery and unstable—that which was in the beginning and which has been proclaimed through two millennia of Christianity and more is now perceived as uncertain, its discourses merging and beyond hermeneutic reason. Thus we finish with a brief image of two poets in the Jewish tradition, Celan and Edmond Jabès, facing each other in a conversation that moves beyond words and into a questioning of self, in a loss of confidence which lies at the heart of the postmodern.

So, we end with a question mark, and an open book. Perhaps the important thing for the serious student of religion and literature is that questions are asked and that awkward, embarrassing, and even unlikely eventualities are faced—for this may be the way that the deepest issues of religion may be uncovered, even more than through the traditional methods and places of church, liturgy, or sermon.

Sociopolitics of the Body, Race, Sexuality, and Age

MICHÈLE ROBERTS,
THE WILD GIRL

Michele Roberts was born in 1949 and is part English, part French. A poet, playwright, and novelist, perhaps her best-known work to date is *The Wild Girl* (1984), a kind of fifth Gospel written by Mary Magdalene. She uses the figure of Mary to explore themes of the body and sexuality in the Gospel tradition, commenting in her Note at the beginning of the book: "A narrative novel creates a myth in the same way [as the Gospels]. I wanted to dissect a myth; I found myself at the same time recreating one."

The brief extract given here is taken from the end of Mary's narrative, when she is reflecting back on her life as a prostitute, as the lover of Jesus, and her attempt to build an "enclosed garden" of love. God's call, however, is different and demands an absolute obedience. As a feminist writer exploring issues in women's spirituality, Roberts leaves the tensions between body and the spiritual life unresolved at the conclusion of her novel.

From The Wild Girl

The sound of my own voice woke me up.

There was no mother. There was no unity. The dream of harmony shattered the pieces like an earthenware jar thrown across the floor of my room. A clay envelope broken, the edges of true words jagged and sharp, incomprehensible. And no healing unguent inside, to flow out and heal me. Just odd words in pieces. Fragmented memories and desires.

I could not lie still. I got up, and went to the door and looked into our little courtyard, to reassure myself where I was. Then I knelt down and tried to pray. But the past, all my memories of cruelty and torment, which I had sought to bury and transform into a safe, enclosed garden of fruit and flowers, thrust themselves upwards like weeds, broke through my green hedge and threatened to spoil my harvests. And the visions in the dream pulled at my hair and fingertips and would not let go.

Dawn glimmered at the window. The light beckoned me outside. I sat in the dewy grass under the apricot tree. I tried to face this new summons, God calling me to finish my book and to leave my home, my earthly paradise, and to travel anew, through cities and deserts and the wilderness, to proclaim the Word. I wept and groaned. For all my fine words before my dreams, I did not feel ready for this great change, did not wish to accept it.

Your will be done, God, I shouted eventually.

Then I went inside to make breakfast.

157

TONI MORRISON,
BELOVED

Toni Morrison (b. 1931) grew up in Ohio and studied at both Howard University and Cornell University. Since then she has taught at SUNY (State University of New York) at Albany, and most recently at Princeton University. In 1993 she became the first black American to win the Nobel Prize for Literature. Her novels include *The Bluest Eye* (1970), *Song of Solomon* (1977), *Tar Baby* (1981), *Jazz* (1992), and *Beloved* (1987)—excerpted below—which won a Pulitzer Prize. She also writes drama and literary criticism.

In an interview Morrison has spoken of the necessity to "reinhabit" the lives of slaves and former slaves in America. *Beloved* does this by telling the story of Sethe and her daughter, who is known as "Beloved." At the beginning of the novel is a Bible verse, Romans 9:25: "I will call them my people, which were not my people; and her beloved, which was not beloved." The biblical writer of this passage is Paul, who is rephrasing a verse from Hosea 2:23. Just as Paul reappropriates this older verse, so Morrison reappropriates the same Bible verse that was used to justify slavery. By telling the story of Sethe and Beloved she is also retelling the story of a people "which were not my people," reclaiming a "lost" people.

The term used by Morrison to accomplish this reappropriation throughout *Beloved* is "rememory." Rememories are something like memories that exist outside a person's memory; they have an existence on their own. Thus, in the story, the daughter Beloved is dead but comes back into existence and inhabits the life of her mother and sister in an altogether real way. The epilogue excerpted below hints at *Beloved*'s use of memory and forgetting, of the rememory of storytelling and its ability to put back together what was fragmented and dismembered.

From Beloved

There is a loneliness that can be rocked. Arms crossed, knees drawn up; holding, holding on, this motion, unlike a ship's, smooths and contains the rocker. It's an inside kind—wrapped tight like skin. Then there is a loneliness that roams. No rocking can hold it down. It is alive, on its own. A dry and spreading thing that makes the sound of one's own feet going seem to come from a far-off place.

Everybody knew what she was called, but nobody anywhere knew her name. Disremembered and unaccounted for, she cannot be lost because no one is looking for her, and even if they were, how can they call her if they don't know her name? Although she has claim, she is not claimed. In the place where long grass opens, the girl who waited to be loved and cry shame erupts into her separate parts, to make it easy for the chewing laughter to swallow her all away.

It was not a story to pass on.

They forgot her like a bad dream. After they made up their tales, shaped and decorated them, those that saw her that day on the porch quickly and deliberately forgot her. It took longer for those who had spoken to her, lived with her, fallen in love with her, to forget, until they realized they couldn't remember or repeat a single thing she said, and began to believe that, other than what they themselves were thinking, she hadn't said anything at all. So, in the end, they forgot her too. Remembering seemed unwise. They never knew where or why she crouched, or whose was the underwater face she needed like that. Where the memory of the smile under her chin might have been and was not, a latch latched and lichen attached its apple-green bloom to the metal. What made her think her fingernails could open locks the rain rained on?

It was not a story to pass on.

So they forgot her. Like an unpleasant dream during a troubling sleep. Occasionally, however, the rustle of a skirt hushes when they wake, and the knuckles brushing a cheek in sleep seem to belong to the sleeper. Sometimes the photograph of a close friend or relative looked at too long—shifts, and something more familiar than the dear face itself moves there. They can touch it if they like, but don't, because they know things will never be the same if they do.

This is not a story to pass on.

Down by the stream in back of 124 her footprints come and go, come and go. They are so familiar. Should a child, an adult place his feet in them, they will fit. Take them out and they disappear again as though nobody ever walked there.

By and by all trace is gone, and what is forgotten is not only the footprints but the water too and what it is down there. The rest is weather. Not the breath of the disremembered and unaccounted for, but wind in the eaves, or spring ice thawing too quickly. Just weather. Certainly no clamor for a kiss.

Beloved.

AUDRE LORDE,
"SISTER OUTSIDER"

Audre Lorde (1934–1992) published nine volumes of poetry, all concerned with themes of politics, sexuality, and race. She writes as a black woman, mother, lesbian, feminist, and visionary. Throughout, her lyricism calls for changes in attitudes in all these areas of human experience, in rhythms that are often more oral than literary and link her verse with a universal poetics. Above all, as in the poem here quoted, Lorde sustains a hopefulness and a sense that things will change for the better, in spite of all and in the face of all discouragement.

Sister Outsider

We were born in a poor time
never touching
each other's hunger
never
sharing our crusts
in fear
the bread became enemy.

Now we raise our children
to respect themselves
as well as each other.

Now you have made loneliness
holy and useful
and no longer needed
now
your light shines very brightly
but I want you
to know
your darkness also
rich
and beyond fear.

DOUGLAS COUPLAND,
LIFE AFTER GOD

Douglas Coupland (b. 1961) is best known for his 1991 book, *Generation X*, a book that helped define a generation that had been undefinable (hence, the "X" in the title). He was born on a Canadian NATO base in Baden-Söllingen, Germany, but has spent most of his life in Vancouver, Canada. Since his first book, he has written several unorthodox novels in an attempt to express life in contemporary culture. As the youngest author anthologized here, Coupland's inclusion may be seen as bringing to light certain questions of generational difference and how this affects the status of religion and literature.

Life after God might be considered a follow-up to *Generation X*. It describes the peculiarities of life in Western society after major institutions such as religion have disappeared. Coupland portrays a life without boundaries, only seemingly to come to the end of the book and claim a need for some structure. Both the dangers and the excitements of freedom, of life without structures, are given expression in Coupland's book. The excerpt below, from the final chapter in the book, becomes a quasi-confessional statement about what it's like to live a "life after God." A swimming pool, "the temperature of blood," is a place to play, a place of freedom, but in the final words it becomes a hoped-for return to a warm, secure place.

From Life after God,
1,000 Years (Life after God)

As suburban children we floated at night in swimming pools the temperature of blood; pools the color of Earth as seen from outer space. We would skinny-dip, my friends and me—hip-chick Stacey with her long yellow hair and Malibu Barbie body; Mark, our silent strongman; Kristy, our omni-freckled redheaded joke machine; voice-of-reason Julie, with the "statistically average" body; honey-bronze ski bum, Dana, with his nonexistent tan line and suspiciously large amounts of cash, and Todd, the prude, always last to strip, even then peeling off his underwear underneath the water. We would float and be naked—pretending to be embryos, pretending to be fetuses—all of us silent save for the hum of the pool filter. Our minds would be blank and our eyes closed as we floated in warm waters, the distinction between our bodies and our brains reduced to nothing—bathed in chlorine and lit by pure blue lights installed underneath diving boards. Sometimes we would join hands and form a ring like astronauts in space; sometimes when we felt more isolated in our fetal stupor we would bump into each other in the deep end, like twins with whom we didn't even know we shared a womb. . . .

Life was charmed but without politics or religion. It was the life of children of the children of the pioneers—life after God—a life of earthly salvation on the edge of heaven. Perhaps this is the finest thing to which we may aspire, the life of peace, the blurring between dream life and real life—and yet I find myself speaking these words with a sense of doubt.

I think there was a trade-off somewhere along the line. I think the price we paid for our golden life was an inability to fully believe in love; instead we gained an irony that scorched everything it touched. And I wonder if this irony is the price we paid for the loss of God.

But then I must remind myself we are living creatures—we have religious impulses—we *must*—and yet into what cracks do these impulses flow in a world without religion? It is something I think about every day. Sometimes I think it is the only thing I should be thinking about. . . .

Now here is my secret:
I tell it to you with an openness of heart that I doubt I shall ever achieve again, so I pray that you are in a quiet room as you hear these words. My secret is that I need God—that I am sick and can no longer make it alone. I need God to help me give, because I no longer seem to be capable of giving; to help me be kind, as I no longer seem capable of kindness; to help me love, as I seem beyond being able to love.

I walk deeper and deeper into the rushing water. My testicles pull up into myself. The water enters my belly button and it freezes my chest, my arms, my neck. It reaches my mouth, my nose, my ears and the roar is so loud—this roar, this clapping of hands.

These hands—the hands that heal; the hands that hold; the hands we desire because they are better than desire.

I submerge myself in the pool completely. I grab my knees and I forget gravity and I float within the pool and yet, even here, I hear the roar of water, the roar of clapping hands.

These hands the hands that care, the hands that mold; the hands that touch the lips, the lips that speak the words—the words that tell us we are whole.

Science

ITALO CALVINO,
"ALL AT ONE POINT"

Italo Calvino (1923–1985) was born in Cuba, grew up in San Remo, Italy, and studied in Turin. Working as a journalist, he first wrote fiction of a political nature. His later fiction has been compared with the "magic realism" of Jorge Luis Borges (see above, chapter 5), playing with ideas of time and space, the nature of the text and reading, and exploring the conundrums of contemporary science. His works include *Invisible Cities* (1972), *If on a Winter's Night a Traveller* (1979), and *Mr. Palomar* (1983), this last collection exploring the tiniest fragments and details of experience.

In his unfinished Eliot Norton Lectures of 1984, Calvino wrote: "My confidence in the future of literature consists in the knowledge that there are things that only literature can give us, by means specific to it." The lectures concentrate on five "values, qualities, or peculiarities of literature"—lightness, quickness, exactitude, visibility, and multiplicity. The extract below is from his collection of stories entitled *Cosmicomics* (1965) and was originally published in *Playboy* magazine. Using scientific symbols as names for his "characters," Calvino takes us back to the "time" before time and the "big bang," playing with the paradoxes of space using absurd images of sociability, relationships, and sexuality as constructions of what we have come to call our reality.

From *"All at One Point"*

Through the calculations begun by Edwin P. Hubble on the galaxies' velocity of recession, we can establish the moment when all the universe's matter was concentrated in a single point, before it began to expand in space.

Naturally, we were all there,—*old Qfwfq said,*—where else could we have been? Nobody knew then that there could be space. Or time either: what use did we have for time, packed in there like sardines?

I say "packed like sardines," using a literary image: in reality there wasn't even space to pack us into. Every point of each of us coincided with every point of each of the others in a single point, which was where we all were. In fact, we didn't even bother one another, except for personality differences, because when space doesn't exist, having somebody unpleasant like Mr. Pber^t Pber^d underfoot all the time is the most irritating thing.

How many of us were there? Oh, I was never able to figure that out, not even approximately. To make a count, we would have had to move apart, at least a little, and instead we all occupied that same point. Contrary to what you might think, it wasn't the sort of situation that encourages sociability; I know, for example, that in other periods neighbors called on one another; but there, because of the fact that we were all neighbors, nobody even said good morning or good evening to anybody else. . . .

It was what you might call a narrow-minded attitude, our outlook at that time, very petty. The fault of the environment in which we had been reared. An attitude that, basically, has remained in all of us, mind you: it keeps cropping up even today, if two of us happen to meet—at the bus stop, in a movie house, at an international dentists' convention—and start reminiscing about the old days. We say hello—at times somebody recognizes me, at other times I recognize somebody—and we promptly start asking about this one and that one (even if each remembers only a few of those remembered by the others), and so we start in again on the old disputes, the slanders, the denigrations. Until somebody mentions Mrs. Ph(i)Nk$_0$—every conversation finally gets around to her—and then, all of a sudden, the pettiness is put aside, and we feel uplifted, filled with a blissful, generous emotion. Mrs. Ph(i)Nk$_0$, the only one that none of us has forgotten and that we all regret. Where has she ended up? I have long since stopped looking for her: Mrs. Ph(i)Nk$_0$, her bosom, her thighs, her orange dressing gown—we'll never meet her again, in this system of galaxies or in any other. . . .

Mrs. Ph(i)Nk$_0$'s great secret is that she never aroused any jealousy among us. Or any gossip, either. The fact that she went to bed with her friend, Mr. De XuaeauX, was well known. But in a point, if there's a bed, it takes up the whole point, so it isn't a question of *going* to bed, but of *being* there, because anybody in the point is also in the bed. Consequently, it was inevitable that she should be in bed also with each of us. If she had been another person, there's no telling all the things that would have been said about her. It was the cleaning woman who always started the slander, and the others didn't have to be coaxed to imitate her. On the subject of the Z'zu family—for a change!—the horrible things we had to hear: father, daughters, brothers, sisters, mother, aunts: nobody showed any hesitation even before the most sinister insinuation. But with her it was different: the happiness I derived from her was the joy of being concealed, punctiform, in her, and of protecting her, punctiform, in me; it was at the same time vicious contemplation (thanks to the promiscuity of the punctiform convergence of us all in her) and also chastity (given her punctiform impenetrability). In short: what more could I ask?

And all of this, which was true of me, was true also for each of the others. And for her: she contained and was contained with equal happiness, and she welcomed us and loved and inhabited all equally.

We got along so well all together, so well that something extraordinary was bound to happen. It was enough for her to say, at a certain moment: "Oh, if I only had some room, how I'd like to make some noodles for you boys." And in that moment we all thought of the space that her round arms would occupy, moving backward and forward with the rolling pin over the dough, her bosom leaning over the great mound of flour and eggs which cluttered the wide board while her arms kneaded and kneaded, white and shiny with oil up to the elbows; we thought of the space that the flour would occupy, and the wheat for the flour, and the fields to raise the wheat, and the mountains from which the water would flow to irrigate the fields, and the grazing lands for the herds of calves that would give their meat for the sauce; of the space it would take for the Sun to arrive with its rays, to ripen the wheat; of the space for the Sun to condense from the clouds of stellar gases and burn; of the quantities of stars

163

and galaxies and galactic masses in flight through space which would be needed to hold suspended every galaxy, every nebula, every sun, every planet, and at the same time we thought of it, this space was inevitably being formed, at the same time that Mrs. Ph(i)Nk$_0$ was uttering those words: ". . . ah, what noodles, boys!" the point that contained her and all of us was expanding in a halo of distance in light-years and light-centuries and billions of light-millennia, and we were being hurled to the four corners of the universe (Mr. Pber^t Pber^d all the way to Pavia), and she, dissolved into I don't know what kind of energy-light-heat, she, Mrs. Ph(i)Nk$_0$, she who in the midst of our closed, petty world had been capable of a generous impulse, "Boys, the noodles I would make for you!," a true outburst of general love, initiating at the same moment the concept of space and, properly speaking, space itself, and time, and universal gravitation, and the gravitating universe, making possible billions and billions of suns, and of planets, and fields of wheat, and Mrs. Ph(i)Nk$_0$s, scattered through the continents of the planets, kneading with floury, oil-shiny, generous arms, and she lost at that very moment, and we, mourning her loss.

TAMIKI HARA,
"THE LAND OF HEART'S DESIRE"

Tamiki Hara (1905–1951) was born in Hiroshima. He wrote poetry from his school days. In 1945 he was exposed to the atomic bomb dropped on Hiroshima, but he survived. He wrote his finest work after this experience but committed suicide in 1951.

The work from which this extract is taken, *Shingan no Kuni* (The Land of Heart's Desire) is anthologized by the Japanese Nobel prize-winning author Kenzaburó Ōe in a collection of Japanese stories about Hiroshima and Nagasaki, *Fire from the Ashes*. Ōe wrote of Hara: "The work he left behind . . . is filled with profound insights for us who must continue to live in the nuclear age. Machine-centered civilization, having introduced nuclear devastation, then pushed forward madly along a course of development fueled by nuclear energy. Toward this vigorous pursuit—that could lead to global annihilation and, in any case, faces an 'unknowable future'—Hara harbored profound misgivings."

From "The Land of Heart's Desire"

I am drifting off to sleep when a sudden shock like lightning strikes my head, which unfolds in an explosion. A sharp spasm seizes my body, then all is still, as though nothing had happened. Opening wide my eyes, I check over my senses: nothing seems to be wrong. What was it then that, independently of my conscious will, had made me explode just now? Where did it come from? *Where?* I don't really know. . . . Could it be all the countless things I have failed to do in my life, bottled up inside me till they exploded? Or could it be the memory of that moment on the morning of the atomic bomb, coming back to assault me after all these years? I cannot really say. So far as I know the horror of Hiroshima did not affect me mentally. Could it be, though, that the shock of that time has been constantly eyeing me and my fellow victims from a distance, awaiting its chance to drive us mad?

Sleepless in bed, I summon up a vision of the earth. The night cold creeps shuddering into my bed. . . Why should I be so utterly chilled as this, my body, my existence, my innermost self? I decide to appeal to the earth that gave me being. And dimly, a vision of the earth rises up within me. O wretched globe! O warmthless earth!—Yet this, it seems, is the earth millions of years hence, an earth of which I have as yet no knowledge. And before my eyes there arises, a dim mass, another earth. At the very heart of its sphere, a mass of crimson fire simmers and whirls. What could exist inside a furnace such as that? Substances yet undiscovered, mysteries yet unconceived—such things might well be mingled there. And what will happen to our world when these things spew out, all at once, onto the earth's surface?

All men, I feel sure, have their own vision of the treasures stored beneath the earth, as they face their unknowable future, with its destruction, its salvation . . . I myself have long cherished a vision of an age when harmony would come to the earth, when deep in men's hearts would sound the quiet murmur of a spring, and there would be nothing to snuff out individual existences any more.

MARK C. TAYLOR,
NOTS

Mark C. Taylor (b. 1945) is one of the most influential theologians alive today. Taylor teaches at Williams College, Massachusetts, and since the early 1980s has written a number of books that have come to define "postmodern theology." His 1984 book, *Erring: A Postmodern A/theology*, has become the starting point for almost every work of theological writing attempting to deal with the current "postmodern" culture. In *Erring* Taylor claimed that the move into postmodern theology entails (1) the death of God, (2) the disappearance of the self, (3) the end of history, and (4) the closing of the book. Since then he has gone on to express an "a/theology"; that is, not simply a theology without God, but a theology that leaves open the question of God. To do this Taylor has turned to literature and the arts and found strong points of expression for postmodern theology there.

In the excerpt below from his 1994 book *Nots*, Taylor moves into a poetic style that tells of his own experience of giving himself insulin injections. The experience, through the poetic style of writing infused with religious language, becomes a liturgical experience.

From Nots

I remember all too well (how could I ever forget?) the first time I suffered by my own hand the wound of a syringe. It was not the pain I dreaded, though there was that, but the violence, the violation of my body. Its wounding, puncture, bleeding; the injection of a foreign, synthetic, artificial agent. I felt that I was betraying the body that had betrayed me. Wound upon wound, betrayal upon betrayal. What would it all solve? What would it cure? I drew the syringe slowly, carefully, deliberately, and watched the mesmerizing trickle of the chemical substance. Numbers and lines, small numbers and fine lines. Always fine lines that must not be crossed. A mistake, a misreading, a miscalculation could prove fatal. When the agents reached the proper line on the syringe, I paused long enough to forget what I had to do. Then with a suddenness that startled me, I sank the needle into my flesh, deep into my flesh, and emptied the contents of the syringe into my body. Much to my surprise, I felt *nothing*—no pain, no pleasure, no relief. Nothing but a slight trace of blood marked the site of my transgression. The text of the body can be read in the silent trace of blood.

Now there was nothing left to do but to wait. Doing nothing is never easy, and never more so than when waiting for test results. Distractions do not distract, diversions fail to divert. In the midst of the noise around me, all I could hear was the silence of the telephone whose ring promised a message I hoped would never arrive. When tests are vital, uncertainty is not always to be feared and certainty not always desired. Sometimes the only thing more terrifying than uncertainty is certainty itself.

"Yes, I see.
I understand.
No, no, I'll be alright.
No need for that.
At least, not now.
Thank you.
Goodbye."

Names and numbers that only yesterday I had never heard today are a matter of health and sickness, life and death. When all is said and done, it comes down to codes and numbers—input and output, positive and negative feedback, communication and miscommunication. Pluses and minuses do not cancel each other, input and output never balance. Thus, messages inevitably fail to arrive or arrive mistakenly. It makes no difference. God, it seems, is no mathematician or geometer, and the world is no book waiting to be read. My body, which, of course, is not my own, is a text that remains unreadable for me as well as the others who watch over it. Numbers, angles, things never add up; they are never right—never have been, never will be right. There is irony—bitter irony—in the numbers inscribed on the syringe. The more careful I am to be sure I do not make a mistake, the more I realize that mistakes are unavoidable; the more I struggle to achieve "reasonable control," the more I am forced to admit that control is neither reasonable nor possible. *Things are always out of control.*

In time, it all becomes ritualized, which is not to say regularized. The pulse of life as well as disease: fluids flowing in and out, out and in. Insulin in, blood out; codes and numbers in, codes and numbers out. Rituals are often violent and bloody. There is something hypnotic, even addictive, about the ritual of a syringe: the care for the instruments, the deliberateness of the preparation, the solemnity of the administration. As in any ritual worth repeating, there is a moment when death draws near. In this moment, the fluid, the sacred fluid of life, can quickly become fatal—a few more numbers, a few more lines, a few more drops. The ritual turns on the point of excess and control: too much and/or too little, never just enough, never equilibrium, never harmony. To stop or to go on? And what would it be to stop? Or to go on? When the impossibility of control becomes overwhelming—and it does become overwhelming—the excess of death is no more fearful than the painless prick of a sharp needle. Would it really be a betrayal to betray the body that has always already betrayed me?

"This is my body
broken"

Nothing ever balances . . . *nothing ever balances.* Betrayal is unavoidable, cure impossible. Disease is neither a mode of being nor of nonbeing but is a way of being not without not being. The dilemma, the abiding dilemma to which we are forever destined, is to live not.

Intermediality

JOHN CAGE, "OVERPOPULATION AND ART"

John Cage (1912–1992) was one of the twentieth century's greatest avant-garde artists. He was foremost a music composer, but his theories and practices of music cannot be separated from his work as a visual artist, poet, philosopher, and cultural critic. Cage grew up in Los Angeles, where as a teenager he wanted to be a minister in the Methodist Episcopal church as his grandfather had been. Instead, he entered Pomona College at the age of sixteen, dropped out at age eighteen, and set off for a travel and "independent study" time in Europe. While in Europe he immersed himself in the artistic traditions of the continent and practiced and studied painting, poetry, and architecture, and he began to learn music. When he returned to the United States, Cage studied with Arnold Schoenberg (who had emigrated to the United States), and he began to meet other artists who together had a profound impact on the arts in general in the twentieth century.

Later in Cage's life he turned to the practices of Zen Buddhism and incorporated Zen concepts into his life and work. Even in the short passage that follows, which is excerpted from a long "lecture-poem" he wrote and delivered not long before his death, we can trace the influence of both Christianity and Buddhism. Significantly, these religious influences are brought to interact with artistic creation and social problems. Cage, here as elsewhere, envisions an artistic and religious sensibility that affects the way humans live in the world.

Of his work as a composer and poet, Cage has written, "I have been less concerned with institutions and laws, more confident in the efficacy of the individual human mind when it is demilitarized and invigorated by the poetic spirit." Evident in "Overpopulation and Art" is his famous practice of "chance operations" and also the connections between his writing of poetry and his music. In addition, reading the poem is a highly visual experience as the eye is drawn both across the page and vertically up and down.

In Cage, literature is highly sensual and physically disturbing, while his ideas of aesthetics are very liturgical and communal. We see him here drawing upon the literature of the Bible, specifically the incident of Jesus walking on the water (Matt. 14:22–27; Mark 6:48–50; John 6:15–21).

From "Overpopulation and Art"

N   'phone rings
                              reViving
                           practicE
                           of chRistianity
                                 sPlit the stick
                                 O
                                 sPit the stick and there is
                           jesUs
                           waLking
                     on the wAlking
                           on The
                           wrIting
                                 O
                           oN
                           the wAter
                                 oN the water as though
              nothing happeneD
        the snow the white Animal asleep safely
              asleep in the tRee
                           no Traces left
A   O
                           reViving
                           practicE
                           whetheR meditation or nonmeditation
                                 Pleased

                                 Or
                           disPleased
                     won't bUrn
                     the metaL ones won't burn
                                 is A
                                 is The
                                 Is
                                 Of
                     is emptiNessfullness
                           prActicality
              all creatioN
                           enDless
                     interpenetrAtion

whispeRed
Truths

N   the necessity tO find new forms
         of liVing
            nEw
         foRms of living together
      to stoP the estrangement between us
            tU overcome
         the Patriarchal thinking
         the aUthoritarian structures
      and the coLdness
            humAn
            noI togetherness
      the necessIty
            tO develop a culture
         that coNsciously opposes the ruling culture
            A culture which we create
      we determiNe   which overcomes the passive consumers
            attituDes
               And
      which is not Ruled
         by profiTeering

LEO STEINBERG,
*THE SEXUALITY OF CHRIST IN RENAISSANCE ART
AND IN MODERN OBLIVION*

Art historian Leo Steinberg's book *The Sexuality of Christ in Renaissance Art and in Modern Oblivion* caused a stir when it was first published in 1983. In it, Steinberg explores the seemingly scandalous tendency in Renaissance devotional art to give demonstrative emphasis to the genitalia of the Christ Child, or of the dead Christ. He argues that this "showing forth," or *ostentatio genitalium,* made a serious theological statement about the Incarnation, and that the subject, having been "tactfully overlooked for half a millennium," continues to be avoided in our modern oblivion.

Steinberg's book was republished in a much expanded form in 1996, with lengthy essays that engage in debate with his many critics from the worlds of art, literature, and history. His style is witty and deliberately punning, and Steinberg powerfully reveals the importance of debates across disciplinary boundaries—indicating that the business of literature and theology quickly and inevitably expands into a conversation that includes art, cinema, popular culture, and many other forms of discourse and critical discussion. In order to explore the sacred, nothing remains unspeakable. The book's closing page refers to some disturbing images of God the Father accepting the sacrifice of the Son.

From The Sexuality of Christ in Renaissance Art and in Modern Oblivion

What makes the images I am citing rare and psychologically troubling is the Father's intrusive gesture, his unprecedented acknowledgment of the Son's loins. Nothing in received iconography sanctions it; and common intuition proscribes it. Joyce's Stephen Dedalus speaks of the steadfast bodily shame by which sons and fathers are sundered. He perceived their severance, the distancing of their persons through shame of body, as the way of all flesh. And precisely this shame caves in now before our eyes. Natural distance collapses in this coalition of Persons wherein the divine Father's only-begotten is (as theology has it) a virgin, virginally conceived; enfleshed, sexed, circumcised, sacrificed, and so restored to the Throne of Grace; there symbolizing not only the aboriginal unity of the godhead, but in its more dramatic, more urgent message, a conciliation which stands for the atonement, the being-at-one, of man and God. For this atonement, on which hinges the Christian hope of salvation, Northern Renaissance art found the painfully intimate metaphor of the Father's hand on the groin of the Son, breaching a universal taboo as the fittest symbol of reconcilement. Such a symbol can only have sprung from an artist attuned to the deep undertow of his feelings. And it would not surprise me if its originator turned out to be, once again, Rogier van der Weyden. It is perhaps more surprising that a handful of painters, engravers, and carvers understood the metaphor well enough to adopt and to imitate it—before everybody was educated into incomprehension. But this incomprehension—the "oblivion" to which the title of this essay refers—is profound, willed, and sophisticated. It is the price paid by the modern world for its massive historic retreat from the mythical grounds of Christianity.

A few words more. The field I have tried to enter is unmapped, and unsafe, and more far-reaching than appears from my present vantage. Much of what I have said is conjectural and surely due for revision. I can hardly claim, as St. Bernard does in closing his eighty-second sermon on the Song of Songs: "We need have no regrets for anything we have said; it is all supported by unquestioned and absolute truth." But I have risked hypothetical interpretations chiefly to show that, whether one looks with the eye of faith or with a mythographer's cool, the full content of the icons discussed bears looking at without shying. And perhaps from one further motive: to remind the literate among us that there are moments, even in a wordy culture like ours, when images start from no preformed program to become primary texts. Treated as illustrations of what is already scripted, they withhold their secrets.

Postmodern Fiction and Literature

SAMUEL BECKETT,
MALONE DIES

Samuel Beckett (1906–1989) is best known as a playwright for such works as *Waiting for Godot* and *Endgame,* linked with the theater of the absurd, and yet also in the great tradition of Irish drama. But he was also an accomplished novelist, particularly in the trilogy of which *Malone Dies* (1958), first published in French in 1951, and later translated by Beckett himself, is the central part, and in which he explores the fictional possibilities of language in a way that anticipates much later, so-called postmodern writing.

Malone is dying, and in the last words of the book, excerpted below, language finally disintegrates as reference, narrative, and temporal structures fall apart. The novel's great predecessor is James Joyce's *Finnegans Wake,* and its grim humor looks forward to postmodern fiction of the last years of the twentieth century. Can language take us into the actual experience of death itself?

From Malone Dies

Lemuel is in charge, he raises his hatchet on which the blood will never dry, but not to hit anyone, he will not hit anyone, he will not hit anyone any more, he will not touch anyone any more, either with it or with it or with it or with or

or with it with his hammer or with his stick or with his fist or in thought in dream I mean never he will never

or with his pencil or with his stick or

or light light I mean

never there he will never

never anything

there

any more

EDMOND JABÈS,
THE BOOK OF MARGINS

Edmond Jabès (1912–1991), was born in Cairo, but lived in France from 1956 until his death. A major Jewish thinker and philosopher, he is also one of the most important poets of the postmodern and postholocaust period. Mark Rudman, in the *New York Times Book Review,* situates Jabès "in the spiritual company of Kafka and Beckett. The three inhabit the same no-place, which is everywhere, creating works that miraculously cleave to the essential while avoiding the generic."

Jabès offers commentaries on most of the important figures within postmodernism, from Blanchot and Bataille to Levinas and Derrida, but also on major poets, and in particular Paul Celan. At the same time, he looks back to ancient wisdom, in particular the wisdom of the desert and mysticism.

This brief extract is taken from *The Book of Margins,* originally published in 1975, and as an exchange with holocaust survivor and fellow poet Celan, gives focus to the postmodern themes of language and time.

From The Book of Margins
"Memory of Paul Celan"

That day. The last. Paul Celan at my house. Sitting in this chair that I have right now been staring at for a long time.

Exchange of words, closeness. His voice? Soft, most of the time. And yet it is not his voice I hear today, but his silence. It is not him I see, but emptiness, perhaps because, on that day, each of us had unawares and cruelly revolved around himself.

FURTHER READING

Anderson, Laurie. *Stories from the Nerve Bible: A Retrospective, 1972–1992.* New York: HarperCollins, 1994.

Beal, Timothy K., and David M. Gunn. *Reading Bibles, Writing Bodies: Identity and the Book.* London and New York: Routledge, 1997.

Bell, David, and Gill Valentine. *Mapping Desire: Geographies of Sexuality.* London and New York: Routledge, 1995.

Boyarin, Daniel. *Intertextuality and the Reading of the Midrash.* Bloomington: Indiana University Press, 1990.

Cahoone, Lawrence, ed. *From Modernism to Postmodernism.* Oxford: Basil Blackwell Publisher, 1996.

Caputo, John D. *The Prayers and Tears of Jacques Derrida: Religion without Religion.* Bloomington: Indiana University Press, 1997.

Chametzsky, Jules. *Our Decentralized Literature: Cultural Mediations in Selected Jewish and Southern Writers.* Amherst: University of Massachusetts Press, 1996.

Detweiler, Robert, and William G. Doty, eds. *The Daemonic Imagination: Biblical Text and Secular Story.* Atlanta: Scholars Press, 1990.

Hassan, Ihab Habib. *The Dismemberment of Orpheus: Toward a Postmodern Literature.* New York: Oxford University Press, 1971.

Hawking, Stephen W. *A Brief History of Time: From the Big Bang to Black Holes.* Toronto and New York and London: Bantam, 1988.

Hayles, N. Kathryn. *Chaos Bound: Orderly Disorder in Contemporary Literature and Science.* Ithaca, N.Y.: Cornell University Press, 1990.

Ingraffia, Brian. *Postmodern Theory and Biblical Theology: Vanquishing God's Shadow.* Cambridge and New York: Cambridge University Press, 1995.

Jasper, David, ed. *Postmodernism, Literature and the Future of Theology.* London: Macmillan Publisher Ltd., New York. St. Martin's Press, 1993.

Jencks, Charles. *The Postmodern Reader.* New York: St. Martin's Press; London: Academy Editions, 1992.

Kundera, Milan. *The Art of the Novel.* Translated by Linda Asher. London: Faber & Faber; New York: Grove Press, 1988.

Martin, Joel W., and Conrad E. Ostwalt, Jr., eds. *Screening the Sacred: Religion, Myth, and Ideology in Popular American Film.* Boulder, Colo.: Westview Press, 1995.

May, John R., and Michael Bird. *Religion in Film.* Knoxville: University of Tennessee Press, 1982.

McKnight, Edgar V. *Postmodern Use of the Bible.* Nashville: Abingdon Press, 1988.

Miles, Margaret R. *Carnal Knowing: Female Nakedness and Religious Meaning in the West.* Boston: Beacon Press, 1989.

————. *Seeing and Believing: Religion and Values in the Movies.* Boston: Beacon Press, 1996.

Taylor, Mark C. *Erring: A Postmodern A/theology.* Chicago: University of Chicago Press, 1984.

Wellworth, George E. *Modern Drama and the Death of God.* Madison: University of Wisconsin Press, 1986.

Postscript:
From Modernism
to Postmodernism

One of the most significant, and more obvious, of the themes permeating this anthology is the transition from modernism to postmodernism, seen not merely as contemporary experience but as a shift acknowledged in literature from ancient times. Its central characteristic is the move from the rational and the organized into the fear of chaos and disorder—a fear felt, perhaps, by the scribes and Pharisees who listened to the words of Jesus in the Gospel narratives and found the foundations of their world threatened, this disorder lodged within the very order on which they had built their trust and security. "Do not think that I shall accuse you before the Father; your accuser is Moses, on whom you have set your hope" (John 5:45). The deception lies within the law itself.

Focusing for a moment on another great text of the ancient world, Euripides' tragedy *The Bacchae*, one of the most powerful of all acknowledgments of the transition from the modern to the postmodern, we are drawn into a crucial marker of that move, the bewildering atmosphere of deceit. The play's focus is on the divine figure of Dionysus, the very epitome of deceit and trickery. After Pentheus has insulted the god by his failure to recognize him, Dionysus takes his revenge by deceiving him, and it is by deception that the young king meets his grisly death at the hands of his own mother, who is, in turn, deceived in her madness. The consequence of this is the deadly ritual of sparagmos, a rending and fragmentation of the body parts as punishment for hubris and the failure to recognize the god and give him due honor. Throughout the play, irony piles on irony in a spiral of humiliation and violence in which, in the words of the final Chorus, "Gods manifest themselves in many forms, Bring matters to surprising ends."

The characteristics of the moment of transition have been all too clear in our own time, in the trauma of the First World War, the horror of the holocaust, and the blind madness of the Vietnam War, all of which quickly prompted their own literatures reflecting the sense of betrayal as the sense of order and hope are replaced by dismay at the capacity of humanity for fetishized violence and cruelty. From the biting fictions of deception in Thomas Mann's *The Confessions of Felix Krull* and the blandness of mid-European society in Robert Musil's *The Man without Qualities*, we shift rapidly to the horrors of war and the human capacity for maiming in Vir-

174

ginia Woolf's *Mrs. Dalloway*, to the novels of the holocaust, and the post-Vietnam short story of Tim O'Brien, "The Sweetheart of Son tra Bong," in which Mary Ann Belle, the innocent and virginal girl fascinated by warfare, wears around her neck a necklace of dried tongues—an ornament apparently favored by the GIs who saw action in Vietnam.

Dionysus makes a pathetic fool out of his regal subject Pentheus before subjecting him to sparagmos—and we have been made fools of by our century of violence, technology, and consumerism. For one of the ironies of the transition from modernism to postmodernism is that postmodernism's obsession with technology (as Heidegger has so ably shown) is the infatuation that now threatens to encompass and devour us. As our reality slips into a "virtual" reality in the explosion in communications, we become both instigators and victims of an impending apocalypse, both guilty and pathetically innocent, in an atmosphere familiar not only in the "real" theaters of war, but in the celluloid wars of the cinema and mass culture. As the French critic Jean Baudrillard has pointed out, as we watch Francis Ford Coppola's film of the Vietnam War, *Apocalypse Now*, it becomes impossible to distinguish between the filmic mass spectacle of the film and the war—both are overwhelmed by their own technology, violence, and sacrificial rituals of dismemberment, both mental and physical.[1] In danger of being led astray by our own technology, our terrible and compulsive lust for voyeuristic information is exemplified in J. G. Ballard's novel *The Atrocity Exhibition*, once described as the "exemplary psychotic novel." Again the biblical words ring with uncanny power from the so-called "little apocalypse" of Mark 13:5–6: "Beware that no one leads you astray. Many will come in my name and say, 'I am he!' and they will lead many astray."

Yet our anthology presents itself as an indication that not only do literature and art continue to be creatively produced and to stand witness within this crucial transition, but the processes of interpretation also flourish, and it is imperative that we continue to *read*. Our religio-moral responsibilities to translate the implications of the texts before us remain, challenged by the paradoxes, aporias, and urgencies of these texts. And if contemporary hermeneutics have shifted from the ancient hermeneutics of the community to the anxious readings of the individual, at the same time they have moved from a hermeneutics of trust to what Ricoeur calls a hermeneutics of suspicion. Perhaps this is always a necessary move for the postmodern, serving both to alert us to those traits of deceit and irony which surround us in the very fabric of what we perceive as order and to allow the release of our collective, repressive denials. For there will come many who will lead us astray.

O'Brien's short story violently confronts us with a representation of an America that was seduced by the violence enacted in Vietnam. The "innocent land" is aroused by a history of violence, giving itself over to death and the excitement of violence. This is an apocalypse also given over, paradoxically, to innocence: in its sense of itself as a defender of goodness, it is capable of the most atrocious acts of violence. And as technology has "advanced," this may have been even more true of the recent Gulf War, watched by millions of us in the "safety" of our homes as the missiles struck home, like images on a computer in games played by children. What is striking with both the Vietnam and Gulf wars is the intensification of a national self-consciousness that expresses itself as an extreme objectification, a sense of noninvolvement in a filmic "hyperreality"; these hardly encourage communal self-examination, a willingness to bear responsibility for our violent ways, the ability to mourn them, or the determination to overcome them.

The transition from modernism to postmodernism is accomplished at a cost. Can we interpret this transition in terms of a Christian perspective? Especially since we are here designing a literature and religion anthology, our interpretation should attempt to illustrate the important differences that a religious viewpoint can make. For there are clear connections between *The Bacchae* and the Gospel narratives of the Passion: the characteristics of fragmentation, deception, revelation, apocalypse, and irony. In the liturgy of the Eucharist, Christ's body is "broken" as a memorial of his sacrifice on the cross. The Gospels are a drama of his warfare against the archdeceiver, Satan, and there is the final irony, his deception of his enemies as the true nature of his Messiahship is revealed in the resurrection appearances. Defeat is victory, death is life, the foolishness of God is proved wiser than our modernist wisdoms.

The postmodern world, infatuated by computers and microchip technology, purveys its gospels—and these, it may be, have great potential for humane purposes as well as for the demons that beset us. That would be a welcome apocalypse, one that would bless rather than destroy, and we would have our poets such as Wallace Stevens to thank for it. For the Gospels, and their story of the redemptive death of Christ, are pervaded by ironies that the traditions of theology have too often had neither the will nor the ability to recognize ("recognition" as *anagnorisis* is, of course, another great moment in the Aristotelian tragedy), and for that reason we have continually to turn to the poets and artists to identify and remind us of the grand irony at the heart of the greatest of all narratives—a truly postmodern moment at the heart of our program for religion and literature, which may offer a way through the human web of deceit and violence even yet.

We have mentioned specifically Wallace Stevens, since his poem "Sunday Morning" is nothing less than a poetic response to the postmodern condition. It consists of a dialogue between a virginal questioner, inspired by the poem's worshiplike and almost liturgical atmosphere (it is, after all, Sunday morning) to ask herself the profound questions regarding death, immortality, and an afterlife, and a harsh, almost brutal negation. To the romantic vision of the questioner, Stevens offers an alternative, powerful and robust in its imagery. It is declared in the seventh stanza:

> Supple and turbulent, a ring of men
> Shall chant an orgy on a summer morn.

Their vision might well be mistaken for a projection of popular "masculinist" mythologies, but the intention is serious. The community of men that counters the timid feminine queries is intended by Stevens as a forthright, Nietzschean declaration of the freedom from the modernist, theological defenses of death and immortality—postmodern not in its defense via a separation of the sexes but in the very assertion of its rightness. It is assertive in its masculinity and also its acknowledgment of the feminine. The interaction of the sexes in this highly erotic interplay demands a gender empowerment, and not a defense or accommodation of them. The ring of chanting "savage" men is, in fact, a counter to the androgynous frenzy of sparagmos dramatized in *The Bacchae,* and it suggests a healthier, more graceful substitute for them. There is no "ancient sacrifice" that the girl recalls from just as there is no randomness or autism, traits prominent here by their absence.

"We live in an old chaos of the sun" asserts the poet in the final stanza of "Sunday Morning." Here truly is a "kenosis," an outpouring or self-emptying (compare Phil. 2:7) of divinity that is the natural evolution of the death of God. The vocabulary of kenosis is deep within the Christian tradition and the imagery of the passion narratives, but in the words of the poet is far more radical than any conclusion dared by most theologians. Perhaps Christ himself, though not the articulate tradition that appropriated his memory, ventured this utterly postmodern moment that the poet knows. Perhaps the greatest literature has always been within this moment of transition, speaking to us yet beyond us in fictions that we know to be fictions yet, imaginatively, know also to be true. Such literature can, in spite of all, realize the "divinization" of our world in an apocalypse that we have barely begun to appreciate. Writing of the poet William Blake, the radical "death of God" theologian Thomas Altizer expresses this moment powerfully:

> Blake belongs to a large company of radical or spiritual Christians, Christians who believe that the Church and Christendom have sealed Jesus in his tomb and resurrected the very evil and darkness that Jesus conquered by their exaltation of a solitary and transcendent God, a heteronomous and compulsive law, and a salvation history that is irrevocably past. Despite its great relevance to our situation, the faith of the radical Christian continues to remain largely unknown, and this is so both because that faith has never been able to speak in the established categories of Western thought and theology and because it has so seldom been given a visionary expression (or, at least, the theologian has not been able to understand the radical vision, or even perhaps to identify its presence).[2]

In poems like Stevens's "Sunday Morning" and many of the texts anthologized in this volume, we may be led to ask the questions once put by Altizer himself, "Is it postmodernism itself which will release a truly new and yet profoundly or primordial 'understanding of the resurrection'?" In the interplay of literature and religion we may continue to live imaginatively within this moment of transition, acknowledging the horrors and yet also envisioning the glory as the word continues to be spoken and written, and reading, in the most serious sense of the word, continues to offer possibilities of redemption and prompt revisions of thought which lie not in the darkness of "the tomb in Palestine" (Stevens's words again) but in an apocalypse that is truly a genesis of spirit and understanding. This is a mighty aspiration, but we hope that this volume, at least in a modest way, will keep that spirit alive and the hunger fresh.

NOTES

1. Jean Baudrillard, "Apocalypse Now," in *Simulacra and Simulation*, translated from the French by Sheila Faria Glaser (Ann Arbor: University of Michigan Press, 1994), 59–60.
2. Thomas J. J. Altizer, "William Blake and the Role of Myth," in Thomas Altizer and William Hamilton, *Radical Theology and the Death of God* (London: Penguin Books, 1968), 182.

Study Questions

CHAPTER 1. HISTORY OF THE FIELD
AND THEORETICAL ISSUES

1. What are the distinguishing features of a sacred text? The Bible has been described as the basic book of our civilization, in both religious and literary history. In what sense do you think this is a true claim?

2. William Wordsworth writes of the affinities between religion and poetry, but he also warns of the dangers that beset those "who betake themselves to reading verse for sacred purposes." What do you feel are the dangers inherent in the study of literature and religion, and what are the gains to be made?

3. Søren Kierkegaard uses a variety of different "voices" when he writes, rarely speaking directly with his own persona. The poet Emily Dickinson wrote that we should "Tell all the Truth but tell it slant." Why should it be important that poets and writers seek indirect ways of exploring religious matters?

4. In 1935 T. S. Eliot maintained that it was important for "Christian readers to scrutinize their reading, especially of works of imagination, with explicit ethical and theological standards." Could this still be argued today? What differences in our society might make this statement seem outdated or unacceptable?

5. Having read through the passages excerpted in this chapter, how would you define the future of the study of literature and religion? Why does this field of study remain important for us today?

CHAPTER 2. THE EXPLORATION OF ORIGINS

1. If science has "disproved" the stories of creation in the first chapters of Genesis, what value remains in such stories? How can

poetry and literature give us insights into our "origins"? In what sense is the pursuit of the mystery of our origins a religious quest?

2. Assess the significance of the story "The Woman Who Fell from the Sky," particularly the relationship between the woman and her husband. How do you feel about it?

3. Mark Twain's *Extracts from Adam's Diary* retells the story of Adam and Eve in a humorous way. What is the effect of adding a comic element to the biblical story? A poet once expressed a fear that John Milton's retelling of the same story from Genesis was presumptuous and risked the "ruin of sacred truths." Why would a "secular" writer attempt to rewrite the Bible in this way?

4. D. H. Lawrence abandoned his early Christianity and wrote novels and stories that celebrate the physical world. Compare his short novel "The Man Who Died" with John 11:1–44, noting the differences and the similarities.

5. "In the beginning was the Word." Can anything be said to exist before language? Why do you think that stories about origins from widely divergent cultures are so remarkably similar? What is the "truth" of these stories?

CHAPTER 3. THE INTERPRETIVE TRADITION OF LITERATURE AND RELIGION

1. No text is ever entirely original; it is always a comment on and an interpretation of an earlier text. If this is the case, what do you understand by the term "inspiration"?

2. What is the "meaning" of a text? Should we not rather speak of meanings in the plural? Why?

3. It is sometimes said that the interpreter of a text is trapped in the hermeneutic circle. In a writer like Hildegard of Bingen does the sacred text give rise to doctrine, or does doctrine provide a means of interpreting the text?

4. Teresa of Avila remarked that we would understand the words of Jesus Christ in the Gospels "if it were not for our own fault." Would it be true to say that the interpretive tradition arises out of our failure to understand what is there in the text rather than from the difficulty of the texts themselves?

5. Compare Kierkegaard's versions of the story of Abraham and Isaac with Genesis 22:1–14. Do you think that Abraham is a monster or a man of faith? Could he be both?

6. What is the role of the imagination in interpretation?

CHAPTER 4.THE LANGUAGE AND LITERATURE OF WORSHIP

1. In what sense is the language of Jesus at the Last Supper in the Gospels of Matthew and Luke poetic? Would it be possible to replace this with literal language? What is the difference between the poetic and the literal?

2. Why does Soyinka call his version of *The Bacchae* a Communion Rite?

3. What is the importance of paradox in Donne's sonnet "Batter my heart, three-personed God"?

4. Give a close reading and analysis of Father Mapple's sermon. What does it teach us? (Try reading the sermon aloud and listen to the physical sounds of the words.)

5. John Updike's character begins his sermon with the words "Forgive me." In what sense is literature a form of confession and how does it have the effect of "cleansing us"?

CHAPTER 5.THE LITERARY STRUCTURES OF RELIGIOUS TEXT GENRES

1. Could the book of Job be described as a tragedy? Why is tragedy such an important genre in literature? What is the relationship between tragedy in literature and religious experience?

2. The novelist Iris Murdoch has written of the primitive force of stories, claiming that "stories about human beings are best told in words, and that 'best' is a matter of response to a deep and ordinary need." Using examples from biblical narratives, explore these claims. Why are stories so important in the Bible?

3. Find other examples of "the passion story" in literature, and compare them with the Gospel narratives (e.g., Herman Melville's *Billy Budd,* Nikos Kazantzakis's *Christ Re-Crucified,* William Faulkner's *A Fable*).

4. Why do you think that apocalyptic literature is so important for us today? Find other examples of apocalypse in contemporary literature, art, and film, and compare them with Ezekiel 1. (You will find some in chapter 7 in the section entitled "Visions of the End.")

5. "Every piece of writing is a kind of something. It takes its place within a particular formal tradition and in itself exemplifies that tradition" (John B. Gabel and Charles B. Wheeler, *The Bible as Literature*). Identify five different kinds of writing in the Bible,

and find examples of these genres in later literature (e.g., parable, lyric, etc.).

CHAPTER 6. RELIGIOUS DIMENSIONS OF
LITERARY TEXT GENRES

1. The poet and artist William Blake wrote: "The reason Milton
    wrote in fetters when he wrote of Angels & God, and at liberty
    when of Devils & Hell, is because he was a true Poet and of the
    Devil's party without knowing it" (*The Marriage of Heaven and
    Hell*). What do you think Blake meant?

2. In his poem "The Garden of Love," Blake writes in very nega-
    tive terms of the priest. Why do you think poets write so often
    in this way of priests? Can you think of biblical examples of this
    antagonism?

3. Why does Sylvia Plath compare herself with Lazarus, whom
    Jesus brought back to life in the Gospel of John, chapter 11?

4. In what ways is Yeats's poem "The Second Coming" prophetic
    of the twentieth century? What is the particular significance of
    the image of the last two lines?

5. "Though your sins are like scarlet, they shall be as white as
    snow" (Isa. 1:18). Look up this passage in Isaiah and compare it
    with Peter Meinke's poem "Liquid Paper." Do you find this
    poem funny, reassuring, disturbing?

CHAPTER 7. THE GREAT THEMES OF
LITERATURE AND RELIGION

1. What are some of the important differences between the death
    of Orpheus as described by Ovid, and the death of Jesus as
    described in the Gospel of Luke, chapters 22–24?

2. Why do you think Emily Dickinson describes death as she does?
    Comment on the theme of time in her poem "Because I could
    not stop for Death."

3. How would you define the nature of "sin" as it is addressed in
    Baldwin's *Go Tell It on the Mountain*? What is the "truth" that Eli-
    sha and Ella Mae are accused of straying from? Assess the *tone*
    of Baldwin's narrator in this passage.

4. Why is it so important that Elie Wiesel describes his experience
    of the death camps in such terrible detail? Is this an image of the
    death of God, or is it possible to read this passage from *Night* in

another way? How might different religious perspectives affect a reader's interpretation?

5. In what sense is Ballard writing "scripture" in *The Atrocity Exhibition*? What is the relationship between his original text and his later "commentary" on it? Can this tell us anything about the nature of biblical commentaries?

CHAPTER 8. INTERACTIONS: NEW CHALLENGES TO AND FROM OTHER FIELDS

1. What are the problems with calling Michèle Roberts's *The Wild Girl* a "fifth Gospel"? Can literature add another "Gospel" to the four in the Bible?

2. "It was not a story to pass on." Why does Morrison insist on this, having told the story of Beloved at such length? What is the importance of memory in literature and religion?

3. Angels are important figures in the Bible. (E.g., the visit of the angel Gabriel to Mary in Luke 1, and the message of the angels to the shepherds in Luke 2.) Why do angels continue to be so important in literature? Find other examples of angelic visits in modern literature and film.

4. Science and religion have not enjoyed an easy relationship in the past two hundred years. How can literature help to draw their themes and concerns together?

5. Much of the literature in this chapter works by either amusing us or shocking us. How can this help religious reflection?

Acknowledgments

William Wordsworth, "Essay, Supplementary to the Preface to *The Lyrical Ballads*," in *Poetical Works*. Edited by Thomas Hutchinson. New edition revised by Ernest de Selincourt. Oxford: Oxford University Press, 1969.

David Friedrich Strauss, *The Life of Jesus Critically Examined*. Translated by George Eliot, 1846. Edited by Peter C. Hodgson. London: SCM Press, 1973.

Matthew Arnold, "The Study of Poetry," in *Essays in Criticism*, Second Series (1888). *Selected Prose*, edited by P. J. Keating. London and New York: Penguin Books, 1970.

Søren Kierkegaard, *The Point of View for My Work as an Author*. Translated by Walter Lowrie. In *A Kierkegaard Anthology*, edited by Robert Bretall. Copyright © 1946, renewed 1974, by Princeton University Press. Reprinted by permission of Princeton University Press.

T. S. Eliot, "Religion and Literature." Excerpts from *Selected Essays* by T. S. Eliot, copyright 1950 by Harcourt, Inc. and renewed 1978 by Esme Valerie Eliot, reprinted by permission of the publisher. And used by permission of Faber and Faber Ltd.

Paul Tillich, *Theology of Culture*. From *Theology of Culture* by Paul Tillich. Copyright © 1959 by Oxford University Press, Inc. Used by permission of Oxford University Press, Inc.

Nathan A. Scott, Jr., *The Wild Prayer of Longing*. New Haven, Conn.: Yale University Press, 1971. Copyright © 1971 by Yale University. Reprinted by permission of Yale University Press.

Northrop Frye, *The Great Code: The Bible and Literature*. Excerpts from *The Great Code*, copyright © 1982, 1981 by Northrop Frye, reprinted by permission of Harcourt Brace & Company.

Popol Vuh: The Sacred Book of the Ancient Quiché Maya, English translation by Delia Goetz and Sylvanus G. Morley, from the translation of Adrián Recinos (Norman: University of Oklahoma Press, 1950). Copyright © 1950 by the University of Oklahoma Press. Reprinted by permission of The University of Oklahoma Press.

Paula Gunn Allen, "The Woman Who Fell from the Sky." From *Spider Woman's Granddaughters* by Paula Gunn Allen. © 1989 by Paula Gunn Allen. Reprinted by permission of Beacon Press, Boston.

Ovid, *Metamorphoses*. "Chaos Transformed into the Ordered Universe," Book 1, translated by Mary M. Innes. New York and London: Penguin Classics, 1955, pp. 29–31, 36–38. © Mary M. Innes, 1955. Reproduced by permission of Penguin Books Ltd.

Mark Twain, *Extracts from Adam's Diary*. New York: Harper & Brothers, 1904.

Joseph Addison, "Ode" (1712).

D. H. Lawrence, "The Man Who Died", in *Love among the Haystacks and Other Stories*. Harmondsworth: Penguin Books, 1960, pp. 127–28. Reproduced by permission of Laurence Pollinger Limited and the Estate of Frieda Lawrence Ravagli.

Walter Ong, *The Presence of the Word*. New Haven, Conn.: Yale University Press, 1967. Copyright © 1967 by Yale University.

Augustine of Hippo, *City of God*. Translated by Henry Bettenson. London and New York: Penguin Classics, 1972, pp. 659–60. Copyright © Henry Bettenson, 1972. Reproduced by permission of Penguin Books Ltd.

Hildegard of Bingen, *Scivias*. From *Hildegard of Bingen* translated by Mother Columba Hart and Jane Bishop © 1990 by the Abbey of Regina Laudis: Benedictine Congregation Regina Laudis of the Strict Observance, Inc. Used by permission of Paulist Press.

Teresa of Avila, "The Seven Dwelling Places," from *The Interior Castle*. Translated by Kieran Kavanaugh, O.C.D., and Otilio Rodriguez, O.C.D. Classics of Western Spirituality Series. New York: Paulist Press, 1979.

Martin Luther, *Table Talk*, translated by Theodore G. Tappert. Vol. 54 of Luther's *Works*. Philadelphia: Fortress Press, 1967.

Søren Kierkegaard, *Fear and Trembling* (1843), translated by Walter Lowrie. Princeton, N.J.: Princeton University Press, 1968, prelude.

Jacques Derrida, *The Gift of Death*. Chicago: University of Chicago Press, 1995. Copyright © 1995 by The University of Chicago. Reprinted by permission of The University of Chicago Press.

Isaac Bashevis Singer, "Jachid and Jechidah." Excerpt from "Jachid and Jechidah" from *Short Friday* by Isaac Bashevis Singer. Copyright © 1964 by Isaac Bashevis Singer and copyright renewed © 1992 by Alma Singer. Reprinted by permission of Farrar, Straus & Giroux, Inc.

Paul Ricoeur, "The Bible and the Imagination" (1981). Reprinted in *Figuring the Sacred: Religion, Narrative and Imagination*, edited by Mark I. Wallace. Minneapolis: Fortress Press, 1995.

Wole Soyinka, *The Bacchae of Euripedes: A Communion Rite*. From *The Bacchae of Euripides: A Communion Rite* by Wole Soyinka. Copyright © 1973 by Wole Soyinka. Reprinted by permission of W. W. Norton & Company. And by permission of Leavy Rosensweig & Hyman, New York, for the author.

R. C. D. Jasper and G. J. Cuming, *Prayers of the Eucharist: Early and Reformed*. Copyright © 1987 by The Order of St. Benedict, Inc. Published by The Liturgical Press, Collegeville, Minn. Used with permission.

"The Order of the Administration of the Lord's Supper or Holy Communion." From *The Book of Common Prayer*, 1662. Excerpt from R. C. D. Jasper and G. J. Cuming, *Prayers of the Eucharist: Early and Reformed*, 3d ed. New York: Pueblo Publishing, 1987.

Prasna Upanishad, from *The Upanishads*. Translated by Juan Mascaró. Penguin Classics, 1965, pp. 72–73. Copyright © Juan Mascaró, 1965. Reproduced by permission of Penguin Books Ltd.

Julian of Norwich, *Revelations of Divine Love*. Translated by Clifton Wolters. Penguin Classics, 1966. Copyright © Clifton Wolters, 1966. Reproduced by permission of Penguin Books Ltd.

Thomas Merton, *The Seven Storey Mountain*. Excerpt from *The Seven Storey Mountain* by Thomas Merton, copyright 1948 by Harcourt Brace & Company and renewed 1976 by The Trustees of The Merton Legacy Trust, reprinted by permission of the publisher. And by permission of Sheldon Press, London.

John Donne, "Batter my heart, three-personed God," in *John Donne: The Complete English Poems*, A. J. Smith, ed. New York and London: Penguin, 1986.

George Herbert, "Love" (1899).

Herman Melville, *Moby Dick: Or the Whale*, 1851. London and New York: Penguin Books, 1972.

John Updike, *A Month of Sundays. A Month of Sundays* by John Updike. Copyright © 1974, 1975 by John Updike. Reprinted by permission of Alfred A. Knopf Inc. Also reproduced by permission of Penguin Books Ltd.

Archibald MacLeish, *J. B.* Excerpt from *J. B.* Copyright © 1956, 1957, 1958 by Archibald MacLeish. Copyright © renewed 1986 by William H. MacLeish and Mary H. Grimm. Reprinted by permission of Houghton Mifflin Company.

John Bunyan, *Grace Abounding to the Chief of Sinners*. London: Everyman's Library, 1966.

William Blake, "And did those feet in ancient time," from preface to *Milton*, 1804. In *Complete Writings*, edited by Geoffrey Keynes. Oxford: Oxford University Press, 1966.

Patrick White, *Riders in the Chariot*. From *Riders in the Chariot* by Patrick White. Copyright © 1961, 1989 by Patrick White. Used by permission of Viking Penguin, a division of Penguin Putnam Inc. And by permission of Barbara Mobbs, agent and literary executor for Patrick White's work.

William Shakespeare, *All's Well That Ends Well*. Act 2, scene 1, lines 129–44.

R. Vay, "The Parable of Simeon and Bar Kappara," from *Midrash Wayyikra Rabbah*, edited by M. Margulies, reprinted in David Stern, *Parables in Midrash*. Cambridge, Mass.: Harvard University Press, 1991.

Franz Kafka, "Before the Law," in *The Trial*, 1925. From *Franz Kafka: The Complete Stories* by Franz Kafka, edited by Nahum N. Glatzer. Copyright © 1946, 1947, 1948, 1949, 1954, 1958, 1971 by Schocken Books Inc. Reprinted by permission of Schocken Books, distributed by Pantheon Books, a division of Random House, Inc. By permission of Random House UK Ltd. for Secker and Warburg.

Jorge Luis Borges, "The Gospel According to Mark," from *Doctor Brodie's Report*, translated by Thomas di Giovanni. New York: Dutton, 1972.

Acknowledgments

Malcolm Lowry. Copyright renewed 1975 by Margerie Lowry. Reprinted by permission of HarperCollins Publishers, Inc. Reprinted by permission of Sterling Lord Literistic, Inc. Copyright 1963 by Malcolm Lowry.

Peter Meinke, "Liquid Paper," from *Liquid Paper: New and Selected Poems*, by Peter Meinke, © 1991. Reprinted by permission of the University of Pittsburgh Press.

Peter Meinke, "M3," from *Poetry*, copyright 1997 by the Modern Poetry Association. Reprinted by permission of the editor of *Poetry*.

Ovid, *Metamorphoses*, "The Death of Orpheus," Book 11, translated by Mary M. Innes. New York and London: Penguin Classics, 1955, pp. 246–47. © Mary M. Innes, 1955. Reproduced by permission of Penguin Books Ltd.

Emily Dickinson, "Because I could not stop for Death," circa 1862. Reprinted by permission of the publishers and the Trustees of Amherst College from *The Poems of Emily Dickinson*, Thomas H. Johnson, ed., Cambridge, Mass.: The Belknap Press of Harvard University Press. Copyright © 1951, 1955, 1979, 1983 by the President and Fellows of Harvard College.

T. S. Eliot, *Murder in the Cathedral*, in *The Complete Poems and Plays*. London: Faber and Faber, 1969. Excerpt from *Murder in the Cathedral* by T. S. Eliot, copyright 1935 by Harcourt, Inc. and renewed 1963 by T. S. Eliot, reprinted by permission of the publisher. Also reprinted by permission of Faber and Faber Ltd.

Augustine of Hippo, *Confessions*, Book 8, chapter 12. Translated by R. S. Pine-Coffin. New York and London: Penguin Classics, 1961. Copyright © R. S. Pine-Coffin, 1961. Reproduced by permission of Penguin Books Ltd.

James Baldwin from *Go Tell It on the Mountain* by James Baldwin. Copyright 1952, 1953 by James Baldwin. Used by permission of Doubleday, a division of Random House, Inc. Also by permission of the James Baldwin Estate.

William Butler Yeats, "Adam's Curse," from *In the Seven Woods*, 1904, *Collected Poems*. London: Macmillan, 1950. Reprinted by permission of A. P. Watt Ltd. on behalf of Michael B. Yeats.

John Milton, *Paradise Lost, 1667*, edited by Douglas Bush. London: Oxford University Press, 1966, Book 1, lines 81–127.

Elie Wiesel, *Night*. New York: Hill and Wang, 1958. Copyright © 1958 by Les Éditions de Minuit. Reprinted by permission of Georges Borchardt, Inc.

Also reprinted by permission of Hill and Wang, a division of Farrar, Straus & Giroux, Inc.: Excerpt from *Night* by Elie Wiesel, translated by Stella Rodway. Copyright © 1960 by MacGibbon & Kee. Copyright renewed © 1988 by The Collins Publishing Group.

J. G. Ballard, *The Atrocity Exhibition*, 1970. Annotated Edition. London: HarperCollins, 1993. The extract from *The Atrocity Exhibition* by J. G. Ballard is reproduced by permission of the author c/o Margaret Hanbury, 27 Walcot Square, London SE114UB. Copyright © 1993 J. G. Ballard. All rights reserved.

Samuel Taylor Coleridge, "Kubla Khan," 1798, in *Poetical Works*, edited by Ernest Hartley Coleridge. Oxford: Oxford University Press, 1969.

Flannery O'Connor, *Wise Blood*. Excerpt from *Wise Blood* by Flannery O'Connor. Copyright © 1962 by Flannery O'Connor. Copyright renewed © 1990 by Regina O'Connor. Reprinted by permission of Farrar, Straus & Giroux, Inc. And by permission of Faber and Faber Ltd.

Michèle Roberts, *The Wild Girl*. London: Minerva Paperback, 1991. © 1984 Michèle Roberts. Reprinted with the permission of Gillon Aitken Associates Ltd. And by permission of Random House UK Ltd.

Toni Morrison, *Beloved*. New York: Alfred A. Knopf. Reprinted by permission of International Creative Management, Inc. © Toni Morrison 1987.

Audre Lorde, "Sister Outsider," in *The Black Unicorn: Poems*. New York: W. W. Norton & Company, 1978. "Sister Outsider" from *The Black Unicorn* by Audre Lorde. Copyright © 1978 by Audre Lorde. Reprinted by permission of W. W. Norton & Company, Inc.

Douglas Coupland, *Life after God*. New York: Simon & Schuster/Pocket Books, 1994. Reprinted with the permission of Simon & Schuster from *Life after God* by Douglas Coupland. Copyright © 1994 by Douglas Campbell Coupland. Published by Simon & Schuster London and New York.

Italo Calvino, "All at One Point" from *Cosmicomics* by Italo Calvino, copyright © 1965 by Giulio Einaudi editore s.p.a., Torino, English translation by William Weaver copyright © 1968 and renewed 1996 by Harcourt Brace & Company and Jonathan Cape Ltd., reprinted by permission of Harcourt Brace & Company. And by permission of Random House UK Ltd.

Tamiki Hara, "The Land of Heart's Desire," in *Fire from the Ashes: Short Stories about Hiroshima and Nagasaki,* edited by Kenzaburō Ōe. London and Columbia, La.: Readers International, 1985. Reprinted by permission of Shueisha Inc.

Mark C. Taylor, *Nots*. Chicago: University of Chicago Press, 1993. Copyright © 1993 by The University of Chicago. Reprinted by permission of The University of Chicago Press and the author.

John Cage, "Overpopulation and Art," in *John Cage: Composed in America*, edited by Marjorie Perloff and Charlie Junkerman. Chicago: University of Chicago Press, 1994. Reprinted by permission of The John Cage Trust, New York.

Leo Steinberg, *The Sexuality of Christ in Renaissance Art and in Modern Oblivion*, Second Edition. Chicago: University of Chicago Press, 1996. © 1983, 1996 by Leo Steinberg. Reprinted by permission of The University of Chicago Press and the author.

Samuel Beckett, *Malone Dies*, 1958. London: Calder and Boyars, 1968. © Samuel Beckett, 1958. Reprinted by permission of Grove/Atlantic, Inc. and by permission of The Samuel Beckett Estate, and the Calder Educational Trust.

Edmond Jabès, "Memory of Paul Celan," in *The Book of Margins*, translated by Rosemarie Waldrop. Chicago: University of Chicago Press, 1993. © 1993 by The University of Chicago. Reprinted by permission of The University of Chicago Press.